Shakespeare's Tragic Skepticism

Shakespeare's Tragic Skepticism

Millicent Bell

Yale University Press   New Haven and London

Published with assistance from the foundation established
in memory of Oliver Baty Cunningham of the
Class of 1917, Yale College.

Published with assistance from the foundation established
in memory of Amasa Stone Mather of the
Class of 1907, Yale College.

Printed in the United States of America

Library of Congress Cataloging-in-Publication Data
Bell, Millicent.
Shakespeare's tragic skepticism / Millicent Bell.
p.   cm.
Includes bibliographical references.
ISBN 0-300-09255-5 (alk. paper)
1. Shakespeare, William, 1564–1616—Tragedies.   2. Shakespeare,
William, 1564–1616—Philosophy.   3. Skepticism in literature.
4. Tragedy.   I. Title.
PR2983 .B45   2002
822.3'3—dc21   2002003122

A catalogue record for this book is available
from the British Library.

The paper in this book meets the guidelines for permanence and
durability of the Committee on Production Guidelines for Book
Longevity of the Council on Library Resources.

10 9 8 7 6 5 4 3 2 1

For all my loves:
Gene, Tony, Meg, Kiki, Tim,
Michael, Georgia, Rebecca, Alex

Contents

Preface

Shakespeare's Tragic Skepticism has an ambitious aim. In writing it, I have tried to mark out a pathway across a trampled field, discussing plays more commented on over four centuries than anything else ever written except the Hebraic-Christian Bible. But in the case of Shakespeare, there is always something true and important that seems not to have been said before. As for the inevitable dependencies and derivations, everyone who has ever written about Shakespeare knows that it is really not possible to acknowledge fully the diverse influences of past criticism upon one's present thinking. So in writing this book I have avoided massive annotation. I have also tried to restrain myself from trumpeting my own discoveries too confidently or pointing insistently to my differences from others. The originality I may have achieved will be evident, I hope, to the fellow scholar whose business it is to keep track of such things. But the book is also addressed to the general reader who may or may not be interested in that sort of claim.

I was, of course, first prompted to write this study of *Hamlet, Othello, King Lear, Macbeth, Julius Caesar,* and *Antony and Cleopatra* by the realization that much previous discussion tended to confine and reduce their variousness and contradictions. There has always been a simplifying readiness to impose the critic's own con-

ventional ideas about life and its meaning upon Shakespeare—
to make expectable, generally consoling stories out of the strange
sequences of episode and language that actually present themselves. But those plausible stories, those familiar ideas that reassur-
ingly "make sense" of experience for the majority of mankind in
each generation—especially ideas about the definition and stability
of human character and the moral significance of behavior, or
even about the discoverable links to one another of human events
—these were not always sustained by the plays. I began to suspect, as some others have, that Shakespeare's was one of those rare
minds that get around to the other side and see the moon's other
face, where, until space travel, no crater had a name. I discovered
that I wanted to show the prevailing importance in his greatest
plays of a skepticism that has been noted only in a partial, cur-
sory way when it has been noted at all. If the plays express his
thinking, he may have been someone who took seriously skeptical
challenges erupting in his time, challenges that put received convictions into question. He seems to have shared with Montaigne,
his near-contemporary, not only general doubts of what had long
been assumed about the universe and mankind but also doubt concerning the reliability of our own power to perceive and conclude
anything. Montaigne's ideas, expressed in the famous essays Shakespeare certainly read, became a repeated reference in my book as
representation of a general skeptical viewpoint emerging in the sixteenth and seventeenth centuries. I have felt it important, however, also to note that what we witness as the poetry and action
go forward in these plays is a nostalgic attachment to those very
convictions skepticism denies. In these dramatic explorations one
can sometimes come upon a denial of denial itself. The result is a
contest of feelings and ideas. Contradicting effects come into view
as we discover the theatricality of life in *Hamlet,* epistemological
anguish in *Othello,* the view that man is a stripped animal in *Lear,*

the collapse of the sense of time's sequential order in *Macbeth,* or the revelation of history's duplicity in the Roman plays.

Criticism has tended to overlook the apparent inconsistencies, gaps, and contradictions in Shakespeare's tragedies which I see not as faults of craft but as part of Shakespeare's poetic-dramatic version of reality and expressions of a skeptic viewpoint. At the start of the twentieth century, the most influential of modern critics of Shakespeare, A. C. Bradley, insisted that "the center" of Shakespearean tragedy "may be said with equal truth to lie in action issuing from character, or in character issuing from action." But unlike many less keenly observant critics who have come in Bradley's wake, he himself admitted that this idea "was an exaggeration of a vital truth" because "it is a tragic fact" that "men may start a course of events but can neither calculate or control it." Bradley understood that the fearful and mysterious quality of tragic experience in these plays was not to be seen adequately as the operation of a benevolent moral order in which human choice always plays a role. Nor as the consequence of blind accident, either. Critics have rarely admitted that Shakespeare leaves the dilemma unresolved.

I am very grateful to have found encouragement for my own views in a dissenting strain of modern criticism. After the mid-point of the twentieth century, the notion that Shakespeare was a sort of existentialist or absurdist gained attention (partly as a result of Peter Brooks's 1962 production of *King Lear,* which had drawn inspiration from Beckett's *Endgame*). Readings began to appear, like that of Wilbur Sanders (*The Dramatist and the Received Idea,* 1968), which challenged the dominating "providential" interpretation Bradley had clung to despite his awareness of its dubious truth. William Elton, in his learned *King Lear and the Gods* (1966) buried the idea that *King Lear* was "optimistically Christian." Nicholas Brooke, in his 1979 edition of *King Lear,* observed that in this play "all moral structures, whether of natural order or Christian redemption, are invalidated by the facts of experience." Going further in the next decades, a new English school of "cultural materialists" soon questioned the presence in *King Lear* not only of the idea of universal divine governance but also of the humanist faith in the heroic self. Jonathan Dolliver, in *Radical Tragedy: Religion, Ideology, and Power in the Drama of Shakespeare's Contemporaries* (1984), said that the play "repudiates the essentialism which the humanist reading of it presupposes." I have been influenced by this view, though I feel that it overlooks the *agon* which makes for tragedy, the struggle *for* a selfhood that we witness not only in *King Lear* but in the other plays.

I have remained impressed by Norman Rabkin's pioneering suggestion, in *Shakespeare and the Common Understanding* (1954) as well as his more recent *Shakespeare and the Problem of Meaning* (1981), that Shakespeare's complexity was more than the "ambivalence" prized by the New Criticism. It was, Rabkin suggested, a species of "complementarity" analogous to the state of matter described by the physicist Oppenheimer. Rabkin observed: "What is problematic in *Hamlet* is not accidental but rather lies at the center of [Shakespeare's] intention. . . . It is critical fideism [or] . . . 'bardolatry' to assume that every 'ambiguity' we can find is a mark of the poet's genius. . . . But . . . virtually everything in the play is problematic." I have found it useful to go back to see how Shakespeare's relation to his sources often itself illustrated the problem as it was duplicated for the playwright in the creation of his plays. My perception that this relation was often an ironic one had been strengthened when I read Howard Felperin's chapter on *Hamlet* in *Shakespearean Representations* (1977). Though my "archaeological" interest in sources is different from Felperin's, I have agreed with him that Shakespeare's plays "inhabit the gap between things and the pre-ordained meaning of things, between experience and inherited constructs of experience." Stephen Booth, in *King Lear, Macbeth, Indefinition, and Tragedy* (1983), argues that *King Lear* "refuses to fulfill the generic promise inherent in its story." According to Booth, Shakespeare demonstrates in his treatment of character "the impossibility of definition," and that "all human perception of pattern is folly"—and yet manages to assert pattern and order through language and makes the audience "think in multiple dimensions." *Macbeth,* Booth writes, is a play in which "finality is regularly unattainable," and "characters will not stay within limits," and "cause and effect do not work"; the play manipulates the audience to experience conflicted responses.

I have also tried to speculate about the origins of the plays in what existed in Shakespeare's outer world. In a period of unprecedented social mobility and personal refashioning, the inconstancy of personal identity was felt by persons who would never have formulated such a matter so abstractly. Uncertainty about the explanation of events large or small, whether the succession of the crown or a failed harvest or a child's death, made obscure, however unphilosophically, the very meaning of cause for ordinary men and women. I have trusted my feeling that the plays richly incorporate an awareness of many specific *historic* issues that entwine with more general problems. Mundane conditions of shifting social power, or of problematic class, gender, race, and generational relations, can be glimpsed in each play. One cannot write about Shakespeare's great tragedies without taking account of the presence of such immediate historic realities as threats against the crown, the appearance of a new class of homeless persons, the eruption of the witch mania, racial encounters promoted by travel and urbanism, or increasing tensions between the old and the young. These specific social matters project themselves, for a mind like Shakespeare's, upon ultimate questions, and promote the response of skepticism—as well as the resistance to it.

Like everyone writing about Shakespeare today, I have learned much from the no-longer-so-new "New Historicist" argument that social power and its associated ideology work to determine the meaning of Shakespeare's plays as of other works of the literary imagination. But the debate still waged about the role of "subversion" seems unresolvable to me, for I believe that the complex of dominant orthodoxy is not easily simplified, nor is dissidence as obviously "contained" as some suppose. In Shakespeare the battle of contrary viewpoints is, as the witches say in Macbeth, both "lost and won." And in this way Shakespeare stands outside any system that presumes the imperatives of a culture to be inherent in the nature of things—though the New Historicist Stephen Greenblatt probably would deny that there is any possible way of standing entirely "outside." Shakespeare, one might almost propose, is an early–seventeenth century New Historicist of sorts, bounded by his own time and place yet enabled by his skepticism to view his culture with detachment.

Greenblatt's *Renaissance Self-Fashioning* (1980) established a possible chart of the ways personal identity was constituted in sixteenth-century England, and this book has strengthened my acceptance of the view that personhood is invariably a construct of available models. But it is also my conviction that this very perception is at the heart of Shakespeare's plays in a peculiar way. That essential interiority is implied by Hamlet's statement that he has "that within which passeth show" has been claimed by some modern scholars who attribute to Shakespeare and the Elizabethan sonneteers the invention of the modern psyche. But this view is contested both by the mostly American New Historicists and by the Cultural Materialists, mostly English (Dollimore and Alan Sinfield and others, like Francis Barker, Anne Barton, and Catherine Belsey). I find that Shakespeare's tragedies are themselves stagings of this debate. In *Hamlet* the new personal will that is the maker of the self is forced into tragic contest with imposed social selfhoods but cannot find any other mode of being than the ones they offer.

One modern critical work bears a title I nearly borrow, Graham Bradshaw's *Shakespeare's Scepticism* (1987). Bradshaw's book has been an inspiring groundbreaker of my subject, though his coverage is different. He devotes most attention to works I don't discuss and deliberately declines concern with the context of Renaissance Early Modernism, its material conditions, and its war of ideas. But he does employ a concept he calls "perspectivism" to describe a relativism resulting from such unresolved contrasts of viewpoint as that of Othello and Iago. I have been interested further in the effect of uncertainty upon such polarities, however; in the case of Othello and Iago, I have wanted to show the origin of Othello's "fall" in the dissolution of these fixities, a dissolution that seems to validate Iago's own skepticism about the self. And I have insisted more than Bradshaw on the "tragic" element that I want to recognize in my own title—the effect of a skeptic view that is imposed upon idealism only at a terrible cost and after awful struggle.

My procedure has been a "close reading" of Shakespeare's words and of the succession of scenic effects, the accumulations and subtractions that establish or disestablish our impression that these resemble things happening to real persons. Consequently, among the scholars to whom I have incurred a clear debt there are, most especially, the editors of the editions of the six of Shakespeare's plays I have quoted from—G. R. Hibbard, editor of the 1987 Oxford *Hamlet;* E. A. J. Honigmann, editor of the 1997 Arden *Othello;* R. A. Foakes, editor of the 1997 Arden *King Lear;* A. R. Braunmuller, editor of the 1997 New Cambridge *Macbeth;* David Daniell, editor of the 1998 Arden *Julius Caesar;* and David Bevington, editor of the 1990 New Cambridge *Antony and Cleopatra.* In addition I have consulted other modern editions, like Harold

Jenkins's 1982 Arden *Hamlet,* Philip Edwards's 1985 New Cambridge *Hamlet,* Norman Sanders's 1984 New Cambridge *Othello,* Jay L. Halio's 1992 New Cambridge *King Lear,* Nicholas Brooke's 1990 Oxford *Macbeth,* Kenneth Muir's 1984 Arden *Macbeth,* and Michael Neill's 1994 Oxford *Antony and Cleopatra.* To the annotations of these editors I have resorted at numerous points for enlightenment in the interpretation of Shakespeare's language, though to none of them should my own sometimes dissenting readings be attributed.

Speaking of editions, I should point out that though I have resorted to editions of Shakespeare that generally "modernize" his original text somewhat, I have not followed the same practice with the three most important works from which he drew inspiration in writing the plays I discuss: Montaigne's *Essays* and Plutarch's *Parallel Lives,* both of which he knew in contemporary English translations, and Raphael Holinshed's historical chronicles of English and Scottish history. I have chosen to quote from John Florio's edition of the *Essayes* (1603), Thomas North's of Plutarch's *Lives of the Noble Grecians and Romanes, Compared Together* (1579), and Holinshed's *Chronicles of England, Scotland, and Ireland* (1587) for the language that communicated to Shakespeare Montaigne's speculations, Plutarch's biographies, and Holinshed's historical interpretations. Sometimes even a turn of phrase in these sources enlightens one about Shakespeare's own view of the subject he took in hand.

Obligations are not, of course, confined to the influence of books. I am proud to declare my particular gratitude to two brilliant friends who were readers of my manuscript in its early stages, Helen Vendler and Christopher Ricks. They not only offered me warm interest and approval of what I had tried to do but gave my manuscript scrupulous reading and provided suggestions for improvement or development. Such encouragement also came from another prepublication reader, Michael Goldman. And portions of the book written when it had hardly got under way had a fortunate reception for which I am grateful from the editors of the journals that published them in earlier form: *Yale Review* ("Othello's Jealousy," Spring 1997, pp. 120–136), *Hudson Review* ("Hamlet, Revenge!" Summer 1998, pp. 310–328), and *Raritan* ("Othello's Moor," Spring 2002, pp. 1–14). I am also very grateful for the care and interest in the book's development shown by my editors at Yale University Press, Lara Heimert and Dan Heaton. Besides these, there has been one constant counselor and affectionate encourager, my husband, Eugene Bell, who also read and expertly critiqued my manuscript.

Shakespeare's Tragic Skepticism

Introduction

Hamlet, Othello, King Lear, and *Macbeth*

Shakespeare is no more ready than Iago to wear his heart upon his sleeve for daws to peck at, and maybe, like Iago, he really has no heart. What he is "trying to say" in his plays is hardly distinguishable in the chorus of ideas that his poetry and dramatic structures make us hear. The Romantics thought he was "myriad-minded"—Coleridge's term. His entertainment of contraries, his apparent self-contradiction, showed the "negative capability" Keats said was the mark of literary genius. In modern times, T. S. Eliot felt that Shakespeare had no general ideas worth talking about. Nevertheless, Eliot offered his own egregious simplification, a "Senecan Shakespeare," while warning against accepting it too seriously: "About anyone as great as Shakespeare, it is probable that we can never be right; and if we can never be right, it is better that we should from time to time change our way of being wrong."

In offering a skeptical Shakespeare, a doubter of many received views about humanity and the universe, I feel the diffidence Eliot urged one to have. I believe that the plays I am examining in this book exhibit the effects of a potent philosophic skepticism verging upon nihilism. Yet criticism always simplifies. It is always an expression of the critic's own bias. Any correspondence I feel between my own doubting mood at the start of a new century and Shakespeare's own fin-de-siècle condition may be an illusion, just as the biases of earlier readers made them discover in Shakespeare their own confidence in a universe in which everything had its place and all meanings were secure and accessible. I know that my extract leaves something behind. Like others today, I may be too sure that an earlier school of critics was too sure that Shakespeare believed in the rule of divine intention and stable order in the cosmos and in human society. "Take but degree away, untune that string, and hark what discord follows" was, for a while—but no longer is—a favorite quotation from *Troilus and Cressida*. We are more likely, now, to think that it may not express the writer's personal view about the knowable design of the world and man's proper place in it. Do *Hamlet, Othello, King Lear,* and *Macbeth* give us confidence even about who one is? One's very soul, that immortal essence once thought to be God-implanted and unalterable, might, these plays sometimes suggest, be so elusive and variable as to bring its very existence into question. Though Shakespeare makes character so vivid that it survives all inconsistency and seems almost to require no proof of itself, I shall argue that the plays flout traditional ideas about human selfhood as a known and consistent quality by which a man or woman is identified. As for the plot of time by which events are linked together—a sequence and relation that makes rational sense of human experience—this, too, may not have seemed self-evident to Shakespeare either. His greatest plays seem to rely upon the commonsense logic that connects what happens with causes in circumstances and character; after all, it is only by believing in that logic that we are able to carry on in life. Yet significant gaps and paradoxes disrupt the sequences of action in these plays and bring such coherence and meaning into doubt. They even, finally, provoke us to wonder what one might really know about these matters or anything else. One might doubt that human perception was a reliable instrument. Shakespearean confidence in that instrument seems hardly secure. Troilus's question in *Troilus and Cressida,* "What's aught but as 'tis valued?" persists in his major tragedies despite Hector's answer to relativism,

> Value dwells not in particular will,
> It holds his estimate and dignity
> As well, wherein 'tis precious of itself.

Shakespeare allows us to put some trust in the prospect of getting at the final truth and worth of things, but he also invites us to question the absoluteness of our ideas and the validity of our impressions in the most radical way.

A working title for this book was *Honest Shakespeare*—meant to give our author a characterization ambiguously awarded to Iago. Although *honest* is also applied to someone like Desdemona—to mean female chastity as well as truthfulness—William Empson, who counted fifty-two occurrences of the word or its cognates in *Othello,* also pointed out years ago that it had an emergent sense as description of a type of person coming into view in the new century, one who was uninhibited by abstract principles. Iago is mistakenly called honest by those, like Othello, who trust him to tell the truth, and the term grows more and more ironic as it is applied to a man who lies continually and whose true feelings, if he has any, are disguised rather than evident. But a further irony may be suggested by the word's meaning as descriptive of a no-nonsense speaker who dispenses with exalted beliefs and declines to differentiate between seeming and being. In a word, a skeptic. Shakespeare, of course, the creator of Hamlet, who seems to see either man or woman not only as a quintessence of dust but also as the paragon of animals—"noble in reason, infinite in faculties, in form and moving how express and admirable, in action how like an angel, in apprehension how like a god"—is hardly himself to be identified with the most cynical and hateful of all his characters. But the Iago who is so cruelly contemptuous of those, like Othello, who think life is more than a shadow-play of illusions, expresses a part of Shakespeare's mind as much as Othello does. And this can be seen in the four great tragedies in which the will to belief in universal coherence and meaning struggles, often unsuccessfully, against skepticism. The title I finally settled on, *Shakespeare's Tragic Skepticism,* stresses more accurately the way *tragedy* results from skeptic disillusion; Hamlet feels *at one and the same time* the wonder of the human creature and the beauty of the world which has become a "sterile promontory" to him. His mood is one of tragic loss from which he sees no recovery. This is a mood very different from that of Iago, who, unlike Othello, has never believed or loved, and whose character belongs to the genre of comedy.

That ideas contend with one another in Shakespeare's writing is a quality he shares with the skeptic near-contemporary with whom I find him comparable, Michel de Montaigne. Montaigne's curiously moving, often evasive, often self-revelatory confessions of alternating belief and unbelief are not merely a feature of his response to the dogmas of his religion. They are duplicated in his attitudes toward numerous other generally accepted assumptions about mankind and the world. Taken as a whole, Montaigne's essays dramatize the unreadiness of his belief to come down on any conclusion without allowing for the possibility of its opposite. It is that representative skeptic method of balancing opposing views which was to be inherited from Montaigne by Pierre Bayle, who, at the end of the seventeenth century, made his famous encyclopedic dictionary a dramatization of the "method of doubt," in which one opinion was posed against another. I am suggesting that Shakespeare's thought, if we can assert anything about it, is, like Montaigne's or Bayle's, dialectic or dialogic. It pits an idea against its opposite. It looks to me as though Shakespeare—writing as he did at a time of cultural crisis when old convictions and new doubts were contending in men's minds—put contrary views into combat to test their strength. His plays are never allegorical—they never dramatize directly the contest of ideas—yet in them ideas contend from line to line in the richest language the stage has ever known. Through the action and language of the plays he invites his audiences to question, from moment to moment, the inherited, standard truths of his time. He also allows his audiences to view fearfully the results of abandoning the prop of such beliefs. This is the hidden structure of argument in Shakespeare's plays. Within these plays there are particular poetic occasions, like the soliloquies, which miniature such a structure. The most famous soliloquy of them all, Hamlet's "To be or not to be . . ." is just such a balancing of alternatives—about the "nobler" course, about the right expectation concerning death's aftermath, about the process of choice itself. The presence of contraries in the one man is, of course, notable in the case of Hamlet—a matter not merely of ideas but of a personality in which so many irreconcilabilities cohabit that he seems, if we watch too closely, to be not one but a dozen separate persons—and only Shakespeare's incomparable way of giving all his hero's speech a certain tone keeps us from noticing. One of the secrets of his high poetry is the way its complex verbal effects both enrich and contradict one another.

Where did Shakespeare's skepticism come from? I believe that the relation of contemporary economic and social turmoil to skepticism about personal definition is salient in *King Lear*. *Othello* may be said to take place in a Venice contemporary with the real London in which social identities might collapse and the self lose its moorings. *Hamlet,* for all its derivation from ancient legends of tribal revenge, exhibits the personal self as something sought rather than securely endowed, a condition that bears a relation to the circumstances of a new age of social mobility. The anxiety produced by the tensions of Elizabethan-Jacobean power struggles has something to do with Macbeth's lost confidence in the progress of events as a comprehensible sequence. Over the whole complex scene in which thought and life interacted and reflected one another, there hung a doubt of the human capacity to perceive life truly. This doubt is expressed with a curious precision in *Othello* but could also have been heard in contemporary witchcraft trials, a parallel I shall have occasion to enlarge upon in my chapter dealing with that play.

Is it too simple to suppose that during the years 1564 to 1616, when Shakespeare was alive, the uncertainty of common life unsettled settled convictions? Shakespeare's plays, as I shall show, reflect anxieties somehow become more intense and universal than previously. To begin with, traditional ideas about an inexplicable correspondence between disturbances in the human and natural worlds seemed confirmed by contemporary phenomena to an extraordinary degree. Such natural disasters as the unusually frequent crop failures that caused universal distress in the 1590s anticipated the development of a world ruled by market forces remote and incomprehensible to the average person. Even a good harvest was perverse misfortune for the hoarder referred to by Macbeth's Porter — an apt illustration of life's non-sequiturs. That Lady Macbeth never explains the fate of those absent children to whom she once gave suck may not have seemed a puzzle to early audiences; only half of London's children survived into adulthood. The sudden death of old as well as young was a constant reminder of the inexplicable. In 1603, around the time when Shakespeare was writing *Measure for Measure* and *Hamlet,* plays full of verbal reference to death and disease, one-sixth of the inhabitants of London — thirty-six thousand persons—died of the plague. The theaters were closed from mid-April of that year to the following April. James I was crowned in the midst of this siege of pestilence during a week in which more than eleven hundred Londoners died of it, and he had had to cancel his inaugural ride of pomp through the city. Like so much of life, the plague was a demonstration that disaster could strike without apparent origin—for so unknown was the source of infection that orders were sometimes given for the slaughter of the city's dogs and cats, though these animals were the population's safeguards against the London rat, the real vector. The secret causes of things were hidden from sight.

The Elizabethan-Jacobean person tended to believe that drought and pestilence were evidences of a universal disturbance. It would be readily felt that the storms that rage in *Julius Caesar* or *King Lear* are not merely poetic metaphor of social and political turmoil but literal symptoms of discord and disorder in all things. Not only had there been an earthquake in London in 1580, but the heavens seemed to manifest the arrest of normal rhythms in the universe by the nova in Cassiopeia in 1572, the comet of 1577, planetary conjunctions in 1583. Eclipses of the sun and moon aroused a peculiar terror. The obliteration of the heavenly regulators of the passage of day and night and of the months of the year was probably profoundly alarming to the average person, who did not understand the causes. Shakespeare seems to refer to contemporary astronomical perturbations and their effect on the public mood in all of his major tragedies. Taking note of the unnatural terrors of various sorts that accompanied the death of the old King Hamlet, Horatio mentions the phenomena supposed to have preceded the assassination of Caesar, recently depicted in Shakespeare's own play. To these portents Horatio adds "disasters in the sun" and the moon's eclipse, reminders to the theater audience of the solar and lunar eclipses of 1589–1601. Maybe G. R. Hibbard, the excellent Oxford editor, goes too far in saying that Horatio's remark occurs only to advertise *Julius Caesar* and "does not advance the action in any way." Catastrophe will come to Denmark in due course, though it will take the whole length of the play for its full measure to arrive. Nature's disorders will be shown to correspond to human disorders.

So the night passed on the battlements of Elsinore, where men barely recognize one another and the ghost appears, is a night like that in *Macbeth* when Duncan will be murdered. There is relief when Horatio, in such exquisite fashion, welcomes the "morn in russet mantle clad [who] / Walks o'er the dew of yon high eastward hill" at the end of the scene. But this mood is temporary. Ahead lie all the deaths, none of which is the consequence of any deliberated human plan—the deaths not only of Gertrude and Claudius, but of Polonius and Laertes and Ophelia, and of Hamlet himself—before the ghost's expectation of revenge is realized. On the night of Duncan's murder, the moon is down, as Fleance observes to Banquo, and he has not heard the clock. All heaven's "candles" are out, though Banquo dismisses this condition with a domestic witticism: "There's husbandry in heaven." More true to the portent of this particular night is the later description by Lennox and Ross of the hours that followed when the earth was "feverous and did shake," and "By th' clock 'tis day / And yet dark night strangles the travelling lamp"—as though there had been both earthquake and eclipse, bringing to mind images of deadly fever and strangulation. *Macbeth*'s setting of darkness lit by guttering lamps, of foul weather that hides the illuminations of sun, moon, and stars, of day turned into night, is not simply a poet's way with gloomy scenic atmosphere but a reference to the terror of real moments remembered by Shakespeare's audience when the regulators of clock and calendar disappeared from the skies. Such phenomena seemed more portentous because human events abounded in sudden change and

inexplicable reversal of normal expectation. In *King Lear,* Gloucester, a representative credulous Elizabethan, fears that "these late
eclipses in the sun and moon portend no good" — reflecting a widespread response to the successive eclipses of both in conjunction
with the Gunpowder Plot in the autumn of 1605. Othello sees his
wife's supposed betrayal as a time when there

> should be a huge eclipse
> Of sun and moon, and . . . th' affrighted globe
> Should yawn at alteration.

Such a sense of cosmic cause beyond mankind's control made
human events seem without origin in the will and character of any
person — and was, indeed, a threat to the idea of moral responsibility. For all his predestinarian convictions, Calvin protested the
determinism implied by astrology and would have accepted not
only Cassius's famous protest, "The fault, dear Brutus, is not in our
stars, / But in ourselves, that we are underlings," but also Edmund's
sneer at his father's astrological notions and Iago's insistence that
" 'Tis in ourselves that we are thus or thus. . . . The power and cor-
rigible authority of this lies in our wills." Calvin called the idea that
"all the evils wherewith the stars threaten us do proceed from the
order of nature" a "phantasy," a way of pleading, wrongly, "that
our sins are not the cause." But the mystery of human causes often
seems in Shakespeare's plays, as it often seemed in common experience, to be impenetrable.

Socially, historians have come to realize, the England of "good
queen Bess" was only fitfully merry for most, and uncertain for all.
Economic dislocation and political instability were as present as
the skies in the minds of English men and women as Elizabeth's
long reign came to an end. Those mysteriously frequent seasons of
drought or blight had combined with the long-time trend of the
enclosure of agricultural land to change the rural world, sending

men and women by the thousands in quest of a new basis of life, reduced to rags and beggary like Lear's "poor, naked wretches" and wandering along England's roads or seeking uncertain reconstitution in the great city of London. It was in 1601 that Parliament passed a poor-relief act obliging local parishes to help the needy, but reluctance to support the poor from other places led to "settlement laws" limiting migration. "Rogues, vagabonds, and sturdy beggars" were subject to whipping, banishment from the realm, or even execution. There was an army of young men in their teens or twenties who came to London from their distant homes seeking apprenticeships and hoping to prosper in the city—lured by the generally delusive myth of Dick Whittington, the dream of a total change of self from low to high. There was a new breed of "masterless men," defined as persons who acknowledged no affiliation to any superior in the medieval ladder of authority.

Others discovered unprecedented opportunity in a volatile economy. The more fortunate or canny achieved a wealth that transported them to styles of life, to senses of selfhood, their parents could not have imagined. As Hamlet remarks to Horatio in response to the jokes of the gravedigger, "The age is grown so picked [concerned with fashion] that the toe of a peasant comes so near the heel of the courtier he galls his kibe"—that is, scrapes his heel. Shakespeare himself was an example of the way wealth and status were accessible in the booming theater industry of a London seething with moneymaking. There was a febrile "culture of consumption" which attracted the newly prosperous from the remotest parts of the land to the great city that was the source of political and economic authority. London grew from 80,000 to 200,000 inhabitants in Shakespeare's lifetime. So conspicuous were these newcomers that official proclamations were issued urging their return to their rural homes to maintain the immemorial order and separations of the commonwealth, for, as King James himself said in 1616, "as every fish lives in his own place, some in the fresh, some in the salt, some in the mud: so let everyone live in his own place, some at Court, some in the Citie, some in the Country." Yet even for the fortunate, there was always the risk of slipping into a limbo of declassification and poverty. Even a favorite at court might fall out of favor, a fortune might be wasted or lost. For so very many, either way, the scheme of life that had once defined what one was and how one would live one's life had so thoroughly disappeared that there was a changeover in the traditional social categories that contain the self, and men and women found themselves behaving in new roles and differently costumed like actors in a play, as Shakespeare himself was likely to say.

During Shakespeare's lifetime, moreover, it was not only new social actualities that placed former assumptions in doubt. The minds of men and women were charged with the effects of cultural reformulations of a philosophic or religious sort. As it has been easy enough for historians to see, the Protestant attack on the institutional authority of the Catholic Church had opened a new source of uncertainty as Protestantism began to multiply the churches. Each was militant for its own creed; there was no longer any unquestionable, universal guide. In England the religion endorsed by the authority of the state in Henry VIII's time began by being Roman Catholic but went to a Catholicism in which the king was the head of the church yet persecuted extreme Protestants as well as "papists"; then the rule of the secular state became decisively Protestant under Edward VI and decisively Roman Catholic again under Mary Tudor; and Protestant again under Henry's third child, Elizabeth. It was also true that though religious faith was more intense than it had been for centuries, this faith had the daunting task of keeping at bay the devastating idea that God did not exist at all. The charge of skepticism was everyone's term of abuse, though Erasmus had defended his readiness to believe the truths of religion precisely because he was a skeptic. He had declared, in *The Praise of Folly*, that "human affairs are so obscure and various that nothing can be clearly known"—so one had best be a Christian Fool and lead a Christian life. To this, Luther had expostulated, "How can he believe that which he doubts?" The Holy Ghost, he said, "is not a skeptic and he has not inscribed in our hearts uncertain opinions, but, rather, affirmations of the strongest sort." Erasmus's skepticism actually merged with the view of the counterreformation Jesuits concerning the necessity of dogma and the renunciation of reason, for both agreed that one could not arrive by one's own powers of mind at true interpretations of Scripture, as the Reformers were saying. But the Protestant leaders wrote tracts attacking the skepticism of Rome. And the Catholic Church said that the Reformers were skeptics in disguise because they invited every man to discover his private truth—howsoever it differed from that of everyone else.

Renaissance skepticism was the special product of a state of belief that required an allowance of faith in the place of rational proof—thus an escape from, not an assertion of, atheism. Before writing his famous essays, Montaigne had translated a book by the fifteenth-century Spanish theologian Raymond Sebond, which was put on the Church's Index of Forbidden Books because it seemed to exalt reason and experience over dogma. Montaigne claimed that he had been prompted to this task by the threat to his Catholic faith of Lutheranism—to which Sebond's writing was a response. But when Montaigne came to write the longest and most famous of his essays, which called itself an "apologie" for Sebond, he himself went beyond his master in radical skepticism. Montaigne argued that reason was only an available aid to faith, as God willed it to be. "It is faith onely, which lively and assuredly embraceth the high mysteries of our Religion." It is the obligation of man to put in the service of faith "all the reason we possesse." Yet our reason is a weak instrument. "All our wisdome is but folly before God; that of all vanities, man is the greatest; that man, who presumeth of his knowledge, doth not yet know what knowledge is." The very weakness of our understanding, if we recognize it properly, leads us to God more readily than our presumption of knowledge. Such skepticism was as far as possible from the modern disbelief that is a kind of certainty in itself. It consisted of a readiness not so much to deny what had always been believed as to say that one could not really know one way or another. Understandably, the Catholic Church has never been at ease about Montaigne. His faith was accepted on its stated terms when his collection of essays was first published, yet his book was placed on the Index in 1676, as Sebond's writing had been a hundred years before. There is no reason to suspect that Montaigne's faith was not sincere—perhaps even passionate—precisely because it existed under threat. The fideist wall against doubt was always in danger of being breached. But his fideist faith is only one side of Montaigne's ambivalence, shared perhaps with Shakespeare when Hamlet vaguely suggests to Horatio that there are more things in heaven and earth than are dreamt of in his philosophy. On the other side there was unredeemable doubt.

Atheism was almost inadmissible in Shakespeare's day, though some accused persons are known to have confessed being *saved* from it. Thomas Harriot, the polymath intellectual whose perfected system of algebraic notation is still used, and who observed sunspots before Galileo with a telescope perhaps devised by himself, had a reputation for impiety though he always declared his religious faith. He had been the tutor of Sir Walter Raleigh—who sent him to Virginia, about which he wrote the first major colonial report—and Raleigh was sometimes suspected of atheism, too. One of the judges at Raleigh's treason trial warned him not to let "Harriot, nor any such Doctor, persuade you there is no eternity in Heaven, lest you find an eternity in hell-torments." As Stephen Greenblatt has pointed out, atheism, an unacknowledgeable or "unspeakable" viewpoint, was always a mark of damnation and otherness. That the accusation was made against Raleigh shows, moreover, that it was associated with the most absolute of political crimes.

Both Shakespeare and Montaigne exhibit, I believe, the effects of the current inclination of thought called Pyrrhonism, after Pyrrho, the third-century B.C. Greek who taught that nothing can be known. Science was about to open an era of self-confident discovery of natural causes, to suggest that not only could the motion of the planets and the sources of disease be discovered but that *everything* could be known. As the seventeenth century went on, the discoveries of science eventually established the very concept of causality. But it was doubt that initiated that search. Descartes's great enterprise started from a universal doubt from which only the famous *cogito* might rescue him. It enabled him to believe both in the existence of the world—about which God would not deceive us—and in God himself and a God-ordered world of first and secondary causes. Newton's *Principia* of 1687 is the culmination of the idea that not only is the universe knowable but that what happens in it can be explained by natural law.

Yet at the end of the sixteenth century this view still had not emerged. Only a few kinds of truth, like mathematical proofs, were practically attainable. Francis Bacon aspired, with his grand inductive program, to the ultimate restitution of "moral certainty," a concept borrowed from theology by which one might be sure of most things after observing and evaluating the facts. Bacon's efforts were directed precisely against that devastating suggestion of Montaigne that nothing could be rationally concluded as true. Montaigne said, "Que sais-je?"—and had the question struck on a medal with a representation on it of a poised balance, calling it his "emblem." The answer was: "Nothing." It was doubt itself and the weakness of the human mind in discerning the meaning and connection of events that sustained such a mind as Montaigne's in a condition of precarious faith.

How complexly doubt and credulity—or faith—contested in the mind is well illustrated by the response even of advanced thinkers to the topic of witchcraft, the obsession of the age. Few disputed the existence and power of witches throughout the seventeenth century. Robert Boyle, the inventor of the vacuum pump and the discoverer of the Law of Gases that bears his name, professed a belief in witches. Joseph Glanville, the author of the *Scepsis Scientifica,* who asserted that the greatest enemy of science was unwarranted belief in what cannot be proved, attested to a belief in witches and employed skeptical arguments to demolish the dogmatism of the critics of the witch belief. Even Montaigne's distinguished French contemporary, the political philosopher and reputed skeptic Jean Bodin, believed in sorcery and urged the burning of witches. It is not surprising that those who flatly refused to believe in witches were identified as atheists; the active presence of Satan might seem to guarantee, after all, the presence of God. Glanville said, "Those who dare not bluntly say, 'There is no God' content themselves (for a fair step and introduction) to deny there are Spirits and witches." But at the same time, witchcraft, with its suggestion that human nature can be inexplicably altered by possession, and the events of life directed into unexpected courses by forces beyond our detection—or visible only by demonic and misleading prophecy—must have attracted precisely the skeptical mind already impressed by the obliquity and mystery of life rather than by its evident meaningfulness. Was Shakespeare's mind so attracted? Perhaps we can only guess about his thoughts about this current intellectual topic, thoughts that may be just barely visible where witches are actually present, as in *Macbeth,* or suggestively referred to, as in *Othello.* In reading *Macbeth* one may suppose that the attraction of the belief in witches to the skeptical mind is to be explained by what the witches betoken—that the cosmos and the social world were not so obviously the expression of a rule of universal order. The witchcraft trials of the day, which Shakespeare must have followed with the same curiosity as everyone else, were, moreover, a demonstration of how inaccessible all truth might seem—a thought that prevails in *Othello*.

About disbelief in witches as a test of one's readiness to set aside irrational ideas, Montaigne was cautious. He does say, in the essay "Of the Force of Imagination," "It is very likely that the principall credit of visions, of enchantments, and such extraordinary effects, proceedeth from the power of imaginations, working especially in the mindes of the vulgar sort, as the weakest and seeliest, whose conceit and beleefe is so seized upon, that they imagine to see what they see not." But he says also, in another essay, "It Is Folly to Referre Truth or Falsehood to Our Sufficiencie,"

> It is not peradventure without reason, that we ascribe the facilitie of beleeving and easines of perswasion, unto simplicitie and ignorance. . . . Forasmuch therefore, as the minde being most emptie and without counterpoize, so much the more easily doth it yeeld under the burthen of the first perswasion. And that's the reason why children, those of the common sort, women, and sicke-folke, are so subject to be mis-led, and so easie to swallow gudgeons. Yet on the other side, it is a sottish presumption to disdaine and condemne that for false, which unto us seemeth to beare no shew of likelihood or truth: which is an ordinarie fault in those who perswade themselves to be of more sufficiency than the vulgar sort. So was I sometimes wont to doe, and if I heard any body speake, either of

ghosts walking, of foretelling future things, of enchantments, of witchcrafts, or any other thing reported, which
I could not well conceive, or that was beyond my reach
. . . I could not but feele a kind of compassion to see
the poore and seely people abused with such follies. And
now I perceive, that I was as much to be moaned my-
selfe: Not that experience hath since made me to dicerne
any thing beyond my former opinions: yet was not my
curiosity the cause of it, but reason hath taught me, that
so resolutely to condemne a thing for false, and impossible, is to assume unto himselfe the advantage, to have
the bounds and limits of God's will, and of the power of
our common mother Nature tied to his sleeve: And that
there is no greater folly in the world than to reduce them
to the measure of our capacitie, and bounds of our suif-
ficiencie.

The passage is as good an illustration as one can find in Montaigne's
Essayes of the character of his skepticism, which regards all things
doubtfully, and even applies doubt to the act of doubting, because
so many things cannot be known.

There is evidence that Shakespeare knew these essays directly.
He could have been reading them in the French editions published
in the 1580s, but we *know* that he read John Florio's translation —
from which I have been quoting — published in 1603, because no
later than 1605 or 1606 Shakespeare wrote *King Lear,* in which a
number of passages echo Florio. In *King Lear,* besides, more than
one hundred words have been counted that Shakespeare never used
in his previous writing but which are shared with Florio. Of course,
every play of Shakespeare's contains words he had not previously
used but had picked up somewhere, perhaps just out of current
talk. But the assimilation of Florio suggested by this degree of lin-

guistic relation is striking. It has even been claimed that Shakespeare may have seen Florio's Montaigne before it got into print but after it had been entered into the Stationer's Rolls in 1600. The general trade in manuscripts, it is now believed, had not yet been displaced by the sale of printed books. And Montaigne was the kind of new stuff—the latest thing around—that might have been talked about and passed about in manuscript among young men just down from the universities, Inns of Court men studying the law but fascinated by the theater, writers and theater people and intellectual young aristocrats often to be caught, like Prince Hamlet, with a book in hand, but often eagerly reading a new work even before the printer got it. It is likely that Shakespeare got at Montaigne that way—a common process by which the thoughts of a dangerous, almost interdicted writer were diffused.

In the same way, in the sixteenth century, Machiavelli's disregard of old beliefs about the sacredness of princely authority might have put off a cautious printer when *The Prince* got to be talked about—more talked about than read or understood—by the English. Machiavelli, like Montaigne, always professed belief in God, but he challenged the view that politics was an expression of heavenly purpose—a skepticism that more and more fitted the modus of the Tudor politician, however much such a thought seemed nearly atheistic. Fear of the Florentine's practical counsel to ambitious men was expressed popularly on the stage in the stock figure of the scheming "Machiavel," although publication of an English edition of *The Prince* did not take place until 1636. But handwritten copies of inaccurate translations traveled from reader to reader before any were published. There is no way of knowing if Shakespeare read Machiavelli directly as Francis Bacon and Walter Raleigh did, but he would have absorbed a Machiavelli influence from the currents of the air he breathed as he wrote his plays and created a wicked Richard III or a Claudius, an Iago, an Edmund, or a Macbeth, in all of whom Machiavelli's ideas about politic conduct and the way to power are reflected.

One can hardly doubt that Shakespeare heard speculative discussions in London stimulated by a new interest in the recently rediscovered writings of classical skepticism, which had already been assimilated by Montaigne. Those meetings at the Mermaid Tavern in which Shakespeare lifted a tankard with Ben Jonson and others, including Raleigh, may be only legend, but Shakespeare could have seen Raleigh's translation of the *Hypotyposes* of Sextus Empiricus. It was circulating—also in manuscript—as early as 1591, when one of the "university wits" Shakespeare undoubtedly knew, Thomas Nashe, read it. The clever young men who caught the latest word on the wind would have been eager to get a look at Montaigne—a writer who knew Sextus but went beyond him in brilliance and daring—as soon as the translation was heard of. Florio himself was in the entourage of the Earl of Southampton; he had been the young lord's Italian tutor. And Shakespeare had dedicated his first published poem, *Venus and Adonis,* and then *Lucrece,* to this same patron who was, possibly, also the "Mr. W.H" to whom the poet dedicated his *Sonnets.* The alternate candidate for the honor of the *Sonnets* dedication has been, of course, another youthful aristocrat with literary interests, the Earl of Pembroke, to whom Shakespeare's theater colleagues, Heminges and Condell, dedicated their posthumous Folio edition of his works. Pembroke, as well, might have connected Shakespeare to Florio. The poet-playwright Samuel Daniel was, as it happens, one of those who had the chance to study Florio's translation in manuscript, for the London printer of the *Essayes* included in the published book a blurb by Daniel, a fulsome poem of praise addressed to his "deere friend John Florio." Daniel had been Pembroke's tutor and remained his friend as he grew older. But even without a connection through this lord, Shakespeare certainly knew Daniel, who would become licenser of the Children of the Queen's Revels, rivals of Shakespeare's own company, the King's Men. Daniel's *Cleopatra,* based on Plutarch, had been published in 1594, and Shakespeare took hints from it when he wrote his *Antony and Cleopatra* in 1606; Daniel then promptly revived and improved his own older play by reciprocal imitation of Shakespeare.

One way or another, we have grounds for supposing that Shakespeare knew Florio's translation before writing *Hamlet,* on stage a year before the book was out and for sale. *Hamlet* adds more words to Shakespeare's known vocabulary that also are in Florio—even a slightly greater number than is the case with *King Lear.* In Ben Jonson's *Volpone* (1605), someone reports that "all our English writers" are ready to "steal" from "Montaignie." If Shakespeare is included in this reference, his interest in Montaigne was already noticed by his contemporaries—or, at least by so perceptive a friendly rival as this fellow-dramatist. But there seems not to have been any more specific notice of the relation of Shakespeare and Montaigne until the eighteenth century, when the editor Edward Capell drew attention to the way *The Tempest* seems almost to put into verse parts of Florio's version of the essay "Of the Caniballes." A Montaigne "influence" has, ever since, been a standard assumption by scholars, who have drawn up tables of close or not-so-close parallel passages purporting to show similarities between ideas expressed in Shakespeare and in other essays in Montaigne's collection. There is even a copy of Florio in the British Museum which contains a Shakespeare signature some think genuine.

But I do not want to insist too hard that Montaigne was what is loosely called a "source." Many of the parallels that have been pointed out are stock proverbial statements or could have come from writers other than Montaigne, and can be lined up in another list of parallels with someone else. The possibility of such gleanings of words or passages is less important than the fact that Shakespeare would have encountered in Montaigne a dissident mind to which his was profoundly responsive as much as or more than to Machiavelli's. It is more important to say that Shakespeare and Montaigne were co-inhabitants of a particular sphere that swung through the space of human life at the time of the birth of the modern world. Others rode with them. Though the *Tempest* connection seems almost certain, it is really more important to notice the common interest Shakespeare and Montaigne had in the theme of the "natural" versus the "civilized," expressed in both the "Caniballes" essay and *The Tempest*—and the cultural relativism the comparison suggested. It was an interest that must have been shared by many in the age of European discovery of the rest of the globe and its peoples. And a relation to Montaigne may be greatest where there are fewest direct traces of specific transfer. *Othello,* written in 1603 or 1604, does not so strongly exhibit those verbal markers of Shakespeare's fingering of Florio to be noted in *Lear* or *Hamlet,* and no specific transmission need be inferred from my argument that Montaigne's unease about the presumption that truth is deducible from appearances is the same unease expressed in *Othello.* But in the "apologie of Raymond Sebond" Montaigne repeats examples given by early skeptics like Cornelius Agrippa and Sextus that a flat painting can appear three-dimensional, that sweet wine tastes bitter to a sick person, and numerous other instances when our senses deceive us. He asks whether the qualities we think we discern in objects are real—and moves from this to a general skepticism about the validity of our perceptions. In a philosophically related way, jealousy, as Shakespeare presents it in this play, is a crisis of epistemological confidence that brings everything into doubt. Of the four plays I consider as Shakespeare's tragic core, *Macbeth* is farthest from Montaigne's cheerfully stoic mood—yet this dark and mysterious work, as I shall try to show, may be an outcome of Montaigne's skepticism—and of Machiavelli's correlative cynicism—pushed to an excruciating intensity that annihilates in particular the linkage of cause and effect, human selfhood and act. It is because I want to identify such companionships of mind belonging to the last years of the sixteenth century and the early years of the seventeenth that I will refer occasionally to Montaigne's essays in particular as a way of pointing up some of Shakespeare's meanings. The demonstration of Shakespeare's skepticism must, in any case, rest on what one can discover directly in the dramatized dilemmas of these plays that arrived in the London theater in such an astounding burst of splendor between 1600 and 1606.

My discussion will go against the grain of much past criticism by concentrating on evidences of what might seem the great artist's bumbles or omissions, his inattentiveness to traditional dramatic requirements. It is a fact that Shakespeare's chief personages often seem to lack clearly defined and consistent characters and motives. The sequence of events in the plays sometimes fails to compose a logical story in which one thing leads to another. Yet criticism, as one knows, often rewrites, failing to see what it is not prepared to see—and these greatest of the master playwright's plays are most often discussed as though the opposite were true. Some few, of course, have faulted Shakespeare for lapses that meaner talents never have had trouble avoiding. The eighteenth-century novelist Charlotte Lennox wrote a book called *Shakespear Illustrated: or the Novels and Histories, on Which the plays of Shakespear are Founded,* stating her actual preference for the way the writers who had given Shakespeare suggestions for his plots had made matters easier to understand than the great playwright had done. The same critique and the same preference were declared by Tolstoy, when he wrote at the beginning of the twentieth century that Shakespeare had "weakened and spoiled" his original stories by leaving his characters without motive. Hamlet's delay in executing revenge; Othello's exaggerated vulnerability to suggestion and Iago's malice; Lear's foolish decision to renounce power and his throne, and Cordelia's refusal to indulge a father who loved her best; Macbeth's unforeseeable disloyalty and murderousness—all these receive more explanation in Shakespeare's sources, Tolstoy complained, than Shakespeare deigned to include in his plays.

But how can one agree with such an elevation of realist sensemaking in plays that sometimes lack it yet leave us wrung with grief and exaltation? Is it really a negative observation that the vastly inferior stories upon which each of these plays was based gave answers and explanations Shakespeare did not reach for? Shakespeare, it would seem, *liked to* reduce rather than fortify the circumstances that explain what his characters do, and he often refused to provide a basis for easy summary of what they are. To Lennox and Tolstoy we might respond that his indifference to such obvious coherence allowed him to express another view of life, a view we call skeptical though it might have seemed tragic to Aristotle, who did not believe that character made for fate. Shakespeare's major tragedies, the four that are the core of my discussion as well as the two Roman plays that "frame" them, sometimes seem like old fairy tales or myths—studies of human adjustment to an unforeseen destiny assigned by the immemorial tale that precedes the person who happens to inherit it. The gap between person and deed illustrates a classical idea of tragedy, the descent of fate, the destined catastrophe for which there has been *no* preparation or explanation.

Early-twentieth century critics, reading the plays like poems, as the Romantics had, declared that Shakespeare provided meaning by something vaguely called "atmosphere." His poetic language, particularly continuous patterns of imagery, tied things together. But Shakespeare does not discard the idea—basic to the way we strive to think about human life—that there are persons and there are events, and that the mind must *strive* to connect the two, however, at times, unsuccessfully. He compels us to share the *effort* toward connection and coherence his dramas still represent under duress, just as his chief characters themselves seek meaningfulness in their lives. Shakespeare works not only to promote the erasure of motive and destabilize character, to disconnect plot and make events inexplicable, and to deny the reliability of human impressions. He also lets us hold onto a sense of human individuality somehow independent of complete demonstration. In *Othello,* despite Iago's irresistible reasoning, the actual representation of personality in the play makes a shambles of his "likelihoods" concerning Desdemona. Iago is a manipulator of appearances; Othello should not have believed him. The narrative of the love of Othello and Desdemona survives Iago's assault. But doubt has been lodged in our minds—there is, to a lingering minor degree, the terrible possibility that there is some basis for Iago's charges. The alternative play written by this rival playwright within the play hovers over Shakespeare's *Othello,* and we experience the shudder that comes from the realization that absolute certainty is not possible. Hamlet, whose "inky cloak" of conventional mourning hides a seeming vacuum, and who seems to act out his revenge as though it has been a wearisome role in a stale play, remains the "sweet prince" whom Horatio blesses at the end. The character of Hamlet illustrates, as we shall see, the effect of a double view that contributes to the often-remarked richness of Shakespearean characterization; he has both a self to which he must be true and no self. Those other great characters of Shakespeare's I will be talking about, also—Lear and Macbeth—are always persons, however complicatedly inconsistent.

Harold Bloom has said recently that Shakespeare "invented" for literature the idea—later so important 'for the novel—of characters who develop rather than unfold, and who are, as Hegel said, "free artists of themselves." It is certainly true that we think Shakespeare's characters "real" precisely because they are not easily confined to a cartoon outline. They contradict themselves and change. They refute definitions of themselves. The mostly formulaic summaries that seem to contain them also seem untrue to what we want to feel about them, and about ourselves—that we are somehow more than any of our conditions, more even than our acts, that ours is a potentiality which life will never completely exhaust. And yet this still leaves them—and us—vulnerable to the skeptical doubt, the terrifying sense that we are nothing in ourselves; only our deeds, however they came about, make us. That we believe in the unenacted possibilities of Shakespeare's characters—as we believe in our own—is one of those leaps of faith art and religion persuade us to make. If Shakespeare is a Renaissance skeptic, he is, like Montaigne, also a believer who sustains himself by faith alone.

But still—after acknowledging that Shakespeare allows chaos and mystification to get in where we are looking for order and explanation, am I not claiming a unifying intention in what may have been only inattention? Didn't Ben Jonson say that Shakespeare was careless? I anticipate that I may be accused of trying to discover artistic meaning where there is simply artistic defect—if so, guilty of a version of what used to be called "bardolatry." And how securely, anyway, can we argue for unifying intention from Shakespeare—who may not have valued consistency and total meaningfulness in what he wrote? These plays which have been so often searched for the author's single viewpoint may not even be the result of one man's will alone. Recent studies of the Elizabethan theater have described the complex collaboration of playwright, actors, theater producers, and audiences that is not made visible simply by the discovery that someone else wrote some part of the text, like the interpolated Hecate scene in *Macbeth*. These plays that are the product of one of the greatest of individual imaginations are less personal than we have supposed.

The master playwright was probably more accommodating to the ideas of others than we like to think. That Shakespeare's meanings are multiple and elusive and even compete with one another—that he is "myriad-minded"—may have an explanation the Romantics did not reach for in their exaltation of the unique vision of genius. I have said that the plays allow us to discover in them contending viewpoints. These may not have all been Shakespeare's own but those of other wills and tastes that merged with his unknown separateness, perhaps sharing his vision, perhaps arguing with it, but still accommodated by his own act of composition. That these accommodations were made in a spirit of active hospitality may be possible. What Shakespeare seems to have been persuaded to "leave out" or decided to leave out without prompting is often as significant as what he admitted into his writing. I shall be looking at this matter particularly in the case of *Macbeth,* whose discontinuities are sometimes attributed to supposed theater cuts in the only text we have of that play. But the argument for Shakespeare's preference for a certain indefiniteness may be made just as plausibly where we have more than one authoritative text, as in *Hamlet.* There, the least Shakespearean, though earliest, text seems to clarify matters made obscure in the two versions on which we mostly depend for the more authentic intention of the playwright, and the play appears to travel on to its final version toward not a more visible but a more obscured logic. In looking at these and other instances in which uncertainty occurs, I hope to discover, after all, that meaning often lurks just where it seems to break down. Stephen Orgel has observed recently that the instability of Shakespeare's texts seems to "release" his characters from our expectations of credibility and psychological consistency. The curious thing is that this very release seems to invite a skepticism that the playwright could have been willing to let us entertain. *Hamlet,* as I shall begin by showing, represents a mind that could have resembled the playwright's own in its contesting engagement with received ideas of self and destiny. *Hamlet* gives us more insight than any other work of the age into a great artist's struggle to be impossibly free, and his subjection in the end to others' expectations—a struggle which is itself a mirror of the always-threatened human enterprise to discover a final and independent self and an interpretable life.

To the argument rounded out by my discussion of *Hamlet, Othello, King Lear,* and *Macbeth,* I have added an extra chapter. Somehow the door would not quite shut as I came to the end I had anticipated. I found that I wanted to look again at the "Roman plays" that enclose these four in the sequence of Shakespeare's production to see what relation they bear to the great tragedies. When *Hamlet* was first presented in 1599, *Julius Caesar,* written earlier in the year, was fresh in the theater public's mind. Horatio's description in the opening scene of the prodigies that had preceded Julius's assassination is a reference that the audience must have picked up right away to similar descriptions in the earlier play. When Polonius boasts that in a college production he "did enact Julius Caesar [and had been] killed i' th' capital," there could have been a shudder of anticipation in seeing that this Polonius, soon to be killed by Hamlet, had been Caesar weeks before and that the leading actor vividly recalled as Brutus was now Hamlet. *Macbeth* was probably written about the same time as the later Roman play. Though their atmosphere is very different, there are passages that suggest that Shakespeare was thinking of both at once, as when Macbeth says that he fears Banquo, and observes, "My genius is rebuked, as it is said,/ Mark Antony's was by Caesar"—referring to a remark in *Antony and Cleopatra.* This play may have been completed shortly *after Macbeth;* it bears signs of Shakespeare's retrospect of all the previous tragedies, including *Julius Caesar,* which had not only produced a Roman sequel but had also forecast *Macbeth* as a play about political assassination.

That *Julius Caesar* and *Antony and Cleopatra* were different from the famous four was obvious. Tragic they were, but not tragic in the same way as the others. Yet still, the issues of personal destiny emerge more profoundly in this pair than in either Shakespeare's previous history plays or the plays of his final period after 1607. It is probably significant that their chief source is the greatest he ever drew upon—the historian Plutarch. It was in Plutarch that Shakespeare found the hint that Cassius was an Epicurean—a follower, that is, of a classic skeptic, some of whose ideas reappear in Montaigne—and this helps us to understand how Cassius came to stand as a model for the development of Iago. But above all, I think, it was Plutarch's struggles to rationalize the accidents of Roman history and the contradictons of historical record that inspired Shakespeare. As in Plutarch, the relation of social power to self-definition seems already unresolvable in *Julius Caesar* and continues to be a difficult issue in what he wrote during the next few years. It is an issue that receives its most ironic treatment in *Antony and Cleopatra*. The dispersed viewpoint that is almost a structural difficulty when Shakespeare seems unable to take the perspective either of Caesar or of Brutus is continued in the relativity that makes for skepticism in all the later plays, and most extravagantly in *Antony and Cleopatra*. And so, the Roman plays frame the four that are my central subject in this book.

I

Hamlet, Revenge!

When, at the end of the second act, Hamlet bawls, "Bloody, bawdy villain!/ Remorseless, treacherous, lecherous, kindless villain!/ O, vengeance!" the audience laughed, I guess, the way modern audiences laugh when viewing Mel Brooks's *Young Frankenstein.* They recognized a horror-thriller style old-fashioned enough to be funny; this was the way the Revenger hero of Thomas Kyd's *Spanish Tragedy* had ranted on the stage fifteen years before. Shakespeare's modern editors disagree about the "O, vengeance," which appears only in the 1623 Folio. The editor of the Arden *Hamlet,* who commits himself to the earlier Second Quarto, where it is missing, thinks it must have been put in later by someone else, probably an actor. It jars, he feels, with the brooding self-reproach Hamlet has just expressed after hearing an actor orate about the avenging of Achilles by his son Pyrrhus and about the grief of Hecuba over slaughtered Priam. The editors of both the Oxford and the New Cambridge editions think Shakespeare wrote it himself, and they take it very seriously, the Cambridge editor remarking: "This cry, the great climax of the rant with which Hamlet emulates the Player, exhausts his futile self-recrimination, and he turns, in proper disgust, from a display of verbal histrionics to more practical things."

I, too, think it was Shakespeare's, but I disagree about its tone and intent. It is really a nudge to the funny bone of the sophisticated theatergoer of 1601. It resulted from the irrepressible leaking out of the playwright's satiric impulse in the midst of high seriousness. If so, it is a small sign of what happens elsewhere in *Hamlet*. The elocutionary set piece that has moved Hamlet to this exclamation is itself an imitation of the style of a creaky older play about Queen Dido of Carthage. Hamlet is not put off by its stiff rhetoric; the mercilessness of the blood-smeared Pyrrhus and Hecuba's lamentation stir him profoundly by their application to his case. But the theater buffs in the audience must have been amused. And perhaps also by "The Murder of Gonzago," which the company of strolling players soon puts on according to Hamlet's instruction. This is, apparently, another Revenge Tragedy, as the type is called—one, like Kyd's, with a Spanish setting—but it will represent his own father's murder and so cause his uncle to acknowledge his crime. Its character as parody is indicated by Hamlet's impatient exclamation to the actor who comes on as the murderer: "Pox, leave thy damnable faces and begin. Come—'the croaking raven doth bellow for revenge.'" Hamlet is asking for recollection of a line in *True Tragedy of Richard III*, which had been on the stage ten years before. That raven and its bellow strike the very note, now become comical, of the old Revenge plays. And this was not merely a matter of the wearing-out of theatrical motifs. In Shakespeare's time, we must remind ourselves, the ancient revenge theme remembered in medieval traditions of tribal feud was already an archaic idea. With the ascension of James I in 1603, an analogy could be made between the situation of Shakespeare's Hamlet and that of the new king. Though James was the son of an executed royal mother who had been a hereditary claimant to the English throne, he did not consider reprisal against her enemies at the English court. Familial blood-feud must have seemed a cause no longer relevant to the program of a modern head of state.

"The Murder of Gonzago" is, I would say, a fictitious play invented by Shakespeare as an example of the kind of dramatic entertainment he makes fun of at various points in *Hamlet*. Though Hamlet is supposed to have added some lines, there is no evidence of the voice we know him by in the fragment we hear before a terrified Claudius rises from his seat. It is stale bombast cast into out-of-style couplets, unlike the naturalistic dialogue enclosing it. Shakespeare seems to have wanted to exaggerate its theatricality. He sets it in contrast with the reality of a modern—though medieval—Denmark. At the same time, Shakespeare is letting the audience know it is going to see the unfolding in his play, despite its realism, of just another such tale of teeth-grinding and bloody setting-to-rights as those it used to find so thrilling. The *Hamlet* world is a contemporary realm, and the thought behind it belongs to that latest Renaissance moment Shakespeare shares with Michel de Montaigne. Yet it deliberately frames its modernity within an archaic kind of story ultimately finding its model in Seneca, that of its probable source, a lost Revenge Tragedy, also by Thomas Kyd. This "ur-Hamlet," as the scholars call it, was undoubtedly the play remembered by a contemporary as including a "ghost who cried so miserably at the Theatre like an oyster-wife, *Hamlet revenge!*" Shakespeare's *Hamlet* has all the prescribed features of the once-popular genre (and its surprising retro success helped bring the genre back into popularity). It has a ghost who demands revenge for a murder and a hero who promises to achieve it, pretends to be mad, indulges in philosophic soliloquies, and does not succeed in his purpose till the end of five acts. Even a play-within-a-play is a favorite of older plays of this kind. Moreover, like *The Spanish Tragedy*, which has all the features just mentioned, *Hamlet* also has a secondary revenge plot which brings about the completion of the main plot; it is Laertes' drive to avenge the death of *his* father, Polonius, which takes the action to its finish. The audience would recognize these reprises and wait for the turn Shakespeare would put on them.

What he did was employ them all with a difference—make the play-within-the-play an ironic giveaway, make a teasing mystery of the delay of the execution of revenge which once had served just to extend suspense, make his hero's detached soliloquies exceed in profundity and poetry anything the theater had ever heard, make the madness the Revenger is supposed to feign to conceal his purposes an occasion for paradoxical wit and cynic philosophy as well as a symptom of the hero's real mental anguish, introduce in Laertes the model of the effective Revenger yet use Hamlet's relation to the Polonius family as an opportunity to contrast him with "normal," or ordinary, persons. But, as though reminding the audience of his effort to reincarnate the old Revenge persona, as though, indeed, representing his creator's own surrendered skepticism, Hamlet will still shout at the end, when Laertes threatens to outdo him in melodramatic grief for Ophelia, "Nay, an thou'lt mouth, / I'll rant as well as thou."

It has been suggested that Shakespeare himself was the author of the lost "ur-Hamlet," and that what we have is only a revision of his own earlier work. But this seems unlikely. The play we know is consciously set *against* another version of its story and seems to question that version's conspicuous marks of type as though to point out what a different thing Shakespeare was inclined to write. T. S. Eliot decided that *Hamlet* was a failure because he detected in it the signs of an unsuccessful struggle against what he called "intractable material." Shakespeare wanted, he said, to write about something else, the effect of a mother's guilt upon her son, but forced himself to impose this motive on the old revenge story someone asked him to spruce up—and failed. This is wrong unless one accepts Eliot's questionable idea of the play's theme, but he was right to insist on the layered nature of *Hamlet*. There is no doubt that Shakespeare engages his literary model with some irritability. But in doing so, his genius discovered a different interest in the story than Eliot's psychosexual one. He succeeded, I believe, in representing a condition of mind that cannot either dismiss or dispense with models no longer congenial yet inescapable. In his extraordinary hero he represented that condition.

Hamlet's postmodern status as "metatheater"—theater about theater—is obvious enough, and not only because of the way it exhibits its relation to its theatrical precedents. We must suspect that the writer has inserted some reference to himself in the play, reminding us, as he does so, that what we are reading or seeing is only a play, after all, an unreliable representation of that assumed reality we call life. Was not the author himself an actor? Shakespeare was a theater man fascinated by the problems of his craft—and his Hamlet not only knows the theatrical scene of Shakespeare's time but gives judicious advice to actors and can act creditably himself and write a dramatic script or part of one; he loves to see a play put on, quite aside from its possible use as a conscience-catcher. It is not surprising that he thinks in theater terms, seeing himself as an actor who has "the motive and the cue for passion." There are, from the earliest moment to the last, occasions when the curtain between the theatrical and the supposedly real is rent—beginning with Hamlet's remark when the ghost can be heard groaning as it retreats to its purgatorial exile, "You hear this fellow in the cellarage"—*cellarage* being a term that reminds the audience that an actor is making noises down in the space beneath the stage. At a theater like the Globe, where the same company played repeatedly, the audience was always aware of the man playing the part; when Polonius said that he had played Caesar, it would be remembered that, indeed, the actor had done so only recently in *Julius Caesar*—and be prepared for Polonius's death at the hands of the Hamlet who had been Brutus. Metatheatricality is detectable elsewhere in the literature of the Elizabethan stage, and Shakespeare's earlier plays give an emphasis to common terms that suggest the theater: words like *cue*—or *tragedy, play, prologue, perform, show, act, scene,* or *part*—are frequent. But *Hamlet* is particularly rich in such language, as has often been noted. What has not been sufficiently discerned is that Hamlet's theater interest—and all the hints and references to the theatrical in the play—constitute a metaphoric motif and the tracking sign of a dominating theme. Hamlet is a play about a man who recognizes—in a way we can surely relate to in our day—that he lives in a forest of representations of himself, and that there is no sure substance and constancy that transcends this phantasmagoria.

"All the world's a stage," as Jacques says in *As You Like It.* Life is "a poor player that struts and frets his hour upon the stage," as Macbeth says. The idea was an old one. The Globe Playhouse is supposed to have displayed on a sign the words "Totus mundus agit histrionem," attributed to Petronius. The theatrical, for Shakespeare's audience, is what our multiple media are for us— as Michael Almereyda suggests in his recent film by surrounding his twenty-first-century Hamlet played by the young Ethan Hawke with tape machines, video cameras, and television and computer monitors in a skyscraper-housed corporate Elsinore. By such means, and the mind-processes they represent, we perceive the shifting reality of ourselves, projections created by a culture obsessed by the imaging not only of the arts but of all the media of "information" and by the publicity engines of commerce and politics. What being we have, then, may be only what we appear to be on a phantasmic screen.

As a conventional theater piece, "The Murder of Gonzago" challenges the objective status of events that are supposed to have preceded those we have been permitted to witness directly. It also reminds us that these later visible events are themselves the matter of a play, Shakespeare's *Hamlet*. And this flow of theatricality expands outward from the edge of the stage. Those ranks of interested spectators in the Danish court who watch the performance by the visiting players are mirrored by the theater filled with the spectators of Shakespeare's play. Each spectator in either audience is, besides, not only a viewer of the action but an actor, too. An eighteenth-century antiquary by the name of Oldys claimed to have seen a manuscript in which Jonson and Shakespeare exchanged these verses:

> JONSON. If but *stage actors,* all the world displays,
>   Where shall we find *spectators* of their plays?
> SHAKESPEARE. Little, or much, of what we see, we do;
>   We're all both *actors* and *spectators* too.

Within Shakespeare's play itself, actors are often audiences and audiences actors. When Hamlet observes Claudius at prayer, he is the observer posted where he cannot be observed, though he fails to detect the deception in the performance, fails to realize that it is *only* performance, a mere appearance of repentance. Hamlet himself is observed by Polonius from behind an arras both in the "nunnery" scene with Ophelia and the parallel scene with his mother in her closet. The theatricality of the situation may lie in Hamlet's apparent oblivion—as an actor must arrive at a state in which he is only half-conscious of the spectators in the theater. With Ophelia, Hamlet may be "playing a scene" for her alone, unaware of hidden witnesses. But he may be acting a role for unseen viewers whose presence he suspects. Like a script, the constraints of social life and inherited or acquired forms, it is implied, limit the spectator in the theater to a life of prescribed performance. We who watch *Hamlet* are not only spectators but actors in some larger cosmic theater enclosing us. We embrace roles which do not express any essences of our own, any "characters" that maintain themselves beneath appearance and behavior dictated by the parts for which we have been cast.

The theatricality of actual disguise is not present in the play; it is, in fact, to be seen in only one of the tragedies I am discussing in this book, *King Lear,* where, as we shall observe, it plays a major role. Hamlet's feigned madness—if that is what he exhibits—is a disguise like the disguises of a mystery story, but one that does not break down, finally, to reveal the truth being sought. What this appearance of madness conceals or reveals is never clearly evident. But the play is, nevertheless, full of concealment and spying, as in those spectatorial moments I have already compared to the relation of actors and audience in the theater. Polonius, who sends a spy to look into the life abroad of his own son, is ludicrous and inefficient in his surveillance of Hamlet, and dies for his own spying upon the prince. Only when he is dead is he said by Hamlet to be, at last, "most still, most secret, and most grave," an achieved secret-service man. Rosencrantz and Guildenstern deserve Hamlet's contempt for the inefficacy of their prying, and he tells them, "You would play upon me, you would seem to know my stops, you would pluck out the heart of my mystery, you would sound me from my lowest note to the top of my compass; and there is much music, excellent voice, in this little organ, yet cannot you make it speak, 'Sblood, do you think I am easier to be played on than a pipe?" If Hamlet's "mystery" is more—or perhaps less—than the secret plans he is suspected of nursing, it is ultimately unknowable. Yet he himself is a spy among spies; he undertakes to find clear evidence of his uncle's guilt and to confirm the accusation of his father's ghost, an enterprise that may be judged only partly successful.

Shakespeare does not reveal Hamlet's state of mind in the nunnery scene, does not make evident what he really feels about Ophelia, what he knows or doesn't know about the surveillance of Polonius. This is one of the notorious gaps that make the play seem incomplete until performed, and as such it is another sign of the play's uncompromising theatricality. A director soon discovers that something must be done to clarify a situation about which the playwright has given no hints. It has been suggested—without real evidence—that Hamlet has already overheard Ophelia being given instructions to spy on him, and that his "Nymph in thy orisons" greeting is ironic. Most productions of the play try to make it clear that he soon guesses the presence of an observer, in any case, and improvise a rustle behind the arras at which the actor starts before he asks Ophelia where her father is. But it is the theater that imposes a more definite meaning on such a moment though the writer has been more reticent. Such reticence may be the essential nature of dramatic literature, and particularly of Elizabethan drama, but most of all of this great and mysterious play of Shakespeare's.

Of course, such indefiniteness, such irreducible mystery or contradiction that leaves clarification to the performance, is sometimes blamed simply on the state of the text of *Hamlet*. Notoriously, there is more than one *Hamlet* book. The imperfect but earliest First Quarto, which seems based on an actor's recollections of his own and others' parts, contains a few hints about how the play might have been first produced and fills in a few important gaps—perhaps reflecting the effect of a production in making the indefinite definite. It is in this *Hamlet* and not in either the Second Quarto or the 1623 Folio that Gertrude denies any knowledge of her husband's murder. In these other two earliest editions, her complicity remains an unresolved possibility. It is only in the First Quarto, also, that a stage direction says that Hamlet actually jumps into Ophelia's open grave to wrestle with Laertes, a detail that affects our view of Hamlet's personality at so late a moment, emphasizing the startling breakdown of his composure, the revelation of the suppressed romantic passion his Revenger role has not allowed him to express. The Second Quarto, which most scholars think was printed from Shakespeare's preproduction manuscript, is more indeterminate about such matters although it is the longest of the three texts. In this version, nevertheless, Hamlet lets his mother know that he has somehow got wind of the fact that Rosencrantz and Guildenstern are to accompany him to England as "engineers" of his destruction, and that he will "hoist [them] with [their] own petard"—which makes his revenge against them a premeditated engineering on his own part. It is in the still later Folio, which also seems to bear marks of Shakespeare's own revisionary participation, that the connection between act and intent is loosened by the omission of this passage. Hamlet's midnight impulse to open his escorts' sealed letters—by which he learns of their perfidy—arises only aboard ship, out of obscure prompting in the midst of sleepless tossing in his berth. He later remarks, "Our indiscretion sometimes serves us well / When our dear plots do pall," and concludes that human ends are seldom the consequence of our purposes, though some inscrutable divine intent may direct our lives. A more striking Folio deletion is of that scene and soliloquy in the Second Quarto's glimpse of martial Fortinbras and of Hamlet's admiration and intent to emulate him expressed in his outburst, "How all occasions do inform against me." Though this seems illogically placed in Act IV, it expresses very well the hero's respect for the man fit to take over Denmark. But a more indeterminate Hamlet—no longer so simply the dedicated revenger—remains when it is removed.

Until recently editors wrestled to reconcile the elements of the several editions in a single "conflated" text that contains fewer holes of meaning of the kind just referred to. There is something wrong about such an attempt to create what may never have been either written or acted. Each of the versions may represent *Hamlet* at a particular moment. But in the end, Shakespeare may have preferred us to have less rather than more confident knowledge about the explanation of events. It is also true that discrepancies among the early texts may remind us that Shakespeare is incompletely the author of his play. The revamping of the old *Hamlet* was probably a task assigned by his theater company. The testing of production, the inclinations of director and actors in giving representation to what he first wrote, but also the responses of audiences to this revival of the old Hamlet story—all these controlled to some degree his interpretation of his sources, the Latin history of the Danes written in the beginning of the thirteenth century by Saxo Grammaticus and a recent work-up of it in French by François Belleforest, as well as the general Revenge design probably present in the earlier Hamlet play. So—picking and choosing, adding and omitting, Shakespeare leaves a good deal to the actor, but something inherent in this permissiveness remains.

He seems to leave it to the actor representing Hamlet to decide the question of Hamlet's madness in the nunnery scene and elsewhere. In the Revenge tradition, madness is used by the avenger to divert suspicion; in Shakespeare it actually arouses it, so that it has no practical function. Can it then be genuine, after all? Belleforest's Hamlet had good reason to fear a murderer who has killed openly before witnesses at a banquet and who knows that vengeance is on its way unless he finishes off the probable avenger, and such a Hamlet could only hope to protect himself by pretending to be an idiot or a madman. After the ghost's revelation, Hamlet does tell Horatio and Marcellus that he may put on an "antic disposition," but this seems unnecessary, and we are never sure, as time passes, to what degree he is carrying on such a pretense, to what degree he is overtaken by real madness. Shakespeare's Hamlet is not at first in danger from a man who has killed in secret and thinks himself safe from discovery. Claudius, who knows nothing about the ghost, feels so secure that he is even ready to make Hamlet his heir, and hopes for his affection. He is anxious only to defuse Hamlet's resentment of his mother's hasty remarriage. Hamlet's odd behavior actually *alerts* Claudius to his dangerous potentialities. But just because the question is left obscure, Shakespeare is able to suggest something complex and skeptical. For the writer's own will to shape his materials, to make them new even by resisting or undermining their traditional meaning, counts too. Shakespeare's hero is the representation of that resistance, though some submission, in the end, is inevitable for both character and playwright.

That Shakespeare did not take the Revenge plot very seriously is shown by the way he let its coherence lapse. As *Hamlet*'s dramatic motive, revenge may seem to be blatantly present. What more is needed than the set-up of the ghost's injunction taken to heart so solemnly by the hero? That action does not promptly follow intention is partly inherent in the suspense requirement that holds off the final shoot-out. Shakespeare's audience may even have accepted Hamlet's scattered and often inappropriate self-reproaches simply as reassurances that the end to come was still in view, as E. E. Stoll suggested in modern times. But Shakespeare's exaggeration of this delay, which has so often been thought to discredit Hamlet's character—to make him a procrastinator—does not really do so. Instead, this exaggeration makes it appear that there is no necessary connection between his intentions and what he does. A. C. Bradley, whose summary of Shakespearean tragedy has been more influential than that of any other critic for almost a century, declared that for Shakespeare, "the center of the tragedy may be said with equal truth to lie in action issuing from character, or in character issuing in action." But this is exactly what I would dispute. Precisely these lapses of the coherence the standard Revenge story provides, these narrative "weaknesses," open up larger questions of human identity and destiny. Hamlet's slowness to execute revenge against Claudius is not the result of either "bestial oblivion or some craven scruple." Things do not happen because Hamlet is what he is. The whole question might be well displaced from Hamlet's character altogether and seen as just structural. The Revenger plot invoked at the beginning simply stops and starts and is impeded by incident that does not advance it; it is something ultimately inescapable, but operates discontinuously. The play seems to arrive where it must arrive almost without plan or effort on the revenger's part.

As I have already remarked, Shakespeare's contemporaries may have regarded the way the denouement was held off as merely cliffhanger convention. The eighteenth century hardly noticed the delay about which there would later be so much comment. Hamlet's famous slowness to effect revenge, his ineretia, was a nineteenth-century discovery. It was the Romantics who saw it as the consequence of his personality; "a Hamlet" was a cliché of the period: a fatally reflective soul with a disability for doing anything. Such a view sprang from the Romantic schism between introspection and action—something foreign to the Elizabethan way of thinking about human behavior. It is true that Hamlet does occasionally chide himself for dragging his feet. After hearing the actor's Hecuba speech he wonders whether he is not "a dull and muddle-mettled rascal . . . like John-a-dreams, unpregnant of [his] cause" because he does not cry out similarly, and he reminds himself that he "should have fatted all the region kits / With this slave's [Claudius's] offal" before this. But this self-incrimination seems unsustained. Hamlet does acknowledge his delay to the ghost that confronts him a second time in his mother's presence:

> Do you not come your tardy son to chide,
> That, lapsed in time and passion, lets go by
> Th' important acting of your dread command?

The ghost appears as an agent whose task it is to haunt Hamlet with reminder of his Revenger role, and in the closet scene with

Gertrude it appears in order to "whet [Hamlet's] almost blunted purpose." But Hamlet's mind is elsewhere, and what he scolds his mother for is not involvement in his father's murder but her incestuous marriage to his uncle, her "act/ That roars so loud and thunders in the index," for that lubricity she yields to

> in the rank sweat of an enseamèd bed
> Stewed in corruption, honeying and making love
> Over the nasty sty—

After this, delay is not mentioned until the sight of Fortinbras on the way to battle with his soldiers is a belated "spur" to revenge grown dull—the scene dropped out of the Folio.

There is no reason to suppose that Shakespeare meant us to guess at any impediment to prompter action. It has sometimes been said that Hamlet is halted in carrying out the duty assigned him because he feels a revulsion against murder and knows that vengeance is only the Lord's. But no such conflict of primitive blood-for-blood with religious principle is expressed in the play. Indeed, nothing is more *un*christian, as has often been noted, than Hamlet's reason for sparing Claudius when he might do it pat—that killing him in a moment of repentant prayer will save his unworthy soul. What else but admiration is one supposed to feel for fire-eater Laertes' prompt vow to "cut [Hamlet's] throat i' th' church," if necessary?

The impression that Hamlet is the cause of his own history really arises from the fact that his gloom or his "antic" behavior sets into motion the schemes of *others* to make him disclose himself— the nagging and nosing of Rosencrantz and Guildenstern or the use of Ophelia as a bait to make him show his true thoughts. But neither of these attempts succeeds; the plot does not go forward because of them. It is the *chance* visit of the players that prompts Hamlet finally to seize upon the idea that "The Murder of Gonzago" will make the king disclose his guilt and prove the truth of the ghost's story, even though it had already seemed an "honest ghost" on the battlements of Elsinore—just as chance produces the death of Polonius and even, perhaps, of Ophelia, and ultimately, too, of Laertes and, finally, of Gertrude, and of Claudius, whom, alone, Hamlet was supposed to kill. The strategem of the "Mousetrap" does not produce further action. In any case, just before the play is put on, Hamlet is before us with "To be or not to be." The stop of suicide rather than the forward motion of revenge is on his mind, and then the further interruptive "nunnery" scene with Ophelia immediately follows. The effect of the "Mousetrap" on guilty Claudius makes Hamlet ready to "drink hot blood" like a proper old-style revenger, yet he spares the praying king, and his immediate conversation with his mother barely glances at his father's murder. He is not unready to kill Claudius at an unanticipated moment in Gertrude's bedroom when he suspects the king behind the arras and thrusts through his sword. But the man he kills is not his uncle but Polonius—a death we tend to regard almost as Hamlet does, as a bad joke, another interpolation into the serious business of the story. And so Hamlet is bundled off to England; the plot is out of his hands. What he does achieve— the death of those paltry secret agents, Rosencrantz and Guildenstern—is of dubious value to the revenge program he has left behind, and if he comes back to Denmark to take up his destiny, he does not have a plan to bring it about. Ophelia is drowned, perhaps but not certainly having taken her own life because of Hamlet's cold rejection as well as her father's death. Her death is an event that does not either impede or promote Hamlet's progress toward his supposed aim. It is only the end of a "love interest" in which the lovers failed one another. It helps to make Hamlet an actor in the drama of *Laertes'* vengeance for the death of *his* father and of his sister, but Hamlet's own revenge plot achieves itself without his seeking during the duel he fights reluctantly. The fiction of purposive action is mocked.

Still, if the usual explanations fail, there is sufficient interpretation of Hamlet's seeming delay in a First Quarto passage whose profundity has not been appreciated—possibly because it comes out of the mouth of Claudius. Arousing Laertes to seek vengeance for Polonius's death, Claudius warns that time, *inevitably*, "qualifies the spark and fire" of strong feeling.

> There lives within the very flame of love
> A kind of wick or snuff that will abate it;
> And nothing is at a like goodness still;
> For goodness growing to a pleurisy,
> Dies in his own too-much. That we would do,
> We should do when we would; for this "would"
>   changes,
> And hath abatements and delays as many
> As there are tongues, are hands, are accidents,
> And then this "should" is like a spendthrift sigh
> That hurts by easing.

This passage is Shakespeare's poetry at its highest pitch and a philosophic summary as removed as possible from easy moralism. The viewpoint stated is that of a stoical skepticism which sees no persistence in righteous will or any human intention. Human goodness—like all supposed constants of character—is self-consuming, dies of its own excess, and must pass, must change, because "nothing is at a like goodness still." Motive and its enacting are only weakly linked. The passage represents an amoral extremity of view the Elizabethan audience may not have been prepared to accept, for it is cut from the Folio. Yet as the Player King had already said, "Purpose is but the slave to memory, / Of violent birth but poor validity." So though that personal inertia of which Hamlet has been accused is hardly evident, passion passes or lingers on only as a painful sigh of regret, "lapsed in time and passion" by an unavoidable decay and the neglect of mere memory, to which it is "slave."

In contrast with the realist logic operating in his sources, most of the events of the play do not have obvious causes but seem to succeed one another disconnectedly. Not only does character fail to determine destiny, but circumstances themselves seem to be less significant than one might expect. Shakespeare never brings forth the explanation available in his models of the way the revenge plot falters: that it is difficult to get at a monarch surrounded by his guards. Shakespeare omits the guards altogether. Hamlet never complains of lack of opportunity. The events of the play are not strung upon the old string of this-happened-and-then-as-a-result-that-happened we are used to calling plot. Its paratactic structure seems to signify the way events no longer seem attached to one another in a consequential way but are merely "and then" followed by "and then." When, in the last act, Hamlet observes that news from England of the death of Rosencrantz and Guildenstern will soon reach Denmark, he not only concedes that the time is short in which to act against Claudius. He says, "a man's life's no more than to say, 'one.'" We never advance from the count of one to a sequent "two." A skepticism that may reflect Montaigne and even anticipates Hume in its indifference to commonsense presumptions about cause and effect may, for Shakespeare, bring into doubt the linkage of happenings.

Instead, Hamlet's Denmark suffers from a sense that events are separated from one another. The preparations for war about which we hear in the opening scene have produced "post-haste and rummage in the land," the casting of cannons and the labor of shipwrights making "the night joint-labourer with the day," but they are not a prelude to anything. The foreign enemy is soon turned aside by Claudius's diplomacy, and Fortinbras will never be an invader but, instead, becomes at the end the welcomed future king. Paradoxically, time, which will seem to lag, has hurtled obscenely forward before the play begins, without providing a due connection of events. The trouble with the marriage of Claudius and the widow of the late king seems to have been not only the incestuous nature of his wedding of his "sometime sister" but its precipitance, its improper acceleration of natural pace. Claudius's opening formal address to his court attempts to justify his hurry, doing so, however, by employing images that suggest an oxymoronic and monstrous merging of conditions and occasions, his "one auspicious and one dropping eye," his "mirth in funeral" and "dirge in marriage." The queen, for her part, urges Hamlet to cease his grieving for his father since "all that lives must die," the irony being, of course, that the old king's death is, like the marriage that followed, something that arrived before it should have naturally occurred. Hamlet does not yet know about his father's murder; he has not yet met the ghost who will complain that time for repentance and absolution has been denied him: "Cut off even in the blossoms of my sin,/ Un-houseled, dis-appointed, unaneled." But already his first soliloquy inveighs against the collapse of seemly interval represented by the marriage that followed this death:

> But two months dead—nay not so much, not two . . .
> A little month, or ere those shoes were old
> With which she followed my poor father's body. . . .
>   O most wicked speed, to post
> With such dexterity to incestuous sheets!

This is the burden of his exchange with Horatio, who had returned to Denmark for a funeral and found himself at a wedding where, as Hamlet says, "The funeral baked meats/ Did coldly furnish forth the marriage tables."

But after this start, failure to advance the action, to contribute to the continuity of the Hamlet plot, occurs in the play itself, though it is not so obvious that Hamlet delays. The *plot* dawdles. After Hamlet receives his commission from the ghost, the second act opens in a distinctly distracting way to show us Polonius instructing Reynaldo—whom we will never see or hear about further—to keep a watch on unreliable young Laertes, who is on the loose in Paris. Only after seventy lines is Ophelia brought in, with her revelation to her father concerning Hamlet's strange behavior. Such interruptions of the "action" scenario are part of the play of intrusions that gives *Hamlet* its effect of life caught by chance, of that spectacle of the mundane which stays our impatience for tragedy's drive toward outcome. Progression is forgotten also when Hamlet talks about the theater and the art of acting to the players, or when he sports with the dull fop, Osric, for our amusement, and, above all, in the conversation between the clowns in the graveyard at the beginning of the last act. During such intervals time bides its time.

In *Hamlet,* the soliloquies that are so prominent and wonderful as poetic reverie stand even more apart from the action immediately surrounding them than is true in other plays of the Revenge type. The first announces Hamlet's desire for suicide—that his "too too solid flesh would melt"—without obvious prompting beyond his mother's remarriage, for he still has not learned about his father's murder. Hamlet's mood may really be the product of a state of mind that need not have an immediate cause in events—and this condition in itself is a denial of our simplistic assumption that ideas must derive from direct causes in our experience. "To be or not to be" reverts to the theme of suicide so inappropriately that some scholars feel it must have been misplaced in the texts we rely on, the Second Quarto and the Folio. The First Quarto puts the soliloquy earlier, which suggests that it might even have been reordered that way in performance. Or else that the actor who tried to set it down from memory instinctively imposed a logical order on what he remembered. But keeping it where it is in the more "authorial" Second Quarto and Folio, the soliloquy is just another reminder of how the Hamlet-mind stands independent of the action. It can seem, under these circumstances, however, a reflection pertinent to the philosophic substratum of the play—a review of the relation of being and doing, as one may may read the "question" posed in the opening lines.

The same is true of "How all occasions do inform against me" in Act IV, which, as I have mentioned, is to be found in the Second Quarto though dropped from the Folio, along with the preceding encounter of Hamlet with the marching file of Fortinbras's soldiers. It, too, is thought to be misplaced. It renews Hamlet's resolution when the occasion for action may well be passed, prompting eloquent but inappropriate self-reproach, for he can do nothing now to carry out his duty of revenge. He is virtually a prisoner under arms on his way to exile and lacks not only the "will, and strength," but the "means" he claims to possess to carry out his promise to the ghost. Yet now he reverts to an exaltation of action in traditional terms, expressing a heroic view of the human creature he has already called the "quintessence of dust" by saying,

> Sure he that made us with such large discourse,
> Looking before and after, gave us not
> That capability and god-like reason
> To fust in us unused.

The out-of-order character of this expression of resolution is great enough to have prompted various attempts at alteration by critics or editors—either assigning it to some spot earlier in the play or following Shakespeare or his Folio editors by eliminating it—although no stage director will willingly do so. Keeping it where we find it, some believe that it marks a moment of character change, predicting the man who has come back from England hardened to the execution of his duty. Or it reduces Hamlet to the too-simple revenger he cannot ever be. Philip Edwards, the New Cambridge editor, who wants to keep the passage in place, believes that it must be taken to represent Shakespeare's modernist realism about character in presenting Hamlet as someone who is "a tangle of conflicting tendencies." But leaving it out, as the Folio does, allows us to accept a Hamlet who has nearly surrendered his revenge compulsion and will not take it up until compelled. The play is almost over in the last scene of the final act when he finds it necessary to review his grievances against the man who has killed his king and whored his mother, prevented his own election to the throne and even tried to have him killed, and he asks, as though such a question had not long been settled, "is't not perfect conscience / To quit him with this arm?" But he has no plan.

Hamlet himself has come to conclude that human "plots do pall," though "a divinity"—as he vaguely says—shapes "our ends, / Rough-hew them how we will," and makes something of our "indiscretions." *Ends,* here, ambiguously means either purpose or mere outcome, or perhaps both. Hamlet seems to acknowledge that God, or some greater force than ourselves, may not only direct a life but may give it purpose and a conclusion that rounds out its story in a meaningful way. But neither shaping nor purpose has anything to do with human intention. The metaphoric "rough-hew," referring to stonemasonry, is used by Florio to mean a crude bungle. At the last, Horatio warns Hamlet that he will lose the duel with Laertes. But Hamlet, with a new resignation, replies, "We defy augury. There's a special providence in the fall of a sparrow. If it be now, 'tis not to come. If it be not to come, it will be now. If it be not now, yet it will come"—surrendering the effort to find a comprehensible design or predictable outcome to his life, though a divine intention may be presumed, on faith, to have directed it.

Hamlet's stoicism gives over any expectation of illumination and, as with Montaigne, atheism is avoided by a kind of stoic fideism. "The readiness is all. Since no man knows aught of what he leaves, what is't to leave betimes? Let be." I quote this mysterious, often argued-over passage from the recent Oxford edition of the play, which slightly modifies the reading of the Second Quarto: "since no man of ought he leaues, knowes what is't to leaue betimes, let be." This seems to mean: there may be a "special providence" that assigns everything its end, but one cannot anticipate it; there is no sure link between past, present, and future as we know them. No man "knows aught" about the life he will leave, so what does it matter if he leaves sooner rather than later? Some scholarly readers prefer the wording in the text of the Folio: "Since no man ha's ought of what he leaues. What is't to leaue betimes?" which clarifies Hamlet's reflection by making it banal—making death mean only a relinquishing of having, or, as we say, that "you can't take it with you." Shakespeare himself, revising, might have settled for that easier sense. But the earlier text reflects an ultimate denial of knowledge, and it is, perhaps, a better statement of Hamlet's skepticism about the meaning of human existence. Dr. Johnson paraphrased: "Since no man knows aught of the state of life which he leaves, since he cannot judge of what other years may produce, why should he be afraid of leaving life betimes?" The whole passage, especially in its Second Quarto version, has reminded some of Montaigne's remarks in the essay, "That to Philosophie, Is to Learn How to Die": "No man dies before his houre. The time you leave behind was no more yours, than that which was before youre birth and concerneth you no more."

If Hamlet's madness has been genuine, we need seek no further for explanation of his grandly excessive despair. Unless, of course, we agree with Polonius that there is a "method" in his madness. Polonius is all the more convinced of Hamlet's madness because he finds in the prince's fierce wit proof of the "happiness that often madness hits on, which reason and sanity could not so preposterously be delivered of." There is, after all, something about Hamlet's possible degree of genuine madness that taps into the ancient idea of the mad person inspired with a wisdom beyond sanity. The same tradition that made madness a way of accessing sacred knowledge made the madman himself sacred. But from folk tradition also derive the stories of feigned madness as a device of self-protection, as in the biblical account of David's assumed madness at the court of Achish—the motive that Shakespeare inherits from his sources but weakens. The trouble here is that even if Hamlet has only been pretending madness, it is still not so certain that his behavior is part of a plan of revenge. His exhibitions of bizarre humor may be designed to twit the duller minds that surround him.

Or it may express his desperate but sane anguish. It is not impossible that this anguish is philosophical. Still insisting on his sanity, we must take seriously what he says to Rosencrantz and Guildenstern:

> I have of late—but wherefore I know not—lost all my mirth, forgone all custom of exercise; and indeed it goes so heavily with my disposition that this goodly frame, the earth, seems to me a sterile promontory. This most excellent canopy, the air, look you, this brave o'erhanging firmament, this majestical roof fretted with golden fire— why, it appears no other thing to me than a foul and pestilent congregation of vapours. What a piece of work is a man, how noble in reason, how infinite in faculty, in form and moving how express and admirable, in action how like an angel, in apprehension how like a god—the beauty of the world, the paragon of animals! And yet, to me, what

is this quintessence of dust? Man delights not me—no, nor woman neither, though by your smiling you seem to say so.

It is sometimes complained that Hamlet's expression of such thoughts to such auditors, who can only respond with stupid snickers, is preposterous, and that, besides, he does know why he has lost all his mirth—it is because of his father's death and his mother's remarriage, as well as because of Ophelia's betrayal, about which he would not want to speak to Rosencrantz and Guildenstern. The explanation generally offered is that he is trying to throw the two spies off the scent. The play's New Cambridge editor, Philip Edwards, says, "So often pointed to as a brilliant perception of the anguish of Renaissance man in general and of Hamlet in particular, it is a glorious blind, a flight of rhetoric by which a divided and distressed soul conceals the true nature of his distress and substitutes a formal and conventional state of *Weltschmerz*." But it seems to me that we must believe Hamlet when he claims that he does not know why he feels as he does precisely because these are feelings derived from the most general of mental states, not, indeed, to be accounted for by any specific experience or event. I would call the instinctive response of reader or hearer to the power of this famous speech sounder than insistence upon psychologic plot-logic. Hamlet has ceased to be, as he so often ceases to be, simply the character whose motives advance the plot. What he expresses is abstract, yet the root of a skeptic pessimism that can be attributed to him—and, perhaps, to Shakespeare.

Hamlet's "lunacy," as Polonius terms it, was noticed before he heard the ghost's tale. It is obvious he had some cause for gloom in his mother's remarriage, but his response already is exaggerated—as the first soliloquy shows. At this point, already, his loathing for man's sensual nature, which even causes him to wish that his own flesh would melt, exceeds the provocation and has made some psychologically minded critics ready to discover an oedipal obsession driven frantic by his mother's remarriage. That Hamlet is shaken by *ideas* taken seriously is more possible, on the other hand, than is generally allowed. His desire for suicide, which erupts in the midst of the action and seems to have no sufficient explanation in the plot, derives from melancholy observation of the discrepancy between human self-esteem and the reality of human nature and behavior. To lose all one's mirth without apparent cause, as he describes himself, is to be someone whose altered response to life is all-inclusive and goes beyond specific occasions. He is a man of the book, we must remember, like no other in Shakespeare except, perhaps, Brutus. "But look where sadly the poor wretch comes reading," the queen observes. How we wish we knew what he reads! Polonius asks, and is told, "Words, words, words," Hamlet making a postmodernist skeptical distinction between objective reference and language that is quite beyond Polonius.

He has promised the ghost to wipe from the "table of [his] memory all trivial fond records, / All saws of books, all forms, all pressures past," as though acknowledging that memory is a readily erased slate from which the traditions of past forms and pressures of custom, all received wisdom expressed by human language, can be expunged like messages written in chalk. But what can be set down in their place? He resolves, he tells the ghost, that its "commandment all alone shall live / Within the book and volume of [his] brain," as though the meaning of this duty can be given more lasting presence in the book of the brain. But is he not pledged to accept the form and pressure of still another of those "saws of books" that he distrusts, the tradition of Revenge embodied in literature, particularly the literature of the theater itself? Polonius asks helplessly for the "matter" of Hamlet's reading and is mocked with truisms: "The satirical rogue says here that old men have grey beards, that their faces are wrinkled, their eyes purging thick amber or plum-tree gum, and that they have a plentiful lack of wit, together with most weak hams—all which sir, though I most powerfully and potently believe, yet I hold not honesty to have it thus set down; for you yourself sir should be old as I am—if, like a crab, you could go backward." And having hardly referred to what the "satirical rogue" might actually have written, but mocked the end of man in the spectacle of aging Polonius, he throws out his hint of his suicidal thought when invited to "walk out of the air" with his interlocutor: "Into my grave?" he asks. And when Polonius takes his leave, says, "you cannot, sir, take from me anything that I will more willingly part withal—except my life, except my life, except my life."

We have no way of knowing what book Hamlet is reading, but we have some basis for supposing that Shakespeare had been reading Montaigne when he wrote *Hamlet*. As I have noted in my introduction, Montaigne's presence in Shakespeare's mind is at once elusive and beyond question. Of course, *Hamlet* cannot have been written and produced later than 1601, by all calculations, and Florio's translation appeared in print in 1603, but there is some likelihood, as I have argued, that Shakespeare could have already read it in manuscript, and there are passages and vocabulary that suggest such reading. Ticking off words that appear in *Hamlet* for the first time in Shakespeare's writing but are present in Florio, scholars count well over a hundred. Passages that seem similar to some in Florio are seldom what the scholars like to call "borrowings," but there is enough resemblance to seem more than accidental. And in any case, the correspondences between Shakespeare and Montaigne mean something more important than such derivation. They establish a common skeptical view.

Man is, if the ancient hierarchical scheme of creation still holds, the "paragon of animals," but Hamlet says that to him this paragon is only the "quintessence of dust." Montaigne, in his famous "Apologie of Raymond Sebond," elaborated an ironic comparison of mankind with other animals, a comparison that demonstrated our conspicuous failure to exceed them. Shakespeare puts two views, the conventional and the skeptic, into confrontation. Hamlet's doubt about hierarchy extends even to those distinctions of universal order, which we make only according to some subjective measure. As Montaigne says, "Who hath perswaded him [man], that this admirable moving of heavens vaults; that the eternal light of these lampes so fiercely rowling over his head; that the horror-moving and continuall motion of this infinite vaste Ocean, were established, and continue so many ages for his commoditie and service? Is it possible to imagine anything so ridiculous, as this miserable and wretched creature, which is not so much as master of himself, exposed and subject to offences of all things, and yet dareth call himselfe Master and Emperour of this Universe?"

Hamlet also brings Montaigne to mind when he says about Denmark being a prison, "There's nothing good or bad but thinking makes it so"—a reflection expressed in Montaigne's essay "That the Taste Of Goods Or Evils Doth Greatly Depend On the Opinion We Have Of Them." Arden editor Harold Jenkins thinks that Hamlet's remark is not serious, and denies the parallel with Montaigne. But there is good reason to think that it has major importance in the play, linking him with the skepticism of Montaigne as well as with other writers of the early seventeenth century. In "The Progresse of the Soule," John Donne writes, "There's nothing simply good, nor ill alone. The only measure is, and judge, Opinion," and in his "Biathanatos," says, again, "There is no externall act naturally evil." "What's aught, but as 'tis valued," as Shakespeare's Troilus also says. Such subjectivism anticipates Locke.

I have compared *Hamlet* to a mystery story because concealment and secrecy are essential to its suspense, but they serve also to reinforce the idea that appearances are unrevealing of anything but what is shown, while, at the same time, we cannot place absolute trust in our impressions. As I shall be saying, this skeptical view of the uses of perception is central in *Othello,* written soon after *Hamlet,* a play in which the implied model of a judicial trial frames the uncertainty of a demonstration of guilt. To establish guilt in the courtroom is, generally, to provide those linkages of plot and those circumstantial demonstrations of the accused's probable criminality, his character and motive, which attach him to a suspected crime so that a court may convict. But appearances are deceptive; irrefutable evidence hard to come by; only "thinking makes it so." Having heard its story, Hamlet is ready to declare that his father's apparition is an "honest ghost," a plaintiff to be believed, but even then he is not sure, for, as he considers again in "What a rogue and peasant slave am I," a deceiving devil may have told this tale. Claudius appears unmoved by the dumb show that precedes and anticipates "The Murder of Gonzago" and his reaction to this play does not obviously confirm its story, for he says no word as he hurries from the scene. He does not give himself away entirely.

As we will see more amply illustrated by Othello's ordeal, absolute proof is impossible. The murder of Hamlet's father was a murder by poisoning — precisely the kind of crime that often was most difficult to prove legally, most often an unwitnessed crime, like witchcraft or like the adultery of which Iago accuses Desdemona — and so, only to be confirmed by the accused's confession. In the Hamlet story as related by Belleforest, there is no problem of evidence. Unlike the murder in Shakespeare "by which the whole ear of Denmark / Is by a forged process of my death / Rankly abused," as the ghost says, old Hamblet in the French novella is openly killed by his brother at a banquet. Shakespeare's Claudius must be brought to make a public confession; this is the purpose of "The

Mousetrap" set to catch his conscience when others are present. But we are never certain to what degree Claudius recognizes the details of his own crime in the double dramatization. Claudius does confess his "rank offence" that "hath the primal eldest curse upon't—/ A brother's murder," but makes this confession only to God, and Hamlet comes upon him at prayer only after it is uttered. The story of his death told by the ghost himself—the precondition of the Revenge play—thus continues to have a certain dreamlike quality, like a nightmare Hamlet has experienced and never entirely either distinguishes from reality or validates on waking. Hamlet swears Horatio and Marcellus to silence about the ghost's appearance, but does not communicate the narrative he alone has heard. "For your desire to know what is between us,/ O'ermaster't as you may," he tells them. He will tell what passed between himself and the ghost to no one, not to Horatio, his friend, nor to Ophelia, his beloved, nor to his mother, though the ghost appears to him again as he scolds her for her corruption.

Never completely defined or authenticated, the ghost initiates the question of personal authenticity, which is Hamlet's central problem. It seems significant that the play opens with a challenge to identity: "Who's there?" the arriving sentry, Barnardo, calls out into the night, and the man at the post responds with a similar, "Nay, answer me. Stand and unfold yourself." "Who is there?" rings out again as Horatio and Marcellus approach. The subject of their immediate discussion is the identity of "this thing," "this dreaded sight" already twice perceived but not understood—person, apparition, or delusion—and when it appears again it is "in the same figure like the King that's dead" but not necessarily the older Hamlet's ghost, and still not represented by a personal pronoun: "Speak to it, Horatio. . . . Mark it, Horatio. . . . It would be spoke to. . . . Question it, Horatio." Horatio demands,

What [not 'who'] art thou that usurp'st this time of
    night
Together with that fair and warlike form
In which the majesty of buried Denmark
Did sometimes march?

— the true spirit of the dead Hamlet. The "character" of the ghost,
whether it or he *is* the old king, or someone or something else, is
never established beyond doubt, the impersonal "it" suggesting,
in any case, an absolute and irremediable distinction between the
living man and what might survive him after death. Yet it impresses
the beholders on the battlements by a resemblance to old Hamlet
that seems like identity. The philosophic paradox of duplication, of
symmetry, is expressed in Horatio's statement to Hamlet, "I knew
your father;/ These hands are not more like," as he holds up both
his hands, which though similar are never exactly the same. The
ghost is as like the dead man, Horatio has observed to Marcellus,
"as thou art to thyself," a strange statement that asserts identity but
hints that even the single living self can be a matter at best of the
resemblance among different appearances. But Hamlet vows, "Perchance 'twill walk again. If it assume my noble father's person, I'll
speak to it though hell itself should gape." In the end he decides to
give it the name that belongs uniquely to the dead king: "I'll call
thee Hamlet,/ King, father, royal Dane." This is a declaration that
anticipates his own assumption of identity with the father whose
old-style heroic mode he will at the last assume when he shouts in
the graveyard, "This is I, Hamlet the Dane."

    Yet up till this point, his difference from his father is more evi-
dent. What one *is* defines itself by what one differs from as well
as by what one resembles. In *Hamlet* the comparison of uncertain
duplicates is of deep importance, beginning with the questionable
twinship of the ghost with the dead man Hamlet remembers, an

inexact resemblance, like that of a pair of hands. In relation to himself, Hamlet thinks of his father as a model who is not repeatable: "He was a man. Take him for all in all. / I shall not look upon his like again." The mystery of uniqueness is explored in the comparison of the dead King Hamlet and Claudius, the brother who replaced him. In his mother's closet Hamlet produces two pictures, and asks her to look upon them both, "the counterfeit presentment [the pictures themselves being false in pretending to be the men themselves] of two brothers." He contrasts a pair who, though likely to be similar, are opposites. One is the classical heroic man, the ultimate human expression of resemblances to the divine:

> Hyperion's curls, the front of Jove himself,
> An eye like Mars, to threaten and command
> A station like the herald Mercury
> New lighted on a heaven-kissing hill;
> A combination and a form indeed
> Where every god did seem to set his seal
> To give the world assurance of a man.

And the other is "like a mildewed ear / Blasting his wholesome brother"—which refers to the brotherhood of similar ears of corn in a corn-crib, one of which differs so perniciously as to cause disease and death to the other.

The contrast recalls Hamlet's "What a piece of work is man," which sets the heroic ideal represented by epic tradition against the view of man that "delights not" Hamlet. "How like a god," Hamlet had exclaimed, conceiving man in the terms of those comparisons with classic divinities he now employs in describing the dead king. But he also sees himself as different from his father-twin as Claudius is from the old warrior wearing armor even as a ghost. Claudius is "no more like my father / Than I to Hercules," he says, recognizing himself as a modern man to whom the epic ideal no more applies than to this Machiavellian sybarite. It is strikingly significant of the turn on his materials Shakespeare is making that in Belleforest, and even in Saxo, Hamlet is straightforwardly *compared to* Hercules, not contrasted with him. Belleforest called Hamlet a Samson, the "Hercules of the Hebrews." Shakespeare removes this heroization, and converts comparison to contrast. Only at the end, in his death, does Hamlet take on the classic character he has resisted despite his promise to the ghost to wipe away from the table of his memory "all trivial fond records" and let only the ghost's command remain. Fortinbras, who has never been anything but uncontrovertibly heroic, asks for a military funeral for the dead Prince:

> Let four captains
> Bear Hamlet like a soldier to the stage;
> For he was likely, had he been put on,
> To have proved most royally; and for his passage,
> The soldiers' music and the rites of war
> Speak loudly for him.

But Hamlet's assumption of the paternal martial heritage comes late.

What Shakespeare thinks of conventional types is represented in his portrait of Laertes—the prompt avenger of a father's murder, but stupid and not really honorable when he consents to have his rapier poisoned in order to make sure that the duel will be fatal for Hamlet. Osric, the courtier fop, a standard comic type himself, is the spokesman for fading categories when he describes Laertes (in still another passage only in the Second Quarto) in type-casting terms as the "absolute gentleman . . . the card or calendar of gentry; for you shall find in him the continent of what part a gentleman would see." But the audience would have understood the used-up nature of the formula, especially in a period when manufactured "gentlemen" were being created in unprecedented numbers by the official College of Arms—gentry status having become purchasable as the new rich became landed proprietors. The traditional social category based on inherited position and the theatrical type could no longer be taken with complete seriousness.

Uncertainty about characterizing conventions links Shakespeare with Montaigne's reiterated observation of the instability of human personality, which, as the Montaigne scholar Jacob Zeitlin says, "runs as a Leitmotif through all of Montaigne's speculations on the heart of man." In one of the essays, Montaigne echoes Plato's "Know thyself," urging that if one knows what one is, one can direct one's conduct, rejecting "superfluous occupations." But what he seems to counsel by this is the prudent conduct urged by Polonius when he tells his son, "This above all—to thine own self be true," and warns his daughter, "You do not understand yourself so clearly." The self that Laertes and Ophelia must sustain is that code of behavior and course of life to which each was born. Such a social self is not inner, but an outerness, the mold by means of which the self must discover itself as expressed in the injunction, "know your place." Montaigne, nevertheless, understood that one's place could change in the fluid French society he inhabited in a time of virtual civil war. He understood that prescribed forms were not always available. What one's place was became subject to opportunity and the self-fashioning of ambition. It may not be irrelevant to notice that Montaigne, like Shakespeare, was someone who understood personally how the general changeableness of life brought fixed ideas of self and position into question. He himself came from a bourgeois family recently elevated to the nobility.

But it was his philosophic skepticism that also urged him to doubt the existence of an essential self independent of circumstances. He contradicts the implied essentialism of his earlier Platonic "Know thyself" when he says, "Sometimes I give my soule one visage, and sometimes another, according unto the posture or side I lay her in. If I speake diversely of my selfe, it is because I looke diversely upon my selfe. All contrarities are found in her, according to some turne or removing; and in some fashion or other. Shamefast, bashfull, insolent, chaste, luxurious, peevish, pratling, silent, fond, doting, laborious, nice, delicate, ingenious, slow, dull, froward, humorous, debonaire, wise, ignorant, false in words, true-speaking, both liberall, covetous and prodigall. . . . I have nothing to say entirely, simply, and with soliditie of my selfe." Montaigne declares repeatedly in many places in his *Essayes* that personal character is undefinable because inconstant. In "Of the Inconstancie of Our Actions," we read,

> Those which exercise themselves in controuling humane actions, finde no such let in any one part, as to peece them together, and bring them to one same lustre: For, they commonly contradict one another so strangely, as it seemeth impossible they should be parcels of one Ware-house. . . . I have often thought, that even good Authors, doe ill, and take a wrong course, wilfully to opinionate themselves about framing a constant and solide contexture of us. They chuse an universall ayre, and following that image, range and interpret all a mans actions; which if they cannot wrest sufficiently, they remit them into dis-simulaton. . . . *There is nothing I so hardly beleeve to be in man, as constancie, and nothing so easie to be found in him, as inconstancy.* . . . Our ordinary manner is to follow the inclination of our appetite, this way and that way; on the left, and on the right hand; upward and downe-ward, according as the winde of occasions doth transport us: we never thinke on what we would have, but at the instant we would have it: and change as that beast that takes the

colour of the place wherein it is laid. What we even now purposed, we alter by and by, and presently returne to our former biase; all is but changing, motion, and inconstancy. . . . We float and waver betweene divers opinions: we will nothing freely, nothing absolutely, nothing constantly.

Montaigne not only doubts the existence of consistent character, but he reproaches literature for too often "framing a constant and solide contexture of us" — a reproach that may have caught Shakespeare's attention particularly. We are each a crowd of contrary selves, he insists. There is, he says, "as much difference found betweene us and ourselves, as there is between ourselves and other. . . . Esteeme it a great matter to play but one man." Montaigne, too, uses the metaphor of costume to represent the diverse, patchwork contradictions of our selfhoods, which he compares to a clown's motley or a beggar's tattered hand-me-downs in which each piece of the self, separate in its origin, is a kind of actor: "We are all framed of flaps and patches and of so shapeless and diverse a contexture, that every peece and every moment playeth his part."

The idea that personal reality is something not inherent or constant may be suggested when Hamlet facetiously ponders with Polonius over the shapes of clouds. He seems to have in mind the arbitrariness of all our interpretations which impose form and meaning on the meaningless welter of life, but it has been noted that the passage resembles one in *Antony and Cleopatra* when Antony says to Eros, after describing cloud shapes that resemble now this, now that,

> My good knave Eros, now thy captain is
> Even such a body. Here I am Antony
> Yet cannot hold this visible shape, my knave.

I suspect that in *Hamlet* the talk about clouds implies, as in the later play, something about the way our characters seem fixed in one form or another but are really susceptible of infinite change.

Hamlet's appearance of madness—a subject to which one returns in so many connections—is a representation of the fragility of selfhood. The disjunctions of the variable self are not so different from what we think of as madness. Is not madness what we call "not being oneself"—an alienation from the consistency one prefers to believe in? As the play progresses, there is a tantalizing uncertainty that leaves it unclear whether this hero's teasing, disjointed, and surreal talk is assumed or a sign of real derangement. There has been an effort to diagnose him as a clinical case since Polonius decided, on the basis of Ophelia's report, that Hamlet had been driven out of his mind by the repulse she administered at her father's command. He diagnoses the prince as a victim of the Renaissance disease of "love ecstasy." Or, if not that, exactly, it has been proposed, Shakespeare meant to make him an illustration of the disease of body and mind that was called, according to medieval-Renaissance physiology, as it is today, melancholia—or depression. He suffered, that is, from an excess of one of the "four humours"—black bile—which was supposed to manifest itself by the symptoms of sullenness and bursts of anger.

His mother suggests that his claim that his father's ghost stands before them in her chamber is "distemper." It is, she says, "the very coinage of [his] brain. This bodiless creation ecstasy/ Is very cunning in." But Hamlet denies that he suffers from "ecstasy"—a synonym for madness:

Ecstasy?
My pulse as yours doth temperately keep time,
And makes as healthful music. It is not madness
That I have uttered. Bring me to the test,

And I the matter will re-word, which madness
Would gambol from.

If the ghost is this time as genuine as it seems to have been when
attested to by others earlier, madness seems improbable. Hamlet
appeals to the queen to sustain his *pretense* of madness to Claudius,
never letting him know, he says, "that I essentially am not in madness,/But mad in craft." It seems improbable that Shakespeare
wrote the play with no other aim than to offer us an example of
pathology. Except for one thing: Hamlet himself will apologize to
Laertes:

I am punished with sore distraction.
What I have done,
That might your nature, honour, and exception
Roughly awake, I here proclaim was madness.

But by keeping us in continual doubt about Hamlet's madness, suggesting even that Hamlet himself is in doubt—yet allowing his protean personality and his elliptic talk make him seem
really crazy—Shakespeare compels us to consider a skeptic view of
the self such as Montaigne expressed. It is this uncertainty that is
even expressed in Ophelia's authentic mad talk. "Lord, we know
what we are, but know not what we may be," she says. In the mad
man or woman the faculties no longer cohere in one person and
sustain themselves through time. Claudius speaks of Ophelia as
"divided from herself and her fair judgment/Without the which
we are pictures or mere beasts." Shakespeare may, after all, want
us to consider skeptical self-alienation as a part of Hamlet's sober
feeling when he apologizes to Laertes with the excuse of madness.

In the nunnery scene, generally taken as simply abuse of poor
Ophelia, Hamlet offers a commentary on the protean nature of
character. Perhaps pretending to be mad, or else yielding to a desire

to release destructiveness and misogyny in himself, and whether or not he is expressing an attitude he really does not feel, he reproves Ophelia as though she were herself a deceiving person—a woman who "paints" her face—or an actress who has put on makeup: "God has given you one face, and you make yourselves another." Hamlet reduces Ophelia with the abuse against women that was a stock litany. He speaks as though the woman he has begun by greeting as a nymph is a whore. One self has erased another. But he is not altogether wrong when he describes her as an actress, for she is playing a part she has been instructed in by her father. In preparing her for this interview, Polonius advised his daughter to assume a demeanor that would conceal her purpose, as one might "sugar o'er/ The devil himself." Claudius, overhearing this description of dissimulation, recognizes its application to himself. He refers to Hamlet's image of the painted harlot's cheek in admitting to the "painted word" which covers his own deed.

Hamlet claims no greater stability for himself. Hamlet's view of his own variable self reminds one of Montaigne's list of his contradictory identities. His soliloquies abound in self-doubt. "Am I a coward?/ Who calls me villain?" he asks, offering himself and the audience a choice of type characterizations. The metaphor of the stage, so conspicuous in the play, enters inevitably into his questioning of his own identity. In "O what a rogue and peasant slave am I," having just heard the player's Pyrrhus-Hecuba speech, Hamlet reproaches himself because he can "say nothing" to match such passion though it is only an actor's pretense of passion. Then he shifts, illogically, to accuse himself of having been like "a whore" who can only "unpack [his] heart with words." He tells Ophelia not to trust the seeming in men, not even his own pose as a lover: "We are arrant knaves all, believe none of us." He could not be more theatrical even if ignorant of his hidden audience as he spontaneously shifts from one role to another, from lover to castigator of women. He sees himself as a player of various possible parts. He tells Ophelia that he has "more offences at [his] beck than [he has] thoughts to put them in, imagination to give them shape, or time to act them in."

Hamlet is all potentiality. He is capable of Cleopatra's "infinite variety" in a negative as well as positive sense. Is he bold or hesitating, passionate or sluggish, loving or cold, refined or coarse? The evidence for the first term in these pairs is what attracts us to him, yet the evidence for the second set of terms is plentiful—and those many attempts to summarize his character and explain his behavior in a unitary way fail. Some of his negative aspects are off-putting enough to threaten his position as the play's hero. His reluctance to kill Claudius when he was kneeling in prayer—because then he might not send him straight to hell—shocked Dr. Johnson. His contrived killing of his sleazy false friends, Rosencrantz and Guildenstern, has seemed to many to be something that should have been beneath him. He is too brutal and vulgar with his mother and Ophelia. There is no limit to the unenacted, unthought, unimagined "offences" of which he might be capable. Yet we endure these spectacles and possibilities for the glimpses given of that noble nature that Ophelia remembers, his tender filial memory and his appreciation of Horatio's friendship, and his generosity to the rash Laertes, who deals him his deathblow. And we love the elevation of his mind, his play of wit and philosophy, his keen understanding of others and of society. Horatio's loyalty is a warrant we accept, for Horatio is our representative in the play—the sensible, decent, ordinary man who gives his complete support to someone worthy of it. But certainly, Polonius and Claudius and Gertrude and Ophelia, those Hamlet-watchers in the play who each want to understand him, fail completely, and Horatio alone is wise enough not to try.

An actor, it is sometimes said, is a man who wants to play

Hamlet. It is the longest part in Shakespeare and has more occasions than any other when the actor stands alone and communes with himself with only the audience to overhear him, but, above all, no other role gives the actor's ego so much rope. There always seems to be room for still another Hamlet to disengage himself from the company of Hamlets the play allows for. But once the actor has chosen the Hamlet he wants to be, discrepancies may be flattened out or eliminated. The actor need not be oppressed by the fact that his forerunners from Betterton to Branagh have each given the stage a Hamlet of his own. Most productions that cut the unwieldy full text simplify Hamlet's multiplicity, as did Olivier's when he reduced the play by a third to disengage the Melancholy Dane from other possibilities.

But in suggesting Hamlet's variability, Shakespeare has expressed his own recognition of the conventionality of all the ways in which drama represents the self, and also the conventionality and insufficiency of all self-conceptions by means of which men and women carry on in life itself. Hamlet may be only the most striking example among Shakespeare's portraits of someone who finds himself in a role that does not suit our idea—even his own idea, if he conceives it—of what might be his character. In contrast with Hamlet's fugitive sense of self, the outer man and his roles are "too too solid." He seems to wish for a death that might come of itself, for suicide is a sin, but he also implies an impatience with the material actuality of his body and his life. He can find no selfhood outside of prescribed forms, no history but in established plots, the gross, enclosing self of social roles that are like costumes in the theater. He cannot be anything other than the Revenger the play sets out to make him. This is the prison that is Denmark.

Polonius makes use of the costume metaphor when he tells Ophelia that Hamlet's vows wear false vesture (he uses the unusual word *investments*). They plead "unholy suits" while pretending holy intent. Hamlet himself, on his first appearance in the play, comes on stage clothed in the black of mourning, and the queen, speaking metaphorically as well as literally, asks him for a change of mood and clothing, saying, "cast thy blighted colour off." She asks him why death "seems so particular" to him, and he answers,

> Seems, madam? Nay it is, I know not "seems."
> 'Tis not alone my inky cloak, good mother,
> Nor customary suits of solemn black,
> Nor windy suspiration of forced breath,
> No, nor the fruitful river in the eye,
> Nor the dejected haviour of the visage,
> Together with all forms, moods, shapes of grief,
> That can denote me truly. These indeed seem,
> For they are actions that a man might play;
> But I have that within which passeth show —
> These but the trappings and the suits of woe.

This is more ambiguous than appears at first glance. Hamlet may be saying that he has put on a false appearance to cover a true self, "that within which passeth show." *Passeth* has been taken to mean that his grief is so great that it *surpasses* any expression. He does not deny the message of his appearance, for it declares his grief — though inadequately. Yet the way he looks and behaves also constitutes "actions that a man might play" as on the stage, a collection of gestures established by tradition for a customary role and easily enacted by the accomplished actor along with a costume, "trappings and suits," deemed appropriate — here, again, making the play's prevailing reference to the theater. A skeptical reading has been urged by recent "materialist" critics who suggest that the interior of Hamlet cannot be shown because it is a vacancy. If there is an inner truth of some sort in him, it is one that escapes all expression and can hardly be spoken of, for no terms of manifestation exist for it.

It is true that asides and soliloquies, more prominent in this play than in any other of Shakespeare's—or, indeed, in the work of any playwright of his day—seem to suggest an inner personality for Hamlet, however hidden. Some have argued for the idea that inner essentiality is, in fact, donated to Shakespeare's portrait of Hamlet by this means—and achieves the sense of innerness more pronouncedly than had ever been the case before in literary portraiture. But one may object that the status of Hamlet's soliloquies as rhetoric gives them a certain impersonality. As I have remarked, they are inadequate representations of his reasons for action—that nexus Bradley thought was the essence of Shakespeare's tragic insight. "To be or not to be"—in which "I" is not used even once—sounds like the young philosophy student's pondering of abstract questions, with the merest implication of personal emotion to make us try, not altogether successfully, to apply them to his case. They show only an *intellectual* inner man.

Does Hamlet ever come close to accepting entirely—or rejecting without question—the Revenger model? There is one moment when he invokes it consciously—and puts it aside. As he goes to meet his mother in the third act, he stirs himself up with an old-style invocation of dark powers—then dismisses their prompting,

> 'Tis now the very witching time of night,
> When churchyards yawn, and hell itself breathes out
> Contagion to this world. Now could I drink hot blood,
> And do such bitter business as the day
> Would quake to look on. Soft, now to my mother.
> O heart, lose not thy nature. Let not ever
> The soul of Nero enter this firm bosom.

> Let me be cruel, not unnatural:
> I will speak daggers to her, but use none.

"When churchyards yawn" is a reminder to himself of the ghost who returned from the realm of death to lay its demand upon him. Now it is the "witching hour," as we still say, when murdering witches were believed to drink the blood of their victims. It is a moment recalled from the old Revenge play scenario he is momentarily willing to impose on himself. Now, he says with melodramatic excess, he could do the unnameable horror that "the day would quake to look on." But he draws back. He will only "speak daggers" to the queen, not commit matricide. He calls upon something rarely acknowledged in this drama of fabricated selfhood: the promptings of an inalienable human nature. This nature, our original being as biological creatures, had been his explanation, in a Second Quarto passage, of the Danish propensity to drunkenness:

> So, oft it chances in particular men,
> That for some vicious mole of nature in them,
> As in their birth, wherein they are not guilty,
> Since nature cannot choose his origin.

Yet in a few moments he will be telling his mother in another remarkable Second Quarto passage that "use almost can change the stamp of nature" and that the assumed character he urges upon her will be like clothing—customs or costumes—that make the man or woman:

> That monster custom, who all sense doth eat
> Of habits evil, is angel yet in this,
> That to the use of actions fair and good
> He likewise gives a frock or livery
> That aptly is put on . . .

For use almost can change the stamp of nature,
And either shame the devil or throw him out
With wondrous potency.

He declares that he will set a metaphoric "glass" before her in which she may view her "inmost part," a paradoxical image, for the literal mirror exhibits only the external woman. But he also pleads with her to be an actress, with the hope that an outer appearance of virtue will, somehow, create an essence that was *not* there in the first place. This daring passage, with its skeptical denial of personal essentiality, was withdrawn from the Folio. But we may suppose that, as an actor himself, Shakespeare had been often reminded of how the simulated emotion can take over, *become* genuine feeling. Montaigne had recalled Quintilian's report that he had seen "comedians so farre ingaged in a sorrowfull part, that they wept after being come to their lodgings: and of himselfe, that having undertaken to move a certaine passion in another: he had found himself surprised not only with shedding of teares, but with a paleness of countenance." So Polonius remarks to Hamlet as they watch the First Player describe the anguish of Hecuba, "Look whe'er he has not turned his colour, and has tears in's eyes." And as though he were a theatrical rival, Hamlet finds himself in competition with an actor who lacks his own great "cue." "What's Hecuba to him?" he ask, and wonders at his own inability to manifest grief.

Hamlet is in a similar competition, later on, with Fortinbras, in the Second Quarto's fourth act. Fortinbras, who has put aside his original desire to avenge his own father's death and recover his property, now marches to Poland with an army of twenty thousand to gain a worthless scrap of land, finding "quarrel in a straw," while Hamlet, "a father killed, a mother stained," still has not acted. He is stirred and humbled by such an exhibition of pure performance—which is like the actor's—as he watches the soldiers

Led by a delicate and tender prince,
Whose spirit, with divine ambition puffed
Makes mouths at the invisible event,
Exposing what is mortal and unsure
To all that fortune, death, and danger dare,
Even for an eggshell.

The peculiarity of this has not been properly addressed by the critics, I'm always astonished to discover. Ignoring the flagrant *pointlessness* of Fortinbras's Polish mission, most continue to think of him in comparison or contrast with Hamlet because we first hear of him as a son aroused to avenge his father's death. One is tempted to see a parallel between him and Laertes and even ancient Pyrrhus; they seem a trio of examples of filial devotion to the Revenger obligation, and their presence in the play is part of that pattern I have mentioned of siblings that differ, of opposite representations of related selves—Hamlet and his father, his father and Claudius, Hamlet and Claudius. Like Pyrrhus and Laertes, as well as Fortinbras, Hamlet is the son of a slaughtered father. Laertes, however, is only a misguided hothead and Pyrrhus a butcher who makes Hecuba, with her copious tears, a foil to Gertrude, who has dried her own too quickly. They fulfill the Revenger role while undermining the role's value. Fortinbras discards it altogether, disappearing as an avenger with confusing promptness. Claudius sends envoys to Fortinbras's uncle, the King of Norway—and by return mail, one might say, news arrives in Act II, Scene i that this young hothead has promised to give up his personal project and embrace instead an assignment to lead his soldiers elsewhere. His "divine ambition" has an epic quality in being quite motiveless, ready to manifest itself "even for an eggshell."

Has Fortinbras any persisting function in the play? Well, someone has to be there at the end to pick up the pieces and assume the nation's throne; Horatio would hardly do as Denmark's new king; he is not a royal person. The great Harvard Shakespearean George Lyman Kittredge, seeking an explanation for Fortinbras's presence, made the matter simple. The dramatic character of highest rank customarily spoke the speech bringing an Elizabethan play to a close, and so "this accounts for the presence of Fortinbras in *Hamlet*. But for him there would be no one left of sufficient rank to fulfill this office." But there may be more meaning in Fortinbras's presence. There is this resemblance of Hamlet's late envy of Fortinbras to his early envy of the stage actor who performs his part with such noble fervor—an unexpected pairing in this play of significant pairings. In both cases it does not matter that the eloquence of the theatrical actor and the soldier's valor are without personal motive. Their spectacular action for action's sake seems superior to Hamlet's inadequate expression of what he calls "excitements of my reason and my blood." Hamlet's envy expresses an existential dismissal of the idea of essences and repudiates the connection of character and deed, a repudiation which is at the heart of the play. Motive, inner intention, is nothing. Man is no more than "a beast" if his capability and reason are unused. Only acts, in this skeptical view, count, and the noblest measure of motive has no existence compared to the show of those who "find quarrel in a straw / When honour's at the stake." What other reflection is Shakespeare inviting when Hamlet, dying, gives his nod to Fortinbras as the successor who will bring peace to Denmark—Fortinbras who is not shown to have any innerness at all? Fortinbras may represent the return, however merely gestural, of an antique type of epic valor which needs no motive except the desire to manifest itself and is acknowledged by heroic fame. It is such a motiveless ambition that Othello remembers so regretfully when he bids farewell to "the plumed troops and the big wars / That make ambition virtue," action itself giving a "virtue" to ambition rather than the reverse. In his death, Hamlet seems to recover some of this lost epic heroism, and Fortinbras calls for a hero's funeral,

> For he was likely, had he been put on,
> To have proved most royally; and for his passage,
> The soldiers' music and the rites of war
> Speak loudly for him.

Yet despite this expectation of a glory that outlives the man, suggested in these lines, death is the ultimate loss of selfhood. The gravedigger's and Hamlet's quibbles about dead Ophelia play on the ephemeral nature of the identities we bear in life:

HAMLET. Whose grave's this, sirrah?

FIRST CLOWN. Mine, sir.

HAMLET. I think it be thine, indeed, for thou liest in't.

FIRST CLOWN. You lie out on't, sir, and therefore it is not yours. For my part, I do not lie in't, and yet it is mine.

HAMLET. Thou dost lie in't to be in't and say 'tis thine. 'Tis for the dead, not for the quick; therefore thou liest.

FIRST CLOWN. 'Tis a quick lie, sir; 'twill away again, from me to you.

HAMLET. What man dost thou dig it for?

FIRST CLOWN. For no man, sir.

HAMLET. What woman, then?

FIRST CLOWN. For none, neither.

HAMLET. Who is to be buried in't?

FIRST CLOWN. One that was a woman, sir; but rest her soul, she's dead.

In the "To be or not to be" soliloquy Hamlet offered a succession of definitions of death, from the simple "To sleep, / No more," ambiguously suggesting a permanent oblivion, to the idea that death is a sleep in which we may, "perchance," have dreams. He says death is "a consummation / Devoutly to be wished," and by consummation he does not mean, as we might, fulfillment, but merely, as Shakespeare uses the word elsewhere, simply an *ending*. The magisterial *Oxford English Dictionary* chooses this quotation as first illustration of the sense of the word as "a condition in which desires, aim and tendencies are fulfilled . . . a goal," but I think this is a mistake. Mere finality may be, more likely, what Hamlet means. *Consummation* could also be an alternate spelling of *consumation,* a hononym Shakespeare uses elsewhere to mean consumption or annihilation. Florio, spelling the word with one *m,* so translates the French *anéantissement* from Montaigne in the passage that goes, "If it be a consumation of one's being, it is also an amendement and entrance into a long and quiet night. Wee finde nothing so sweete in life, as a quiet rest and gentle sleepe, and without dreames" — which Shakespeare must have read. The ambiguity that lingers in the word is the rub, however, of Hamlet's problem; it is the same uncertainty of meaning that is felt even at the end, when Hamlet speaks of "a divinity that shapes our ends" — ends meaning outcome or even purpose, but also, merely, the stop we come to, finally. *Consumation* may also recall Hamlet's sardonic humor over Polonius at supper, "not where he eats, but where he is eaten," which, again, though it may be a commonplace to say the dead are food for worms, recalls Montaigne in adding, "Your worm is your only emperor for diet." Florio's translation of Montaigne says, only a little differently, "The heart and life of a mighty and triumphant emperor, is but the breakfast of a seely little worm."

Now in the graveyard itself, where, indeed, are those selfhoods of the politician, the courtier, the lawyer, "with his quiddities now, his quillets, his cases, his tenures, and his tricks," of the lady painting herself "an inch thick" to whom he had unjustly compared Ophelia, and of Alexander the Great and Caesar, and of Yorick?

Yet it is precisely at this moment when the awfulness of this final erasure is brought to mind that Hamlet recalls his own childhood when, as a little boy, he was carried on Yorick's shoulders—a reminder of the continuity of selfhood that begins in childhood and may be said to be derived from prior human selfhoods. Hamlet, we hear, was born on the day his father, also Hamlet, defeated the elder Fortinbras. When he leaps into Ophelia's grave to contest with Laertes, it is not only with his declaration of the love he has denied, but with a momentary sense of recovered self. His "This is I, Hamlet the Dane" is shouted in thrilling tones as though to set himself forever in history along with the father he had recognized in the ghost. This renewed identity he embraces is, after all, the rage of the old action-man his father was, and expected his son to be—a role deeply persistent in inescapable tradition no longer to be evaded. To Laertes, Hamlet says in a desire not to be exceeded,

> Woo't weep, woo't fight, woo't fast, woo't tear thyself?
> Woo't drink up eisel, eat a crocodile?
> I'll do't.

Hamlet is ready at last to acknowledge how impossible it is to avoid the impositions of conventional role and character. Describing to Horatio how he had—accidentally—discovered and foiled the plot against him on the ship taking him to England, and sent Rosencrantz and Guildenstern to their deaths, he says, "Our indiscretion sometimes serves us well / When our deep plots do pall." A good many critics have found Hamlet's easy disposal of this paltry pair, "no shriving-time allowed," as somehow too brutal for the "sweet prince" we love, and we wince at the fact that when he kills Claudius at last it is not only with the "envenomed" rapier but by a gratuitous forced swallow from the cup of poisoned wine as well. But Hamlet has by this time accepted the Revenger destiny, and the primitive ruthlessness which goes with it.

There is a tradition that Shakespeare himself took the part of the ghost in performance. In a sense, it is Shakespeare who is both haunting and haunted. Like Hamlet, he himself tries to escape the expectations of his audience—yet, ultimately, cannot really do so. As the play wears on, the ghost quite disappears. At the last, when its long-before appeal for revenge is about to be answered, Hamlet hardly speaks at all about his father. He does mention that he used the dead king's signet (another assumption of inherited identity) to seal the death warrant of Rosencrantz and Guildenstern. He also refers to the murder of the man he now calls, more impersonally, "my king," as one item in his list of charges against his uncle, and mentions the murderer's corruption of the queen. But curiously, he speaks for the first time about a personal motive for killing Claudius—his own frustrated ambition; Rosencrantz and Guildenstern had scented that in Hamlet long before, though, then, one thought, falsely. Finally, as I have noted, he asks if all these wrongs do not deserve to be punished by his own arm, as though the question had not long ago been answered:

He that hath killed my king, and whored my mother,
Popped in between th' election and my hopes,
Thrown out his angle for my proper life,
And with such cozenage—is't not perfect conscience
To quit him with this arm? And is't not to be damned
To let the canker of our nature come
In further evil?

But the word *revenge,* which one would expect to hear at the end, is never sounded, and the ghost does not show up to declare its satisfaction. (In Kyd's *Spanish Tragedy,* the final scene consists in a complacent exchange between the ghost and personified Revenge.) Hamlet, in a last reminder of theatricality, turns instead to the witnesses on the stage when, dying, he says,

> You that look pale and tremble at this chance
> That are but mutes or audience to this act,
> Had I but time—as this fell sergeant death
> Is strict in his arrest—O, I could tell you—
> But let it be. Horatio, I am dead;
> Thou liv'st; report me and my cause aright
> To the unsatisfied.

What account of Hamlet Horatio can proceed to give is not clear. It can be expected that the motive of revenge, which no one else besides Horatio has known about, is to be revealed at last as Hamlet's "cause," the cause of his being what he has been, and/or the cause for which he has striven and died. But we cannot be sure how much Horatio ever knew. The sense of that cause as the explanation of all that has happened, has, in fact, collapsed, and Horatio now speaks only of the plotless "accidental" and "casual" and mistaken chances that produced the carnage on the stage. He does not speak of revenge but promises to tell

> How these things came about. So shall you hear
> Of carnal, bloody, and unnatural acts,
> Of accidental judgments, casual slaughters,
> Of deaths put on by cunning and forced cause;
> And, in this upshot, purposes mistook
> Fallen on the inventors' heads.

Fortinbras has quite forgotten his own revenge cause but says only, "I have some rights of memory in this kingdom." Even the audience in the theater, also made pale and trembling by this ending— and whom Hamlet also addresses in his last, hopeless "O, I could tell you"—cannot be confident that it fully knows why all it has seen took place.

2

Othello's Jealousy

Oh, yes, the chief subject of *Othello* is sexual jealousy. Most dramatic representations seize upon and emphasize the way this condition, like a fatal disease, grows on the hero and destroys him until the recovery of sanity and dignity at the tragic end. The more directly we see and hear him the more we almost share the madness that mounts in his mind until it reaches a point in which he appears to hallucinate, seeing what is not there, writhing before the inner vision of his wife's betrayal. In the 1995 Kenneth Branagh film this inner vision reaches the screen and the viewer is briefly unable to distinguish between what is and what is imagined as he or she sees—for a terrifying moment, like a clip from a porn film—Cassio's lips meeting Desdemona's, their naked bodies twining together. Film's hallucinatory power, its ability to make virtual what words have only suggested, its ability to make us voyeurs who desire to witness the last detail of a scene, particularly an erotic scene, adds something that goes beyond stage presentation. The movie's powerful language of the visible provides—delusively, though we know Othello is deluded—that ultimate visibility which goes beyond the evidence Iago has manipulated to "prove" Othello's love a whore.

But the greater reserve of the play as we read it, and even the reserve of stage presentation, which works such tricks awkwardly if at all, reminds us that jealousy feeds, precisely, upon what is not witnessed but only imagined. Othello, desperately swinging between belief in his wife's innocence and conviction of her guilt, pleads for visible proof—"I'll see before I doubt," he cries. He thinks he can trust Desdemona, and his trust is based on his conviction (which plays upon the double sense of seeing as knowing and beholding) that he himself was rightly seen by her: "for she had eyes and chose me," he tells Iago, who responds with his own reference to what is visible, but only to God:

> Look to your wife, observe her well with Cassio.
> Wear your eyes thus, not jealous, nor secure. . . .
> Look to't. . . .
> In Venice they do let God see the pranks
> They dare not show their husbands.

"Make me to see't," Othello pleads. He groans, "Would I were satisfied!" but his tormentor observes—in an age before hidden video cameras and paparazzi—"but how? How satisfied, my Lord?/Would you, the supervisor, grossly gape on?/Behold her topped?" and summons into inner view the dreadful vision, after all.

Iago is expert in producing an effect of virtual reality in someone else's mind. He has begun his work by arousing Brabantio to racist fury by evoking the embraces of Desdemona and Othello himself. "Even now, very now, an old black ram/Is tupping your white ewe," he says in the earlier Quarto text of the play, the Folio, thought to be Shakespeare's revision, adding a third "now" ("Even now, now, very now") to intensify the present-ness of the vision. It is just such a provocative visualization of the sexual act he induces in Othello, who must imagine his wife in the arms of a white

Venetian aristocrat. Iago will continue throughout the travail of Othello's jealousy to promote hallucinations, to make Othello's own imagination set them forth on his inner stage. The visions multiply. Even as he wishes for the oblivion of ignorance rather than the knowledge his jealousy seems to grant him, he imagines her as an army whore, partner of innumerable couplings with the lowest sort of (probably white) common soldiers, "the general camp,/ Pioneers and all," rather than with himself, their commander. By the time we have reached the opening of the fourth act, the process is complete, and for Othello, inner and outer sight are indistinguishable.

And yet, Iago, with his "How satisfied, my Lord?" has warned him from the start that the sexual actuality he demands sight of is inaccessible, unknowable.

> It is impossible you should see this
> Were they as prime as goats, as hot as monkeys,
> As salt as wolves in pride, and fools as gross
> As Ignorance made drunk.

We may legitimately ask why such a seeing is as impossible as Iago says. Lovers have been caught "flagrantly" in the act of sex before and since. Othello is already driven mad by what, by the force of suggestion, he inwardly sees. But he craves a certainty that can be satisfied only by outward sight—the sense that most convincingly assures us that we know what is before us. Yet Iago tells him that such confirmation is not to be had. Iago will go so provocatively far as to suggest—while forcing Othello to imagine the scene—that even the physical sight of Desdemona and Cassio kissing and naked in bed together would not absolutely confirm the suspicion of adultery, after all:

IAGO. Will you think so?

OTHELLO. Think so, Iago?

IAGO. What,

To kiss in private?

OTHELLO. An unauthorized kiss!

IAGO. Or to be naked with her friend in bed

An hour or more, not meaning any harm?

OTHELLO. Naked in bed, Iago, and not mean harm?

That they might "mean no harm" is an improbability that seems to call for a close-up view of coitus itself such as porn films give, or invites such ludicrous debate as to what are or are not "sexual relations" as one heard concerning the escapades of former U.S. President Bill Clinton!

What Iago's strange remarks suggest is that there is something metaphysical about sex to the jealous mind. The sexual act about which the jealous lover wants the truth must seem, however closely viewed, still to hide something. No knowledge is complete enough to satisfy jealousy, which feeds, as I have said, not on the seen but on the unseen. Jealousy does not require provocation or justification, by its very nature. As the shrewd Emilia rightly says,

> jealous souls will not be answered so:
> They are not ever jealous for the cause,
> But jealous for they're jealous. It is a monster
> Begot upon itself, born on itself.

So Othello's mind is the theater in which belief in the unseen contends with the doubt that demands physical seeing and yet never sees enough. The central utterance in the play is, certainly, Othello's anguished "Be sure of it, give me the ocular proof." Yet Othello is plagued by the realization that truth cannot be directly, positively, known; what we perceive is only *seeming*. For, as Iago says, "Her honor is an essence that's not seen." "Seeming," and "seeing," are significantly repeated ideas throughout the play, yet change places. In the scene in which Othello thinks he witnesses Cassio complacently acknowledging his conquest of Desdemona he is, at last, given what passes for proof removing his last uncertainty. But what he observes even with his senses is only appearance and not actuality. Sexual jealousy is an epistemological crisis in which perception is avid of the incontrovertible. Yet jealousy is so unsure of the meaning of what it sees that faith in reality itself is threatened.

In Shakespeare's tale of one who loved not wisely but too well, there is, too, a caution against any love inordinate in its expectations because the coital beast Iago summons into mental view for Brabantio is a monster created only in an instant of sensual pleasure. The very power of the sexual theme in the play both shows us the awful closeness of sexual love and reminds us of the distance between two human beings. This "beast with two backs" Iago describes is both one and two in all lovemaking. In the closest of human mergers, knowledge of the other must be incomplete. Jealousy is evidence of the doubt that lies at the bottom of love's craving for such knowledge, the doubt beneath love's refusal to accept the difference between one's perception and another's reality. It is this doubt of knowing that comes to Othello, who thinks he discovers that the woman he has married is quite different from the girl he thought he wooed. His young wife's apparent alteration is totally inexplicable to him and a devastating lesson in the deceit of appearances. She comes to seem to him the oxymoronic "fair devil," whose fairness belies her foulness. He raves: "a fine woman, a fair woman, a sweet woman . . . let her rot and perish and be damned tonight." He nearly faints at the memory of her loveliness, and thinking of his own most personal perception of her, he says, "O, the world hath not a sweeter creature: she might lie by an emperor's side and command him tasks." But it is only a moment later that he will utter the terrible, "I will chop her into messes! Cuckold me!"

If we see Othello's fall as a telescoped representation of the mind overtaken by its own distrust of appearances—and the paradoxical reliance only upon appearances—we can see that what overcomes Othello, or rather what is represented through Othello's ordeal, is a trembling of the universal spheres, a perturbation from which recovery comes only at the cost of deadly anguish. In *The Winter's Tale*, perhaps Shakespeare's last play, the jealous Leontes says, like another Othello,

> Is whispering nothing?
> Is leaning cheek to cheek? is meeting noses?
> Kissing with inside lip? stopping the career
> Of laughter with a sigh? (a note infallible
> Of breaking honesty) horsing foot on foot?
> Skulking in corners? wishing clocks more swift?
> Hours, minutes? noon, midnight? and all eyes
> Blind with pin and web, but theirs; theirs only.
> That would unseen be wicked? is this nothing?
> Why then the world, and all that's in't, is nothing
> The covering sky is nothing, Bohemia nothing,
> My wife is nothing, nor nothing have these nothings,
> If this be nothing.

So, too, it is not mere hyperbole that causes Othello to tell Desdemona, out of her hearing, "when I love thee not/ Chaos is come again," to exclaim, "If she be false, O then heaven mocks itself," or to say, in later confirmation of this prediction,

> O heavy hour!
> Methinks it should be now a huge eclipse

Of sun and moon, and that th' affrighted globe
Should yawn at alteration.

The plot of jealousy, which derives from its protagonist's submission to visionary improbability as well as genuine probability, is apt to flout dramatic expectations of coherence and likelihood—and like the victim of jealousy himself we may find ourselves indifferent to gaps in the normal logic of events as we are caught up in such a history. Othello's own noble strength, the slowness to anger that rules his early responses to Brabantio and to the drunken scuffle that awakens him from his wedded bliss in Cyprus, the majesty of his normal language—all fail to prepare us for the speed with which he casts reason and refinement aside and becomes brutal and coarse—and shakes our sense of life's legibility by doing so. Yet we do not balk at this any more than at other unlikelihoods in the play. Iago's perfidy is impossible to explain. Desdemona's failure to attempt to discover the root of her husband's change of temper is unbelievably Griselda-like. Can we really take such characters seriously? Strangely, we do.

Anticipating a postmodernist approach to narrative, E. E. Stoll, who urged that Hamlet's delay and his madness were theatrical conventions and no more, argued years ago that these violations of probability in *Othello* would not have bothered Shakespeare's audience either. Maybe we are wrong to think of Othello or Iago or Desdemona as though they are real persons whose motives must be discernible, whose behavior should seem plausible. Their characters, Stoll insisted, are artificial literary structures and well-worn ones at that—like the type of the Revenger that imposes itself on Hamlet. If the ease with which Othello is influenced seems too great, theatrical tradition enjoined that a calumniator should be believed. In the same implausibly unquestioning way, we shall see, Gloucester accepts Edmund's false accusations against Edgar in *King Lear*—another of Stoll's examples of the operation of convention.

Shakespeare also found a way of utilizing other conventional traditions—not of tragedy at all, but of comedy—to shape his incredible story. Comedy thrives upon abrupt reversals and returns, upon unbelievably effective deceits. How often it employs some of the delusionary tricks that destroy Othello's faith in Desdemona! In Shakespeare's own *Much Ado About Nothing* another ex-soldier, Claudio, is deceived by similar means into believing in the wantonness of his innocent betrothed. Such affronts to probability would threaten tragedy. But comedy has a way of simplifying character, reducing a story to the level of anecdote. The courtship which Othello's and Desdemona's marriage climaxed could, by itself, have been the material of a romantic comedy of the kind Shakespeare had himself already written, a comedy about the triumph of love over confusions and obstacles. In romantic comedies, of course, lovers thrust apart by jealous doubt can rise above delusion and folly and the false persuasions of mischief-makers—and we might almost expect this to happen in *Othello*. But such lighthearted use of deception and revelation was not what now interested Shakespeare or, if it did, it now interested him only ironically, as shown in this play by a marriage sequel in which the lovers are finally united after terrible misunderstanding—but only in death. It is a conclusion that is a bitter mock of those marriage endings that resolve the tensions and frustrations of lovers in *Midsummer Night's Dream, The Merchant of Venice,* or *As You Like It. Othello* is a romance become tragic, like *Romeo and Juliet.*

But a different, *un*romantic comic design even more significantly underlies the story of this marriage which it is too easy to say was perfect until Iago got to work. Iago has only to insist upon those persisting differences between the lovers that Shakespeare emphasizes—of age and experience and race and class—to create the conditions for farce.

Shakespeare altered the story he found in the *Hecatommithi,* a prose tale written by Giraldi Cinthio in 1566 and translated into French in 1584. Cinthio's Othello is young and handsome and an accepted member of Venetian society. That Shakespeare's Othello is much older than Desdemona, that the bloom of youth is gone from him while she is young and beautiful, that he is cruder, or at least, less sophisticated than the man he suspects as his rival— all these threaten to make him the butt of a thousand jokes. As George Bernard Shaw remarked, the plot of *Othello* is a farce plot "supported on an artificially manufactured and precarious trick which a chance word might upset at any moment," but the trick is never discovered. Verdi detected and exploited the farcical potential in Shakespeare's characters, Shaw observed: "Desdemona is a prima donna with a handkerchief, confidante, and vocal solo, all complete; and Iago, though slightly more anthropomorphic than the Count di Luna, is only so when he slips off his stage villain's part. Othello's transports are conveyed by magnificent and senseless music which rages from the Propontick to the Hellespont in an orgy of thundering sound and bounding rhythm. . . . With such a libretto Verdi was quite at home." This reductive summary of Shakespeare's play is a piece of Shavian extravagance, but no one understood better than Shaw the way plot patterns matter. Our responses are affected by the fact that, as Michael Neil has remarked, the final act of *Othello* returns to comic convention rewritten as cruel travesty. The play is framed by two beddings, as farce comedy often is, though the second is a deathbed, "the first clandestine and offstage, the second appallingly public; one callously interrupted, the other murderously consummated."

And yet, despite the conventions, especially the comic conventions that dictate the plot in one way or another, the consistent tragic seriousness of the play has always stimulated a desire to find the source of events in the hero's character. F. R. Leavis was able to make a devastating case against Bradley's view that the hero's perfect nature—virtuous and disciplined—is destroyed by Iago's inhuman malice and intellect (even though this somewhat contradicts Bradley's own generalization that Shakespeare's tragic plots are always generated by the character of the chief person himself). Leavis discovered grounds for seeing Othello as a man infatuated with his own idea of himself, and *self*-destroyed. I would put this differently. Insecurity does lurk beneath Othello's eloquent romanticism. But his vulnerability may be promoted by the fact that he is a stranger, only recently come to Venice, unlike the character in the *Hecatommithi*—as well as the fact that he is a Moor. Shakespeare actually adds to the plausibility of the story somewhat by emphasizing the hero's outsider status, providing conditions Cinthio felt no need to provide, for the *Hecatommithi* had already set up an irresistible force in Iago's persuasive powers. In Shakespeare's play we are on the one hand astonished at Othello's groundless suspicions of Desdemona and yet allowed to suspect causes for a condition of mind he would not be able to name. And these are not only the vulnerabilities of his own nature and particular situation—which Shakespeare permits us to glimpse—but a discovery of universal doubt into which he stumbles as into a depthless hole.

Othello *is* the comic Jealous Husband. He sometimes even seems to see himself as the character in a familiar folk tale who is always feeling his head for horns though his wife is innocent. "I have a pain in my forehead, here," he says. But in such set plots, the jealous one is punished for his folly, and the agent of comic correction is a "joker"—a role Auden recognized in Othello in a famous essay on the play. Othello is, nevertheless, worthy of our respect and pity. His delusion and tragic awakening constitute no joking matter. Shakespeare makes tragedy possible by presenting his hero as a man who has already demonstrated to the world his capacity for a heroic career and noble emotion, and whose fall to horrible folly is the inverse of his previous greatness. "O, the pity of it!" we can say—using his own words about Desdemona's supposed dishonor. Only the depth of his disastrous folly makes us also say, "Yes, he is!" when Emilia cries, "O gull, O dolt, / As ignorant as dirt!" as Desdemona lies dead. The play's ending that compelled Dr. Johnson to write, "I am glad I have ended my revisal of this dreadful scene; it is not to be endured," does not lose its heart-rending quality because it has been reached by a plot of farce. The resemblance of Shakespeare's tragic characters to comic prototypes goes only a little way without breaking down. But the comic vibrates a little beneath the surface of Shakespeare's tragedy for all its wrenching pathos. There are moments when we can see the flattened type figure Jealousy persisting in Othello, making him ridiculous even when we are ready to weep for him. But this hero's feelings transcend mere convention as, from moment to moment, he falls from faith to disbelief. We expect but dread his collapse.

Shakespeare's Iago himself resists explanation to a greater degree than Cinthio's does—the Italian novella dilates on *his* reasons as Shakespeare's play does not, while Shakespeare's Iago, like Don John the Bastard in *Much Ado* or like such serious Machiavellian plotters as Edmund or Richard III, seems to act, as has always been said, out of unfathomable malice. One can even argue—as Bernard Spivack has—that Othello's insinuating undoer derives from still another stereotype represented by the traditional Vice of the old "Moralities" still enacted in the yards of country inns by traveling companies in the sixteenth century. This stage demon had no reason for his behavior besides his pleasure in doing evil. He was a horned imp who gleefully pranced upon the stage as he ruined mankind. Did such a creature need "motives" beyond his own diversion? Othello, baffled, as we are, by the lack of an evident explanation "why" Iago has destroyed him, looks at his enemy's feet, finally, to see if he has hooves. He reminds himself that "that's a fable." The demonic Vice figure does not account for Iago. But no credible explanations for his actions are, in fact, available.

Yet Iago's plot against Othello most closely resembles the comic-satiric plot engineered to punish and reform such a jealous husband as Kitely in Ben Jonson's *Every Man in His Humour*, in which Shakespeare himself had acted a part when it was presented for the first time in 1598. In a sense, Iago is a clever servant, like Jonson's Brainworm, who produces an imbroglio of false appearances for the chastisement of false suspicion. Iago, of course, has no interest in effecting reform. He has no moral aim. But one might say that his sardonic humor is curiously principled in its unprincipled way. His scorn is directed invariably not only against a particular delusion or pretension but against *all* delusion, as he sees it. It is directed against all ideality—love and honor and virtue only being some of the items on a list he keeps of false ideas by which mankind deceives itself. It is often pointed out that Shakespeare exhibits contrasted viewpoints in the language of Othello and Iago. There is the poetic "Othello music," as G. Wilson Knight called it, sounded in words that seem to arise from a sense of a moral cosmos and the hero's place in it. There is the language of Iago, prosaically intelligent without any element of the ideal—a language supposed to be expressively inferior. It is also the language of a *social* inferior, that of the comic *servant* who is cast as a critic of his master. Iago regards Othello's afflatus skeptically. He sees that it verges upon the pompous. And there have even been some students of the play who have felt that Iago has a case when he charges Othello with being someone in love with "his own pride and purposes," someone who evades an appeal he wishes to refuse "with a bombast circumstance/Horribly stuffed with epithets of war." Certainly, it must be said that Othello's is the half of language more vulnerable to skepticism. Iago's version of Othello's tragedy is not the one most readers and viewers of the play embrace—he sees it as farce comedy unconverted to tragedy. He sees it as the leveling of preposterous self-delusion and presumption. But the effect of his vision is not lost upon us, despite our reluctance to accept it.

Othello has no comic subplot, not even the subordinate comic humor visible in *Hamlet* and *Lear,* unless one counts Iago's sardonic snickers and grins. (The momentary bawdy clown scene which opens the third act is so trivial and irrelevant that it is almost invariably omitted in performances of the play.) But by its implication of farce the play detaches itself a little from tragedy, and Othello's collapse constitutes an admonitory lesson that appearances may mislead us—which is often the lesson comedy enforces. Othello, who suspects where he should trust and believes where he should doubt, and Iago, the complete skeptic, are not an unfamiliar pairing in comic plots. But although Othello resembles the comic victim, we are moved by his travail as we could not be by the true comic figure. Shakespeare makes us experience—through Othello's distress—a trauma of disbelief in all meaning, and "chaos is come again." Iago is the agent of that trauma, the representative of unbelief as well as the instigator of it in others, which is why, indeed, no grievance he might offer or we might imagine for him is strong enough to account for his behavior. Nor will he, in the end, account for it himself, despite some unlikely reasons he has tossed at us. In response to Othello's final question as to his own motives, Iago only mutters, "Demand me nothing. What you know, you know / From this time forth I never will speak word." His cryptic statement "I am not what I am" has been taken to mean "I am not what I seem," but it is a declaration of nonbeing, the reverse of St. Paul's "by the grace of God I am what I am."

Iago has often been identified with that gratuitous evil St. Augustine found in himself when he remembered how he had simply lusted to steal, compelled by no need or hunger, and had taken joy not in what he stole but only in the stealing itself. Iago hardly exhibits joy in what he does, however. And the "mystery of iniquity" supposedly illustrated by him becomes an instance of the general mystery of selfhood—satanic or human. If he is without motives it is only because he is the most extreme case of the truth that motives are not as available as explanation of all our acts as we might like to think. That character is less firmly attached to such explanations is evident in the view Shakespeare sometimes gives us of his most appealing characters—as we have seen in the case of Hamlet—and of Othello himself, who begins by being the last person we would expect to do what he does.

Iago occasionally acts as though he is obliged, because deeds are supposed, especially in tragedy, to be furnished with motives, to offer us a few. But it is all "a motive-hunting of motiveless malignity," as Coleridge famously said. Most of his proffered reasons are furnished to his silly gull, Roderigo, to justify his animosity. Shakespeare, himself, is shamelessly cavalier about the whole matter. That Iago was ever in love with Desdemona, as Cinthio says he was, emerges only in one incoherent mutter in the play, an undigested particle of the old plot or a sop to an audience that expected even unfathomable villainy to have its reasons:

> I do love her too,
> Not out of absolute lust—though peradventure
> I stand accountant for as great a sin—
> But partly led to diet my revenge,
> For that I do suspect the lusty Moor
> Hath leaped into my seat.

If he himself suffers from sexual jealousy over the same woman as Othello, we see no sign of it in the play. That Iago resents Cassio for having succeeded with Desdemona is also suggested by Cinthio, but Shakespeare makes nothing of that possibility either. It has at least as plausibly been suggested in recent times that it is Othello whom Iago loves, that it is his homosexual jealousy of Othello's married bliss that he really feels. This was Ernest Jones's idea, and it was the intuition of Laurence Olivier both when he played Othello as a gorgeous, hip-swiveling West Indian and more clearly when he played Iago as a rejected lover, opposite Ralph Richardson. But Shakespeare is not really interested in Iago as a representative of sexual jealousy of any kind. His Iago does not feel the morbid suspicion and thwarted love with which he infects Othello. This is a motive Shakespeare transfers to Othello from Cinthio's Iago, who is undeniably in love with his general's wife. Indeed, *Iago's* frustrated lust for Desdemona is the force that generates the plot of the *Hecatommithi*. Othello comes only incidentally into it. Cinthio's Iago first directs his jealous resentment against Cassio, whom he believes she really loves more than she does Othello, and his Desdemona is killed in the end not by Othello but by Iago, with Othello's connivance, in final fulfillment of his fury at her for having rejected him. If there is any jealousy on the part of Shakespeare's Iago that seems believable, it is his quite unsexual envy of Cassio's promotion in rank, a promotion he feels his own devotion merits — a jealousy *not* mentioned by Cinthio and one that Shakespeare refuses to develop. The tried ensign's disappointment is offered as the cause of Iago's resentment of Cassio and anger at Othello only once, and in the suspect context of his effort to convince Roderigo that he has good grounds for his own hostility. (It would hardly have done to figure himself to this rejected suitor as another rival for Desdemona's favor.) Yet his frustrated social mobility, the ambition that makes him ready to be whatever the occasion demands, makes a motive out of his very denial of consistent selfhood.

So, in Shakespeare's version of the story, Iago provokes a distrust of appearances in Othello by arousing jealousy, but that distrust needs no such provocation in his own case. The removal of motives which makes Iago seem inhuman or unbelievable serves, however, to bring his deep-rooted, *un*motivated skepticism and his scorn of those who do not share it into its astonishing salience. Iago's nihilism links him in Shakespeare's works with Thersites and Edmund—and even, to a degree, with Hamlet, who needed, as I have observed already, no specific motive to prompt his skeptic philosophic viewpoint. Into Iago's mind, as into the black interior of a camera, nothing else but the actually seen can enter; he has no dreams. He both disbelieves in the inner essence of persons and is, himself, without inner qualities. His very lack of apparent motive is an illustration of his own theory that "our bodies are gardens, to the which our wills are gardeners"—or that we are whatever we will to be. He is often seen as one of Shakespeare's versions of the stage Machiavel, but less noticed has been the relation of his true Machiavellianism to a philosophic skepticism that suggested the same deprecation of essences that underlies the writings of Montaigne. If Shakespeare read Machiavelli, this strenuous pragmatic thinker could have argued to him that the practical politician was the maker of his own character to which his will was the gardener— and seeming was all. Machiavelli wrote in *The Prince* that "appearances might be for the Prince himself all that counted practically. . . . He need not have all the good qualities . . . but should certainly appear to have them. . . . He should have a flexible disposition. Varying as fortune and circumstances dictate." Consistency was a positive danger. Iago, of course, gives a contrary impression, for he is always called one thing—"honest." But nothing is more slippery than this term reiterated in the play in various senses, including that sense descriptive of a new type of person, one who had cast off the burden of fixed ideas, to which I referred in my Introduction. It is not clear that he is called this because he is thought to be telling the truth or merely because he is a person without illusions, a matter-of-fact believer that what you see is what you have. If "honest Iago" has this further meaning for the audience (if not always for Othello when he calls him that), a further irony may be suggested by the fact that it describes someone who dispenses with exalted beliefs about the unalterable soul and declines to differentiate between seeming and being.

Iago has been said to suffer from a thwarted sense of superiority—exactly *because* he is free of illusions. *This* may be as much a motive as one can muster to explain his hatred of Othello. His is the special bitterness of the man who sees himself as endowed with a superior freedom of mind, which makes him admire only the few who are like himself. The illusioned—especially Othello, but even the gentlemanly Cassio—enrage him by their fatuous high-mindedness. "The Moor, howbeit that I endure him not,/Is of a constant, loving, noble nature," he says, emphasizing with a snarl of contempt for their hollowness, as I hear him, such words as *constant, loving,* and *noble.* He cannot stand Othello, conceding that his general is just what he himself—disloyal, ignoble—is not. He despises the idealism that sustains Othello's virtues. These he regards as mere show, like Othello's elevated style of speech, which he calls bombast. Or of fatuousness:

> The Moor is of a free and open nature
> That thinks men honest that but seem to be so,
> And will as tenderly be led by th' nose
> As asses are.

His effect upon Othello will be to destroy the very qualities he singles out to despise—Othello's constancy (by making him alter his previous faith in Desdemona), his lovingness and his nobility (by reducing him to a brutal murderer), his free, trusting nature (by making him a monster of suspicion).

He works to destroy belief in unimpugnable essences. We can hear this in the very tone of his own consistently reductive language—a base metal to which Othello's will be converted when he surrenders his own golden tone. Love, Iago regards as merely "carnal stings . . . merely a lust of the blood, and a permission of the will," as he tells Roderigo. Iago's definition of love occurs in a speech that is often praised as the expression of the just rule of reason over the passions. When Roderigo wails that he cannot help loving Desdemona ("It is not in my virtue to amend it"), Iago replies, "Virtue? A fig! 'tis in ourselves that we are thus, or thus." Continuing with the sentence I quote again as a key to his philosophy—"Our bodies are gardens, to the which our wills are gardeners"—he goes on to say, "But we have reason to cool our raging motions, our carnal stings, our unbitted lusts; whereof I take this, that you call love, to be sect or scion." Coleridge thought this "comprises the passionless character of Iago. It is all will in intellect; and therefore he is here a bold partisan of truth, but yet of a truth converted into a falsehood by the absence of all the necessary modifications caused by the frail nature of man." Coleridge is plumping, romantically, for the emotions. But Iago's remarks show us something besides: he sees all human qualities as matters of choice and will. Nothing belongs inalienably to one's nature. What he calls "a fig," a nothing, is not only moral excellence but, in the older sense of *virtue,* character.

Yet also as a Machiavellian, a man who understands the meaning of ambition as the drive toward self-making, and character as what we make of ourselves, Iago has never been taken in by the empty selfhood of reputation. Brabantio's early warning, "Fathers from hence, trust not your daughters' minds, / By what you see them act," predicts Iago's disregard of appearances as a clue to any inner truth, his ultimate skepticism about perception. Iago calls reputation "an idle and most false imposition." Though his words—always adjusted to his hearer—are part of his hypocritical comfort to Cassio, they match his general skepticism that denies the stability of appearance even though appearance may be all that we have. The "reputation" speech seems to counsel an admirable stoicism yet also is a repudiation of Cassio's despair that he has "lost the immortal part of [himself]—and what remains is bestial." Iago tells him, "You have lost no reputation at all, unless you repute yourself such a loser." Iago tells Cassio that the "immortal part" of himself cannot be damaged if his own self-belief sustains his sense that he has lost nothing. Yet so lightly is this considered wisdom offered that Iago will contradict it in his later famous gnomic remarks to Othello about "good name"—surely a synonym for *reputation*—which he tells Othello is "the immediate jewel of our souls." In *this* speech he contrasts "good name" with his purse, which he calls trash, a statement worth examining for its inversion of what one would expect him to say—which is that it is exactly *like* money. "'Twas mine, 'tis his, and has been slave to thousands"; it is money, in this period of the primary accumulation of capital, that already shows its power to reduce all meaning to itself as an empty signifier, the universal abstraction of the power to buy. In truth, for Iago, good name is like rather than unlike the infinitely convertible monetary note that passes from one hand to another and serves any purchase. That Shakespeare allows Iago to say that the opposite is true of one's good name is another instance of that play of contrary views that Shakespeare is prone to admit into his text.

Iago's principle of dissimulation confirms his *devaluation* of appearance when he tells Roderigo in the opening scene,

> When my outward action doth demonstrate
> The native act and figure of my heart
> In complement extern, 'tis not long after

> But I will wear my heart upon my sleeve
> For daws to peck at: I am not what I am.

Yet what "native act and figure" is Iago's is never evident. In this he takes to an extreme the example we have seen in Hamlet, who says he has that within which passeth show, yet never reveals the inner consistency beneath his inky cloak. Iago pretends that he has an essential heart, though it is not worn on his sleeve (again, Shakespeare's favorite clothing metaphor!), but this, too, is part of his pose before Roderigo. He assumes the same pose before Othello when he enacts the role of the man who is resolved to keep his thoughts to himself. "You cannot, if my heart were in your hand, / Nor shall not, while 'tis in my custodie" seems to assert, again, the distinction between that which is inward and hidden and that which is shown — except that, as we realize, his undisclosed knowledge about Desdemona is pretended, along with his pretended hesitation. "I am not what I am," he cryptically says — a statement which, as I have said, denies altogether that he has an essential selfhood rather than that there is an inner man hidden from view. There is a curious contradiction in his statement about his own pretended love for Othello,

> Though I do hate him as I do hell-pains,
> Yet, for necessity of present life,
> I must show out a flag, and sign of love,
> Which is indeed but sign.

Iago's show of devotion for Othello will, indeed, be only a misleading flag to disguise his true hatred, like a deceiving white flag of peace. But unless the comma after "love" is wrongly placed, he seems also to say that love is "but sign" — a mere outward exhibition without inner meaning.

So the self, according to Iago, changes with circumstances or can be made to change. If this is Iago's true view, it may be Shake-speare's own in this play, in which either consistency or motivation in the two chief male characters so often lapses. The case may seem different for others. Cassio is a man whose only aberration is caused by the temporary influence of drink, and Desdemona never changes; it would have been better, we might say, if she had changed from the lamblike character she maintains until she is slaughtered. Perhaps if she had become more indignant, more suspicious and probing, disaster might have been averted. Instead, she is described by Cassio as excelling all others "in th' essential vesture of creation"—that is, her innocent soul, like prelapsarian Eve's, unspoiled by the effects of fallen human life, the falsifying clothing of social roles. Her capacity for dissimulation is minimal—displayed pathetically when she distracts herself by exchanging silly jokes with Iago as she nervously waits for Othello's boat to land on Cyprus. She says, "I am not merry, but I do beguile / The thing I am by seeming otherwise." She is not good at beguiling or belying the thing she is—which suggests that her essential self is invulnerable to change even if she wishes to change it. She lies twice—once when she denies that she has lost the handkerchief and again, when she denies, dying, that Othello is her murderer. The first lie is fatal to her; the second cannot possibly save her husband, even if he should want to be saved from the consequences of his crime.

Nevertheless, Shakespeare allows us to consider the plausibility of some of Iago's slurs. We can understand how Othello might see the logic in Iago's warning that Desdemona would have been ready to deceive him, having already deceived her father, who—though it is hard to sympathize with him—is said to have died later of his grief. She also may have her own racist misgiving about marriage to a Moor. She exclaims, rightly, in Act III, at Othello's loss of the self she thought she knew in him ("My lord is not my lord"). But can we go along with his parallel statement in which he declares that she has ceased to exist also ("I took you for that cunning whore of Venice/That married with Othello")? The answer is, of course, no, yet the imposition of an opposed image upon the Desdemona he has loved and we believe in does infect our imagination a little. The success of Iago's campaign against Cassio and Desdemona is the creation of an alteration in their apparent characters, and in a world in which there is no guarantee of any essence, appearance takes precedence over faith. In the perceptions of Othello, the loyal Cassio is turned into the seducer of his general's wife. The honorable gentleman becomes an unprincipled fornicator. In its action on Othello's mind, Iago's transformative magic is capable of effecting a change in Desdemona that seems real to him—as real as Othello's own schizophrenic breakdown. Iago reflects that he will "turn her virtue into pitch" by making her look guilty. He defines her as an expert at dissimulation, though Othello protests, feebly, "I do not think but Desdemona's honest." But even if she is what she seems, there may be no stability in personal "nature," after all, if Iago's theory about essences is acceptable.

With that "coolness of a preconceiving experimenter" Coleridge noted, Iago will persuade Othello that he sees what he does not really see when this "honest" friend remarks upon Cassio's "steal[ing] away so guilty-like" or when Cassio appears to laugh complacently over his conquest of Desdemona—when actually speaking of his mistress. *Seeming* becomes the term that dominates: "Men should be what they seem," Iago says, "Or those that be not, would they might seem none." But *he* is the master of legerdemain who can make things appear that aren't there and make things that are disappear—a professional prestidigitator who produces a handkerchief where one was not expected, one that has "magic in its web" when it becomes the sign of adultery. So Desdemona's affectionate sympathy for Cassio, her too-vehement in-sistence to Othello that this handsome, graceful friend must be forgiven and reinstated in favor, will look like infidelity.

It is Othello himself, of course, who becomes, despite all our wish to know him as one being, the major illustration of the idea that personality is inconstant or malleable. This is most obviously what the play dramatizes centrally—the way the hero of the open-ing scenes is altered by inexorable stages that succeed one another too readily for belief—and yet Shakespeare imposes a credibility by means of language that shows the intrusion of another rhythm into his majestic calm until he exclaims, vowing his revenge upon the wife he thinks has betrayed him, "O, blood, blood, blood!" In this connection it is interesting to observe the fact that the 1623 Folio removes offensive language like this from Othello's late lines in the Quarto text of the second half of the play—as though to make less terrible the fall in which he seems to give over his own elevated tone and borrows another's. It is usual to attribute this change simply to playhouse censorship caused by the parliamen-tary act against profanity passed in 1606, and it is true that the Folio also modifies Iago's language in the same way throughout. But it is not impossible that Shakespeare (if it was Shakespeare who made the changes in the later text) took the opportunity to pre-serve our sense of Othello's persisting dignity. The Folio even adds more "Othello music" by inserting a passage in the midst of the hero's degradation in which he majestically compares his murder-ous intention to

the Pontic sea,
Whose icy current and compulsive course
Ne'er feels retiring ebb but keeps due on
To the Propontic and the Hellespont.

A less wholesale alteration and less improbability results when he recovers, at the end, some of his original character. The unbelievable discrepancy between the earlier and the later man, as the Quarto exhibits them, challenges the continuity of character in the more radical way, on the other hand, and perhaps this is an effect Shakespeare sought at the beginning.

Iago moves on the process of Othello's alteration as Shakespeare does by his own hallucinatory playwright powers. But it is also true that Othello's whole career can be seen from the perspective of a society in which self-transformation as well as the transformations effected by the influence of others—or by the forces of social change—operate to alter the outlines of the self, shift it from one template to another. Othello has succeeded where Iago has failed in self-transformation. He is already, when we first meet him, a "self-made man" who has made the most of the gifts of Fortune. Before he became the hero who won the regard of the Venetian state and the love of Desdemona, he had been someone we can only dimly glimpse. His life has been a *career* which began by the casting aside of a beginning we never see directly. And yet in the end he cannot sustain the new self. The play is very much about such careers, although we think of it as a play concerned only with the private life.

The curtain rises, to begin with, on a discussion about jobs and how one is qualified for them. Iago's possible envy of Cassio's promotion is not implausible, as I have said, even though Iago expresses this resentment only in a single remark to Roderigo. It serves, in any case, to relate the play to a new social climate which gave rise to uncertainty about personal identity—and gives a historical meaning to the way Iago comes before us as the man who believes that one is only what one appears to be, what role one is able to personate. Iago, the lower-class man who expects to rise, calls the aristocratic Cassio, just appointed lieutenant, a mere class-room soldier,

> a great arithmetician . . .
> That never set a squadron in the field
> Nor the division of a battle knows
> More than a spinster.

Practical field experience is a legitimate requirement for the promotion Cassio has gained — and something different from the mere entitlement of class and even the school theory he has acquired. In contrast, Iago has served in battle with Othello "at Rhodes, at Cyprus and other grounds,/Christian and heathen," and he reminds his commander: "I' the trade of war I have slain men." Iago professes to believe in promotion for merit and resents the arbitrary advancement of the candidate, like Cassio, who has an old boys' network. He also claims the earned rights of seniority in the job rather than preferment gained by letters of recommendation from influential somebodies.

> Preferment goes by letter and affection
> And not by old gradation, where each second
> Stood heir to th' first.

But though he makes his claim by referring to a system of respect for service he calls "old gradation," he himself has tried to go up the ladder by the aid of "letter and affection" and secured the support of "three great ones of the city." He is one of the new breed of men who not only claim advancement by merit but will manipulate and scheme for advancement — and by either means expect to escape assignment to a fixed definition. That he has not received his deserved promotion and must prosper just the same is something he is prepared for as a master of Machiavellian elasticity. He deprecates title and position and even the old division into masters and followers which organizes society:

> We cannot be all masters, nor all masters
> Cannot be truly follow'd. You shall mark
> Many a duteous and knee-crooking knave
> That, doting on his own obsequious bondage,
> Wears out his time much like his master's ass
> For nought but provender, and, when he's old,
>   cashiered.
> Whip me such honest knaves!

Others, the new kind of persons, know the meaninglessness of the identity society assigns one. Taking instruction from Machiavelli, they make the most of opportunity, and, though observing the old boundaries of outer behavior,

>   trimmed in forms, and visages of duty,
> Keep yet their hearts attending on themselves
> And, throwing but shows of service on their lords,
> Do well thrive by them, and, when they have lined their
>   coats,
> Do themselves homage: these fellows have some soul
> And such a one do I profess myself.

But in a mobile society, one is always likely to lose one's footing and become a nobody—that is, to cease to exist in a social sense. The play is full of implicit reference to a milieu in which, as in today's corporate world, there is no longer a guarantee of tenure. Demotion breaks Cassio's heart. Othello remembers with grief how he had "done the state some service" before his replacement as general and administrator of Cyprus.

Unlike Cassio, Othello had been, however, a mercenary from

another world who changed himself into something superior. A Renaissance idea of fame, or of "making a name" for oneself, is invoked in the play, as well as Iago's Machiavellian idea of "thriving." Othello gains the love of Desdemona, makes her put aside the prerequisites of class and race assumed for a proper suitor. He wins her by recounting his exploits—the Odysseyan wandering and the dangers he has overcome in faraway places, his courage in battles, his encounters with strange peoples and fabulous lands, his incredible survivals and escapes—even from the ultimate degradation when, "taken by the insolent foe," he had been "sold to slavery." The stranger from an almost mythical otherness has acquired a place within the order of Venice by his own efforts on behalf of a colonial empire. It is this character he has made for himself that achieves his success in his wooing, though Brabantio, who looks for inherited credentials he understands better in the "wealthy, curled darlings of our nation," calls the telling of such stories "witchcraft." And perhaps such self-fabrication, such transformation by which one of the colonized, an ex-slave, joins the military elite of colonial power, *is* a kind of magic.

Yet nothing can be more fragile than Othello's self-making, which has none of Iago's confidence in being whatever he wills himself for the occasion to be. Othello's attempt to give rebirth to an ancient ideal of epic heroism is vulnerable to the spirit of the later time represented by Iago. As his nobility is erased by rage and despair in the middle of the third act, he mourns,

> O now for ever
> Farewell the tranquil mind, farewell content!
> Farewell the plumed troops and the big wars
> That make ambition virtue! O farewell,
> Farewell the neighing steed, and the shrill trump,
> The spirit-stirring drum, th' ear-piercing fife,

The royal banner, and all quality,
Pride, pomp, and circumstances of glorious war!
And, O ye mortal engines, whose wide throats
Th' immortal Jove's great clamours counterfeit;
Farewell: Othello's occupation's gone.

The strangeness of this wonderful speech is seldom commented on. There is no real reason why Othello should say goodbye at this point to the soldier's profession which has given him an epic selfhood. The terrible crime for which he escapes punishment only by performing his own execution is still ahead of him. But the collapse of personal being he is experiencing is inseparable from loss of occupation. Before he embraces his literal self-destruction at the last, he already refers to himself in the third person, saying "Where should Othello go?" as though the man he was is no longer speaking. Afterward, when Lodovico comes looking for him with "Where is this rash and most unfortunate man?" he replies, "That's he that was Othello? here I am." Then he remembers his former self—the self created by his public career—as having once defended the Venetian state even as, at this ultimate moment of further transformation, he identifies himself with the "circumcised dog" he once killed. Critics are mistaken who have spoken of Othello's "recovery" in the final scene, when he seems to become, again, an epic hero and romantic lover who dies by his own hand. It is hard to admire Othello uncritically once having read T. S. Eliot on this hero's famous final speech ("What Othello seems to me to be doing in making this speech is cheering himself up. He is endeavoring to escape reality"). But Eliot did not observe that what happens at this last moment is acceptance rather than escape, an acceptance of his original status as a racial outsider which neither his military achievements nor his marriage has succeeded in permanently altering.

His marriage has proved to be the theater in which the issues of self-realization, the issues that beset men in society at large, are acted out for Othello on the scale of intimate relations. Marriage to a woman of a rank above one's own has been a universally practiced means, throughout human history, of male self-advancement, of course, but the marriage of Othello to Desdemona has provided a precarious bridge over the gaps of race and culture between them. Shakespeare provides hints that Othello's jealous anguish and distrust of his own perceptions may be caused by the interracial character of his union with a daughter of his Venetian masters. All those reminders by Iago of the impossibility of establishing Desdemona's adultery—a privacy invisible directly—refer one back to a miscegenation over whose consummation a cloud of unknowableness also hangs. The real but *transgressive* relation of Othello and Desdemona is even less easily viewable than the adultery of Desdemona with Cassio that did not take place but was so vividly supposed. This marriage becomes, by implication, something not to be made "ocular," as though it is obscene, as though it is fairly represented only by animalistic metaphor in Iago's description to the shuddering Brabantio at the beginning of the play. Among the play's recent critics, only Stephen Greenblatt, in a bold reading, detects the odor of a sense of fornication in Othello's behavior. He attributes this to a feeling of guilt for uxorious passion, a traditional sin of excess, displacing the love of the divine Creator with love of the creature. He finds this hinted when Iago says that he will "abuse Othello's ear / That he is too familiar with his wife"—"he" generally assumed to refer to Cassio, but taken by Greenblatt as a reference to Othello himself, in whom Iago will instill a misgiving about his own passionate attachment to Desdemona. I think this is not justified; there is no point at which Iago does anything of the sort. Yet Greenblatt discerns something other critics overlook, just the same. Othello may well regard his marriage as a kind of adultery. But it is adulterous because it is a forbidden mixture of opposed racial components.

It seems probable that at this early point, Othello and Desdemona have not yet had the opportunity of consummating the union they have just secretly contracted. But just as he will cause Othello to hallucinate the false image of Desdemona and Cassio locked in naked embrace, Iago rouses her father with his wizard evocation, setting into the mind of the old man the animal coupling that represents racial transgression as black ram and white ewe, or compels him to imagine his daughter "covered with a Barbary horse," or "making the beast with two backs." The play suggests that Othello himself is engaged in deferral of this forbidden act. It is only partly accidental circumstance which keeps the marriage from being consummated. This newly married pair cannot have enjoyed their nuptial rapture for long during their first night in Venice when a midnight summons from the duke posts the bridegroom to the defense of Cyprus. Othello renounces without protest the downy wedding bed that waits for him. I recognize in myself a preference for hard beds, he says. The war-hardened soldier hasn't had much experience of love's soft delights, but now, though Desdemona will go along to the island, he observes that the "young affects" of appetite and "heat" are "defunct" in him. He confesses:

> since these arms of mine had seven years' pith
> Till now some nine moons wasted, they have used
> Their dearest action in the tented field.

He tells Desdemona, as he assumes his new assignment,

> I have but an hour
> Of love, of worldly matter and direction
> To spend with thee. We must obey the time.

Desdemona may still be a virgin when they are reunited after separate crossings to Cyprus; Othello says, "The purchase made, the fruits are to ensue. / The profit's yet to come 'tween me and you," and gives orders for a wedding party while he leads his wife to bed. But the party grows wild and brings Cassio into disgrace, and Othello and Desdemona are interrupted once more—after which Othello lingers on with the wounded Montano, saying to his wife, with some equanimity, "Come, Desdemona: 'tis the soldier's life / To have their balmy slumbers waked with strife." Shakespeare may have wanted us to wonder how well their lovemaking had gone or if it had even got under way, and to sustain the doubt in Iago's earlier question, "Are you well married?" Was Desdemona too quick or he too slow? We may connect the jealousy aroused so readily in Othello with one of those postnuptial awakenings that come to men unprepared for the active sexuality of the women they marry. He will come to say under Iago's influence,

> O curse of marriage
> That we can think these delicate creatures ours
> And not their appetites!

But Shakespeare implies more besides. He makes the racism of an arrogant white society, well illustrated by the imperial Venetian state, useful to Iago as a provocation to Brabantio's rage and his suspicion that Desdemona has been acted on by witchcraft—but also useful to him in his undermining of Othello's belief in her love. Iago resorts to the suggestion that Desdemona has not freed herself from her father's racism. Is not this borne out by a love that began with her vision of her lover's "visage in his *mind*" — rather than in the black face gazing at her? Othello's disclaimer to the duke and senators of Venice of his physical desire for his wife suggests that he, also, fears to imagine the joining of their bodies when he declares that all he looks forward to is "but to be free and bounteous to *her* mind." Othello's renunciation of sexual urgency almost removes his color for his grateful employers as though to refute the racist convention that attributes a more uncontrolled, "savage" sexuality to the black man. "Your son-in-law is far more fair than black," the duke tells Brabantio as Othello without hesitation accepts his mission to Cyprus—and delays his wedding-night happiness. But Brabantio is not convinced; the threat of miscegenation, the classic representation of the social threat of the removal of racial difference, is not held off: "For if such actions may have passage free/ Bond-slaves and pagans shall our statesmen be." Iago will remark a bit later to Cassio, "he to-night hath boarded a land carrack," comparing Othello's sexual conquest to the seizure of a Spanish or Portuguese treasure ship by an English privateer—in other words, an act of social piracy.

When Thomas Rymer said at the end of the seventeenth century that *Othello* was a "caution to all Maidens of Quality how, without their Parents' consent, they run away with Blackamoors," he may have spoken for many of the plays' audiences who felt the same threat as Brabantio. Shrinking from the black "thick lips" Roderigo refers to, however, later audiences preferred not to imagine that Shakespeare really meant Othello to be a black man and often made Othello over into a light-skinned North African. Coleridge wrote: "As we are constituted, and most surely as an English audience was disposed in the seventeenth century, it would be something monstrous to conceive this beautiful Venetian girl falling in love with a veritable Negro." But Othello is always called "the Moor" by others in the play. Though this is a word that also means Muslim, even a convert, Othello remains a black African, identifiable by skin color and feature—and *Moor* was a term equivalent to *Negro* in Shakespeare's day, as the Oxford English Dictionary, assembling quotations from the period, concludes. Coleridge spoke for his own age rather than for the Elizabethans, or even for

Rymer—and in the early period, as today, he was always played as that "veritable Negro." Yet the reconceiving of the late eighteenth and nineteenth centuries did not succeed, actually, in altering the effect of transgressive sexuality inherent in Shakespeare's depiction. It was enough that Othello's goatish lust could be imputed, despite his confession that his sexual urges have slackened with age. His collapse into murderous violence would be an illustration of the way, according to the racist view, the coating of civilization must slide readily off the "savage" personality.

Iago can count on the self-hating that afflicts the victim of prejudice who cannot, himself, believe that he is lovable to the racial other. Othello seems to suffer the insecurity of someone who has crossed the racial line yet feels reproved for it when his white wife is reclaimed by her social and racial world in her supposed affair with Cassio. He has been compelled to hallucinate her intimacy with a white man but can hardly imagine his own union with her. Desdemona's choice of him in the place of

> many purposed matches
> Of her own clime, complexion and degree,
> Whereto we see in all things nature tends,

violates, as Iago points out, a recognized theory of the "natural." She may be expected to retain an inclination for such a familiar species as Cassio. Only moments before she is murdered she will remark upon the Venetian nobleman to whom she is related by blood as well as class, "This Lodovico is a proper man." To which Emilia replies, woman-to-woman, "I know a lady in Venice would have walked barefoot to Palestine for a touch of his nether lip." In marrying Othello, Desdemona also has become a transgressor. When she is called a "whore" by an Othello reduced by his jealousy to the racial enemy's language, Emilia exclaims,

Hath she forsook so many noble matches,
Her father, and her country, and her friends,
To be called whore?

But this is exactly what her social transgression must seem to white society, something more adulterous, indeed, than the affair with Cassio of which she is falsely accused.

The comic foregrounding of sex, as in farce, is invoked and obscured in a play in which so much of the time the marriage bed is at least present to mind even if offstage, just guessed at, though unseen, like the sexual union enacted there. Othello's sexual secret discloses itself, however—rather than being merely suspected or hinted—on the deathbed which has been laid with his and Desdemona's wedding sheets—"sheets" being a synecdoche for the bed and a metonymy for the lovemaking that takes place there. When Iago claimed to hate Othello because "twixt my sheets/ He's done my office," or when he remarked to Cassio on Cyprus, "Well, happiness to their sheets!" the same figure of speech had been employed. Like Desdemona's honor, which Iago thinks of as "an essence that's not seen," her sexual union with Othello, though sanctified by marriage, has not been directly imaginable till now, when it is revealed to the prurient gaze as the curtains of their bed are finally drawn apart. "My mistress here lies murdered in her bed," Emilia announces as though the bed of marriage, with its "tragic lodging" of dead bodies—one black, the other white, lying side by side—is what horrified vision must take in at last. "Lodging" even implies the living together, the cohabiting of the lovers. The change of the word to "loading," in the Folio version of the text recalls Iago's plundered "land carrack." When Lodovico says, "the object poisons sight,/ Let it be hid," the horror he feels is for a forbidden union itself as much as for the deaths this union has caused. To intensify that horror and to emphasize the literal perversity of their sexual relation, there is a hint of necrophilia. Othello tells his victim, "Be thus when thou art dead, and I will kill thee/ And love thee after," and then, having done so, "I kissed thee ere I killed thee. No way but this:/ Killing myself to die upon a kiss."

Despite their aspect as the May-December prototypes of farce, there are no more romantic lovers in all of Shakespeare than the almost virginal warrior and the high-minded virgin Lady whose love he wins by recital of his heroic past. The play makes it seem, even if we are sure of the contrary, that only their deathbed unites their bodies in ultimate union. "Star-crossed" by racial difference, they resemble Romeo and Juliet, their prototypes in the enactment of a *Liebestod* climaxing a forbidden love. We must recall that Othello's anticipations of bliss had prompted thoughts of death:

> If it were now to die
> 'Twere now to be most happy; for I fear
> My soul hath her content so absolute
> That not another comfort like to this
> Succeeds in unknown fate.

It is one of those flights of Othello's hyperbole that suggest too much before the fact, and Desdemona herself reins him in with

> The heavens forbid
> But that our loves and comforts should increase
> Even as our days do grow.

To think that one will reach the peak of happiness—and so be ready to die—is a traditional poetic extravagance, but here more sinister, forecasting as it does the death which will actually be the consequence of their love—and Desdemona's literalism expresses an appropriate caution. And well it might, for in the calculus of their unanticipated difficulties Shakespeare has added in something besides the uncertainty of the untried bridegroom, the too-readiness of the bride. In this play about love and jealousy, which shows how love is a moment's hazardous leap over vast distance, he has included racial difference.

At the last, Othello surrenders himself to the prison of race he thought he had escaped. Like Hamlet, the destined Revenger, he is not able, in the end, to cast away the role and character which social convention prescribes. He recalls an exploit of his adopted Venetian identity when he remembers how "in Aleppo once," he had taken by the throat a "turbanned"—that is, unconverted—Turk (wearer of what Shakespeare calls in *Cymbeline* an "impious turband") who "beat a Venetian and traduced the state." He remembers how he "smote him—thus," as he turns his dagger toward himself. This has generally been taken as splendid *coup de theatre*—but it is more. Reenacting that killing of an infidel by his transformed Christian self, Othello becomes again what he was before his conversion and enlistment in the service of Venice. His magnificent self-making has been undone and he now kills, again, his irreversibly circumcised, unassimilable racial type.

Othello, I find I have argued against most of the play's critics, is, despite its concern with elementary personal emotion, the most intellectual of all Shakespeare's tragedies—including *Hamlet,* which is a play whose hero *is* an intellectual, as Othello is not. Harley Granville-Barker called *Othello* "a tragedy without meaning," and Bradley thought it inferior to Shakespeare's other tragedies for lacking "the power of dilating the imagination by vague suggestions of huge universal powers working in the world of individual fate and passion." The editor of the New Cambridge Shakespeare edition, Norman Sanders, calls it "the most private of the great tragedies," though he insists that "to complain of its lack of supernatural reference or its limited metaphysical range is to miss the point." The spectacle of Othello and Desdemona dead together on their bed at the end is, Sanders says, "the only possible end, because the arena for the struggle the protagonists have lived through is best symbolized by the curtained bed." But I think the play not the less philosophical for that. "Sight" is indeed "poisoned," as Lodovico says—yet not merely because of the spectacle of a love that has made possible such horror, but because this ending has shown the unreliability of our vision of things. Faith in Desdemona's innocence, faith which is lost and recovered by Othello only after doubt has done its fatal work, is not the same thing as religious faith. Yet there is a sense in which love for another human and for God may *both* require the fideist leap. Without it, doubt produces that collapse we witness in Othello. It is precisely because Othello's suspicions cannot either be removed by disproof or justified by proof that his jealousy is a representation of the effects of skepticism. The truth about the virtue of his wife had been as inaccessible to Othello as the truths of religion to the mind infected by contemporary philosophic skepticism. The torment of Othello has been epistemological.

Jealousy, of course, is the source both of doubt and of its opposite, credulity. The jealous person, too ready to lose faith, is likely to jump rashly to a mistaken conviction, to "exsufflicate and blown surmises." Empathizing with Othello, even in his delusion, we see both skepticism and credulity at work in his reception of Iago's demonstration of Desdemona's guilt. He aches for the recovery of his state of deception (when, in fact, he saw Desdemona as she was) and regrets the falling off of scales from his eyes (when, in fact, he is deceived). Iago knows that the fatal handkerchief that will incriminate Desdemona is only one of those

> trifles light as air
> [that] Are to the jealous confirmations strong
> As proofs of holy writ.

The reference to Protestant affirmation of the Bible as the sole source of certainty would have been an ironic reminder to Shakespeare's audience of contemporary religious controversy. Reliance on such "proof" is like Luther's refusal, at the Diet of Worms in 1521, to recant unless he could be refuted by the testimony of Scripture. While the Catholic Church continued to insist on the interpretative truth of pope and councils, "Holy Writ" was the sole source of faith for Luther and the other Reformers—yet here it is the term of comparison for a confirmation of *dis*belief!

Is Montaigne's presence hiding somewhere in *Othello?* We can wonder whether Shakespeare had not got a hint for his character from the description of Montaigne's admirable soldier-father that wanders into the essay "On Drunkenness"—a man who "when he was married . . . was yet a pure Virgine; yet had he long time followed warres beyond the Mountaines, and therein served long whereof he hath left a Journal-Booke of his own collecting, wherein he hath particularly noted, whatsoever happened day by day worthy of observation, as long as he served." But such a connection is tenuous. And Montaigne's influence on *Othello* is not given away by the parallel passages scholars like to seize upon. Maybe Shakespeare had not yet got hold of Florio—though it was already published—when he wrote this play, but this seems unlikely in the light of our observation that *Hamlet* already showed footprints registering Shakespeare's access to a manuscript. It could be that *Hamlet,* written in the first enthusiasm of Shakespeare's encounter with Montaigne, exhibits the influence of the French skeptic directly in the utterances of a student of philosophy just down from Wittenberg. In *Othello,* such ideas may have been so deeply absorbed that they could be expressed undidactically in a simple story of love and tragic error. The important correspondences of thought are more elusive than borrowed phrases. Hamlet's statement that "there is nothing good or bad but thinking makes it so," adapted from Montaigne's essay "That the Taste of Goods or Evils Doth Greatly Depend on the Opinion We Have of Them," is a more significant motto for Iago, corresponding to his "Virtue, a fig!" Montaigne's "Que sais-je?" represents the doubt that infects Othello's thought through the persuasions of Iago. No other of Shakespeare's plays—not even *Hamlet*—is so focused on the problem of knowledge.

And perhaps, I am now going to speculate, the writings of philosophers may have yielded place to another influence promoting Shakespeare's skepticism. The courts of law provided a contemporary staging of the problematics of proof. A system of law is a representation, in any society, of the general view prevailing as to what makes things happen and of how a true account of events may be arrived at. But such explanations had come to seem less available in certain trials over which a growing uncertainty hung, the increasingly numerous and controversial, sensational trials for witchcraft which were taking place all over England and on the Continent as the seventeenth century began. These trials reflected conflicted ideas about truth and perception—about what was knowable and how—while political necessity and popular paranoia made the courts eager to come to judgment in those very cases. Like the stage, the courtroom was a place where changing concepts of the self and uncertainties about the interpretation of events were tested. How one might argue from doer to deed, or reverse the process, was the playwright's problem also. By what evidence might a play connect plot and character? Although this parallel of law court and play can be made in considering the issue of truth and perception elsewhere in Shakespeare, I want to press the analogy of a legal trial to *Othello* more particularly. In this instance that parallel seems to have been the organizing principle of dramatic story and language. It has been overlooked that *Othello* hinges upon the fundamental legal-philosophic issue involved in the establishment of proof in such cases as the trials for witchcraft. Shakespeare's play sets a metaphoric courtroom behind the action as though to put this problem of knowledge to the test in contemporary legal terms.

That Shakespeare had a strong interest in the law has been noticed by scholars—and even felt to support the claim of those who put forward the lawyer-philosopher Bacon as the author of the plays attributed to the Stratford man with his grammar-school education. Shakespeare, we know, spent more time going to law himself than most persons. The record of his life, bare as it is of personal facts, is peculiarly rich in traces of legal battles over property; he was positively litigious. Besides which, he was a frequenter of the Inns of Court, where his plays were sometimes performed, in contact with the gossip and thought of lawyers. He was probably also, like so many, a visitor to public trials, spectacles rivaling the stage itself as dramatic entertainment that created amateurs of the law among habitual viewers as sensational televised trials do now. He must have read published reports of trials for witchcraft and sorcery and the controversial writings concerning them; we know for certain, at least, that he read a pamphlet growing out of a famous case concerning possession and exorcism that took place in 1598, for he borrowed from it the bizarre names of the fiends who plague *King Lear*'s Poor Tom.

In *Othello,* the continuous presence of legal language is so striking as to become an undertone constantly reminding one of the courtroom. When Iago complains that Othello turned a deaf ear to those who urged his advancement, he says that he "nonsuits my mediators"—that is, he rules their case out of court. When he refuses to tell Othello his private thoughts, he asks if anyone has

> a breast so pure,
> But some uncleanly apprehensions
> Keep leets and law-days and in sessions sit
> With meditations lawful,

"leets and law-days" being court sessions to certify the good behavior of the community. Pleading Cassio's case with Othello, Desdemona insists that her husband's nagging about the lost handkerchief is but "a trick to put me from my suit." She soon finds that her "advocation is not now in tune," and chides herself for

> arraigning his unkindness with my soul,
> But now I find I had suborned the witness
> And he's indicted falsely,

a reference to the crime of subornation of perjury. Important to note, among these obscurities, is how words that have a common usage as well as specific legal sense seem to reverberate with a courtroom meaning—as when Othello's handkerchief, the central symbolic object that is the mark of the troth between him and Desdemona, is called "the recognizance and pledge of love," where "recognizance" is the word for a binding bond. Such echoes of the language of court procedure enforce an insistent theme.

Still significant in common law was the old requirement, stated in the Old and the New Testaments, of two witnesses to convict. But many serious crimes are unwitnessed; murder was and is most often committed without living witnesses. The criminal himself may even be absent from the scene; the terrorist can send his bombs through the mail; the poisoner need not administer the arsenic he has deposited in his victim's sugar bowl. As Bacon observed in 1616, "For the matter of Proofs, you may consider that Impoisonment, of all offenses, is most secret, that if in all cases of Impoisonment, one should require Testimony, you should as good as Proclaim impunity." But even more difficult to prove by witnesses was, of course, witchcraft, for the *maleficium,* or evil deed, of a witch was performed by invisible influence exercised remotely, and her nonhuman collaborators were inaccessible to the court. It had to be acknowledged that no one had ever witnessed the signing of a compact between a witch and her satanic master. As with other done-at-a-distance crimes, the two-witness rule was impossible to satisfy in the case of witchcraft. In the place of the witnesses, only the confession of the accused could sometimes satisfy judge or jury. Confession had formerly been extracted by torture, but unlike continental courts, English prosecutions no longer relied on torture. And even unforced confessions could not always be relied on. On the other hand, to prove innocence, an alibi, in the usual sense, is meaningless in such cases.

In 1604 King James's revision of the law against witchcraft made even a witch's damage to property punishable by death, whereas previously there had had to be "proof" of a murder. But as the desire to prosecute witches became more intense and cases multiplied, many, including James himself, called a halt to a process that entrapped victims of personal grudges, the eccentric, and the mad. The trials continued, but now concentrated upon a weighing of such visible effects as the presence of a "familiar" in the form of an animal pet, or a particular mark, "the devil's mark," on the body of the accused.

Above all, the courts resorted to "circumstances" that seemed to connect the accused with the harm that had come, by invisible means, to someone else. For some time, legal proof in English courts had been more "probabilistic," as legal philosophers say. During his trial for treason in 1609 Raleigh had complained, "You try me by the Spanish inquisition," when the two witnesses were not forthcoming. His judge replied, "If one should rush in to the king's Privy Chamber, whilst he is alone, and kill the king (which God forbid) and this man be met coming with his sword drawn all bloody; shall he not be condemned to death?" Raleigh was condemned "by the circumstances." The great jurist Edward Coke, presiding at the trial as attorney general, recalled this response in 1628 in his *Institutes of the Lawes of England* and set down the dictum that "violent [strong] presumption is many times full proof." "Presumption," the reliance upon the circumstantial, is an acknowledgment that absolute certainty is, after all, impossible. Because nothing can be absolutely known, because even witnesses sometimes lie under oath or may have been deluded by false appearances, and even the accused, demented or forced, cannot guarantee to us that they are either guilty or innocent, testimony is ultimately unreliable. In the sixteenth and seventeenth centuries in England there was growing acknowledgment of the need of rigor in legal procedure—for juries, for example, who have no special interest in the case and are not witnesses. But this was accompanied by the increasing suspicion of human perception, which skeptical philosophy was beginning to express more theoretically. Probabilistic proof of guilt had become most necessary in the prosecutions of witches.

Witches such as we discover in Macbeth's medieval Scotland are absent in this play about a sophisticated Renaissance Venice. In his own trial for witchcraft we hear Othello touchingly explain the natural means by which he and Desdemona won each other:

> She loved me for the dangers I had passed
> And I loved her that she did pity them.
> This is the only witchcraft I have used.

But it is no accident that *Othello* begins with an actual witchcraft trial when Othello is charged by Brabantio before the duke and senators of Venice with having used "spells and medicines bought of mountebanks" that "beguiled, [Desdemona] of herself," and calls for the death penalty for witchcraft set down in "the bloody book of law." Brabantio's charge originated in his immediate assumption that Othello had "enchanted" Desdemona,

> For nature so preposterously to err
> Being not deficient, blind, or lame of sense,
> Sans witchcraft could not.

As though aware of the new ideas about evidence, the duke, acting like an English magistrate, takes a conservative view in deciding whether there is a basis for a trial. He rules:

> To vouch this is no proof,
> Without more certain and more overt test
> Than these thin habits and poor likelihoods
> Of modern seeming do prefer against him.

His *modern* in "modern seeming" has been taken to mean "commonplace," but I think it simply refers to the relatively *recent* way of pleading for conviction in prosecutions requiring a probabilistic argument. The duke rejects the argument from "likelihoods" by which Brabantio attempts to prove that Desdemona's love for Othello is "against all rules of nature" and must *therefore* have been induced by witchcraft.

It is not only the actual witchcraft trial of Othello that recalls contemporary witchcraft prosecutions. At the end as at the beginning of the play the shadow of a witchcraft trial falls on the story. The trial that awaits Iago when his refusal to confess his crimes is met by Gratiano's "torments will ope your lips" could turn out to be another real prosecution for witchcraft. Inexplicable malice such as Iago's might seem to require the explanation of demonic agency. Iago has been fertile with false suggestions of the reasons for Desdemona's probable adultery, but one can try to imagine the difficulties involved in his own self-explanations at his coming trial. The consuming enmity that drove him to his crimes would need, somehow, to be accounted for. It would become apparent that the justifications he had mentioned to Roderigo—that he thinks the Moor has seduced Emilia, that he resents the fact that Cassio was promoted in his place, and so on—are so perfunctorily offered that they cannot be genuine. His resolute "I never will speak word" might be taken as a refusal to respond with the incriminating explanation of witchcraft. So Iago might be tried as a witch or wizard, someone whose crime derives from a contract with the devil, the absence of motive being an argument only for demonism. Iago is momentarily seen by Othello, finally, as a hoofed devil, though Othello knows "that's a fable," and we have no reason to expect from Iago one of those dubious confessions extracted by torture in continental prisons. His "Demand me nothing" represents, as I have suggested, a genuine vacuity.

Yet the symbolic presence of magic—if not literal magic—haunts the play, represented by the handkerchief which, supposedly endowed with power to protect love, is lost, and then misused by Iago. We almost feel that Iago may be the wizard agent of demonic power after all, even though this rationalist tells Roderigo, "Thou know'st we work by wit, and not by witchcraft"—echoing Othello's own "This is the only witchcraft I have used." When he and Othello pledge their compact, the sacred rite of matrimony only recently consummated between Othello and Desdemona is mocked and inverted, as though a marriage sacrament is being enacted, just as the sacrament of the Mass is mocked and inverted by a witches' Sabbath. These sly hints of actual demonism are offered and withdrawn as though to suggest that in some transposed, metaphoric way they are still true. Iago *is* the manipulator of appearances. He is the magician who can transform others unaccountably by changing how they are seen. He is the master of the impositions of "seeming."

The main action of *Othello* is not a trial for witchcraft, but it is shaped like one. Desdemona, herself, is not openly accused of witchcraft except in Iago's implication as he reports that

She that so young could give out such a seeming
To seel her father's eyes up, close as oak—
He thought 'twas witchcraft.

As a witch, she would, by his account, have been able to still "give out such a seeming" as to have required infernal aid.

Of course, there is no reason to suppose that Iago really places any stock in the idea of witchcraft in others, despite his accusations. He is, after all, the representative of a modern skepticism that denies all spiritual presence. But Othello's fever of jealousy, his desperate demand for proof of Desdemona's adultery, reflects the epistemological dilemmas of legal evidence in witchcraft trials. How might one attach crime to criminal in such a trial? Shakespeare's play not only shows how a noble man with a spotless history may commit the most horrible of crimes but also makes it possible for him to believe, though falsely, that his irreproachable wife is capable of adultery and deceit. The first unlikelihood is true and the second false. *As though* she were a witch accused of the unprovable crime of witchcraft, Iago admits that Desdemona's adultery might not be a thing for which witnesses and ordinary kinds of evidence were available. As I noted at the start of this chapter, Iago rather curiously insists that nothing is less available than "ocular proof" (how the famous phrase smacks of the legal brief!) of Desdemona's adultery. The direct evidence of witnesses, he claims, cannot be expected—which makes it analogous to witchcraft's invisible operations that made it the most secret of secret crimes. Adultery, *like* witchcraft, cannot be otherwise than unverifiable. Iago urges Othello to watch Desdemona for some self-betrayal, but sets forth, meanwhile, her record as a practiced deceiver who has known how to make *seeing* her perfidy impossible. Incrimination by reference to the accused's known character and past behavior might be enough. Iago cites not only Desdemona's past deceit of her father, "seel[ing]" his eyes, but her likely "Venetian" nature. Othello says, "I'll see before I doubt; when I doubt prove." But Iago responds, "I speak not yet of proof." Only "imputation and strong circumstances . . . lead directly to the door of truth" says Iago in the very language of Edward Coke.

In the courtroom the argument against a person accused in this way of an unwitnessable crime might still be made probable. It could invoke the view taken by acquaintances and neighbors of the accused, though this might not be enough to demonstrate guilt absolutely. Plausibility might be added by presenting, as Iago does, a narrative of events based on Coke's "strong presumption." "Likelihoods" might tell the truth in witchcraft prosecutions. It was now said in the law courts, "Only circumstances do not lie." And unlike human beings, *things* (like a handkerchief found where it had no business to be) do not lie either. Of course, we will disagree with an Elizabethan-Jacobean court's criteria even for probability or circumstantiality — and see prejudice instead of objectivity behind Iago's collection of incriminating conditions. He says to Othello: Consider her type and background; she is an upper-class Venetian woman in a society where women deceive their husbands. Consider her previous behavior; she deceived her father and she virtually seduced you into marrying her. And consider the present circumstances of her marriage; you, her husband, are a man older than herself, a man whose blackness and roughness should have repelled her. Does not all this argue for the perversity of her character? Is it not likely she would soon turn to someone of her own class, age, breeding, or race? It would seem that Desdemona is being tried entirely probabilistically.

In the witchcraft trials, in the absences of witnesses and confessions, as one commentator wrote, "if there is any likelihood, and suspicion, and common fame, that was proof ynough." William Perkins, a Cambridge clergyman, noted in his *Discourse of the*

Damned Art of Witchcraft (1608) that if direct witnesses were demanded, "it will then be impossible to put anyone to death. . . . Hardly a man can be brought, which upon his own knowledge, can averre such things." So another writer, one Michael Dalton, advised the courts in 1618 that review be made of the accused's whole personality and condition, his family, his companions, and his way of life, his dress, and "whether he be of evil fame or report." Certain other circumstances, like the accused's known hostility against his victim or the victim's deathbed accusation, would have made conviction certain even without the confirmation of some visible proof. The very fact of accusation incriminated; God would not have allowed the innocent person to be accused of witchcraft. Confession was not really necessary. A failure to confess guilt was itself confirming of it, an instance of the obduracy implanted by the devil. Under the assault of Iago's argument Othello tries, feebly, to keep hold of his faith in Desdemona's character: "I do not think but Desdemona's honest." But Iago, who sees character as unstable anyhow, is ready with an explanation for inexplicable change. Like an expert in Renaissance abnormal psychology taking the stand, he responds to Othello's protest that Desdemona's betrayal would be a case of "nature erring from itself" by identifying her marriage itself as a true adultery, a mixture of higher with lower, a perversity:

> Not to affect many proposed matches
> Of her own clime, complexion, and degree,
> Whereto we see, in all things, nature tends —
> Foh! one may smell in such a will most rank,
> Foul disproportion; thoughts unnatural.

We know how these suggestions affect Othello, most especially the reference to "complexion." He continues to cling to his faith nonetheless, asking, a little later, for presumptive motive: "Give me a living reason she's disloyal." But Iago, as though the question was no longer important, simply responds that he has observed Cassio relive in sleep his secret moments with Desdemona. And when Othello protests that this was but a dream, Iago says, "this may help to thicken other proofs/That do demonstrate thinly." Iago saw Cassio wipe his beard with the handkerchief. "It speaks against her with the other proofs."

So, as the fourth act opens, Iago provokingly drives the question of proof to its most paradoxical extreme with the assurance that, although absolute knowledge is impossible, circumstances will convict. There is no direct witness to adultery between Cassio and Desdemona, but after all, how could there be if Iago is right that even if you found them naked and kissing in bed together for an hour or more, it would prove nothing. Othello painfully insists, "They that mean virtuously, and yet do so,/The devil their virtue tempts, and they tempt heaven." But Iago still continues, like a wily lawyer, to offer a pseudodefense of the accused that only condemns them: "So they do nothing, 'tis a venial slip." As though the case would be similar, Iago asks if giving a handkerchief away need convict a woman of much—knowing that Othello will conclude that it is as circumstantially damning as the sight of the lovers embracing. Othello is frantic for more than "imputation." And prompt to Iago's purpose, Desdemona drops the handkerchief that Iago will seize and enter into evidence. Light as air it is, but it is a piece of material evidence brought into the courtroom, an article of the accused's clothing found at the scene of the crime. It is "ocular proof"—not of the unwitnessed act itself but, at least, persuasive circumstantial evidence. Iago says, legalistically, "the probation [or determining test] bears no hinge nor loop to hang a doubt on." And here he makes the perverse comparison to "Holy Writ" which I have mentioned. Bible citations were often brought forth in witchcraft trials to reinforce a weak case for conviction.

But the time has come for Iago to offer the confirming proof of confession. Iago will repair the defect in his case, or appear to; Othello will think he witnesses Cassio boasting how "he hath and is again to cope" Desdemona when he is talking about his mistress, who appears on cue, handkerchief in hand. Desdemona, of course, cannot be made to confess adultery or appear to. But it will be no use for her to defend herself. Or for Emilia to protest in a logical way, appealing to circumstantial *im*probability rather than probability. "Who keeps her company? What place, what time, what form, what likelihood?" As defense witness, Emilia arrives too late, discovering her husband's perfidy only after the death of her mistress. Before Othello executes his sentence, he asks Desdemona if she has repented of crime, as condemned criminals generally were asked, for the rescue of their souls and also to confirm the sentence by the strongest of proofs — and warning her against the further charge of perjury. "Take heed of perjury. Thou art on thy death-bed." But she refuses and proves her innocence by her death, having nothing to confess. Iago, who has everything to tell, withholds his confession, but Emilia will discredit the false evidence of the handkerchief by revealing that she stole it for him, and documentary proof (letters from Iago) found on Roderigo, closes the case in keeping with the judicial process that governs the play.

In the trial of Desdemona, Iago is prosecutor and Othello executioner as well as judge under a rule of law aimed not only at punishment but to protect society from further crimes by the criminal. That "else she'll betray more men" may be of improbable concern to Othello, but it would certainly be the concern of a magistrate or jury. When this trial is ended, in a terrible parody of judicial conclusion, Othello enters with a speech of deliberate dignity:

> It is the cause, it is the cause, my soul!
> Let me not name it to you, you chaste stars,

It is the cause. Yet I'll not shed her blood
Nor scar that whiter skin of hers than snow
And smooth as monumental alabaster:
Yet she must die, else she'll betray more men.

A "cause," in the simplest sense, is the reason for an occurrence. Or it may be a purpose for action. Or it may be a high principle to which one is attached, like the cause of a heavenly ideal of chastity for which, Othello suggests, Desdemona must die. All general meanings of the word emerge in Shakespeare's repeated use of it in this play that makes so troubling an exposure of doubts that hide behind our assumptions concerning the origins of human events. But the word *cause* has, besides, legal senses and connotations. A cause may be a suit, as Desdemona called her effort to win pardon for Cassio, acting as his "solicitor." A cause is also a matter for a law court to decide. As he prepares to kill Desdemona, Othello assumes the role of a judge making reference to a charge, a "cause," now finally proven beyond doubt.

Still another sense of *cause* is motive—certainly a prime object of judicial inquiry. Legally, to seek a cause is to seek an appearance of motive to increase the probability of guilt, while the accused may claim that for his deed he had just cause. But putative cause may be deliberately manufactured in the courtroom to justify a crime. Iago's famous motiveless motive-hunting seems the consequence of his desire to give his own malice credibility. His spasmodically expressed and even pretended causes are part of a factitious legal procedure. But this does not prevent him from knowing that others, like Roderigo, will be persuaded by him only if he attaches some appearance of motive to his hostilities. Nor will it prevent him from inspiring in others a belief in false provocations of their own. Othello has no genuine cause for his jealousy; it thrives on a poverty of real proof. When Desdemona wonders at the "cause" for Othello's rage, Emilia rightly says, in the speech I have quoted, that

> jealous souls . . .
> are not ever jealous for the cause,
> But jealous for they're jealous. It is a monster
> Begot upon itself, born on itself.

Iago also stirs up the foolish Roderigo by converting his erotic disappointment into useful hatred of Cassio and Othello while pretending his own just resentment: "My cause is hearted; thine hath no less reason." Cassio is right to remind Othello, at the end, how misplaced have been his reasons—manufactured by Iago— for consenting to the attempt upon this loyal subaltern's life: "Dear General, I . . . never gave you cause." How ironic, then, is the location of these nonexistent or manufactured motives in this play haunted by the image of a legal trial! It has all been a perversion of true legal procedure, after all.

If the legal conceptualization I have been tracing in *Othello* relates it to the whole issue of the nature of truth, it is also, as I have suggested, an ironic parody of genuine inquiry. The search for evidentiary proof is, in fact, constantly mocked despite all the talk of proofs and making the wronged husband "see." Iago's pseudolegal demonstration of Cassio's and Desdemona's guilt is conducted in the Cyprus world of "seeming"—a world that makes such deceptions convincing *as though*, I have observed, by demonic magic. Iago has merely to repeat Brabantio's charges that there was something "unnatural" in Desdemona's love to get Othello's assent to an idea he had serenely rejected in the Venetian court. When he speaks of Cassio's declarations, in sleep, of his love for Desdemona, we may consider that Cassio might, indeed, have dreamt of an impossible love affair with the lady he so respectfully admires. But Iago says that such dreams "denote a foregone conclusion," and it is enough for Othello to have heard that Cassio has the handkerchief to be convinced by false analogy that she would betray him sexually. Othello does not have to hear Cassio's actual conversation with Iago about Bianca to assume that his wife is the subject.

So there is a subtle merger of supposition with ascertainable fact. When Iago says, "What if I had said I had seen him do you wrong?" or heard Cassio "blab" of his conquest, the "what if" glides by as though never uttered. Othello reaches vainly for his sanity: "Hath he said any thing?" Then, Iago slips in "He hath my lord"—only to assure Othello that Cassio, if questioned directly, would deny it. When Othello asks, "What hath he said?" he receives the riddling answer "Faith, that he did—I know not what," Iago breaks off, only to continue, "Lie," and pressed further by Othello's "with her?" replies with a verbal quibble that throws his victim into his swoon, "With her, on her, what you will." As we attend this collapse of logic, the difference between the world of illusion and the real world in which fact and appearance are distinguishable dissolves, for we are ourselves swept along by the play's hypnotic persuasion to jealousy, which banishes such distinctions.

Although he denies the meaning of character and demonstrates its instability in others, although he seems to have no private personality—nothing so personal as a motive—Iago is, one might paradoxically say, the only character in the play. All the others are materials to be worked on and shaped by his imagination. Iago's genius can be described as that of a master of theatrical witchery, a dark Prospero. The metaphor of the theater of life in which men and women are merely players, a skeptical idea which was so important in *Hamlet* with its conscious reference to theater, and to which Shakespeare will return in later plays, is present in *Othello*.

Iago is a playwright—like Shakespeare himself—who invents characters and plot, and a director who casts his actors into his play. Iago casts the other characters in the roles he has written for them. Swinburne and Hazlitt—and, after them, Bradley—noticed that in his early soliloquies Iago, as Bradley said, is the dramatist at work in the composition of a play, "drawing at first only an outline, puzzled how to fix more than the main idea, and gradually seeing it develop and clarify as he works upon it or lets it work"—a creative act that implies that life itself is a play for actors. We watch him at his improvisation. What can be done with these characters, these types and talents? There is the Moor with his "free and open nature/. . . That thinks men honest that but seem to be so," and Cassio who "hath a person and a smooth dispose,/ To be suspected, framed to make women false." "How, how? let me see," he murmurs to himself as he considers the use he will make of them, concluding, in the first act, "I have't, it is engender'd! Hell and night/ Must bring this monstrous birth to the world's light." "Ay, that's the way," he murmurs to himself later as he decides to prompt his wife to influence her mistress on behalf of the disgraced Cassio, and, having urged Cassio to plead his case to Desdemona, then "to draw the Moor apart,/ And bring him jump when he may Cassio find,/ Soliciting his wife"—a scenario exactly followed. And in the fourth act, he literally creates a make-believe scene which Othello watches like the audience in a theater, as Cassio is induced to chuckle over his conquest of Bianca—but seemingly (to Othello) of Desdemona. The other characters of the play—especially Othello, Desdemona, and Cassio—become texts Iago appropriates for rewriting. Othello himself thinks of a transformed Desdemona in terms of literary composition, though he does not realize that Iago has been the author of the lying text he reads. "Was this fair paper, this most goodly book/ Made to write 'whore' upon?" he asks in the passage absent from the Quarto text but added, undoubtedly by Shakespeare, to the Folio. So the play, *Othello,* is the monstrous birth he has engendered.

That Iago is a playwright may account for the curious passivity of Othello, Desdemona, and Cassio, as well as his more obvious tools, Emilia and Roderigo, almost to the end. They show little resistance to his manipulation. Those many viewers and readers who protest that this is the chief thing that makes the plot improbable are justified. I have commented on the fact that we find it hard to believe that Othello would not resist Iago's influence and challenge his persuasions, or that Desdemona does not do more to defend herself. It is just as incredible that the intelligent Cassio is as easily manipulated by Iago as the stupid Roderigo, that sharp-witted Emilia does not question her husband's demand for the fatal handkerchief and sees through him only when it is too late. But they are all only actors in Iago's play. Their qualities are either put to perverse uses or submerged, like Othello's nobility, or covered with the costume of false appearance, like Desdemona's and Cassio's innocence. Emilia's "what place, what time, what form, what likelihood" reminds us of the sleights that the playwright has himself exercised, not the least by that famous deception of "double time" that allows no time or opportunity—though we fail to notice it—for an affair between Cassio and Desdemona, yet permits the charge to have a certain plausibility, subjects *us* to Iago's false logic.

Does playwright Iago have the last word? Is his skepticism shared by Shakespeare? As in regard to Hamlet, another theater man and something of a skeptic, we are tempted to ask this question. And as happens again and again when we ask such questions, we realize their futility. *Othello,* like all Shakespeare's greatest writing, does not contain any authorial spokesman to arbitrate the conflicting attitudes and literary conventions placed into action on his stage—and I have referred to an "honest" Shakespeare only to bring out a viewpoint about life that he could have proposed to himself among the multitude he could conceive. Shakespeare's plays, as I have said, are arenas of contention for many ideas at once. In the end, Desdemona is a martyr of trust and belief who was "heavenly true," as Emilia says. Desdemona's last words, before she is strangled by Othello and before she revives to deny that she has been murdered, are prayer. Her "O Lord, Lord, Lord," appears only in the First Quarto published in 1622—six years after Shakespeare's death—and is dropped from the Folio edition of Shakespeare's plays, published the following year. If, as we now think, Shakespeare had a hand in both texts, he may have written in, then written out this final religious note. I find it difficult to accept, as I have said, that Othello's last speech is that recovery of confident identity it is often assumed to be. And neither does it assert any recovered faith in truth, earthly or heavenly. For the famous line in which he declares, in the Folio text of the play, that he resembles "the base Iudean [who] threw a pearl away, richer than all his tribe," the earlier editions say "Indian." But it is impossible to tell for certain whether the Folio revises the Quarto to make reference to Judas, the betrayer of Christ, or just what role Shakespeare played in such a revision—or whether it is a printer's misreading. When Othello called Desdemona a "strumpet," she had answered, "No, as I am a Christian." She is the only character in the play to call herself one.

But perhaps we should remember that absolute values, religious or philosophical, and such faith in them as Desdemona herself represents, are expressed in the close of the play along with the viewpoint of another female martyr. Emilia is a skeptic of a sort, like Iago. Balanced against Desdemona's faith is Emilia's pragmatism in the exquisitely structured scene that precedes the murder of both women by their husbands. Desdemona and Emilia have been talking, lightly, about the handsome Lodovico for whose kiss, Emilia says, a lady she knows "would have walked barefoot to Palestine." Desdemona appears to ignore this reference to the free sexuality of supersubtle Venetian women, responding only with, "He speaks well." But then she sings her willow song, which ends with the tough-minded

> I called my false love but what said he then?
> Sing willow, willow, willow:
> If I court moe women, you'll couch with moe men.

She follows her singing with the remark that her eyes itch and asks, "Doth that bode weeping?" Emilia, who has no superstitions, answers, "'Tis neither here nor there." Desdemona is still musing, perhaps on Emilia's remark about Lodovico, perhaps on the willow song, perhaps on the accusations Othello has made against her. She asks,

> Dost thou in conscience think—tell me Emilia—
> That there be women do abuse their husbands
> In such gross kind?

When Emilia responds, "There be some such, no question," Desdemona asks, "Wouldst thou do such a deed for all the world?" and repeats her question after declaring that that she herself would not "by this heavenly light."

Emilia answers with a gnomic rhyme, as though becoming the conduit of immemorial common sense: "The world's a huge thing: it is a great price / For a small vice." And she reflects, "Why the wrong is but a wrong i' the world; and having the world for your labour, 'tis wrong in your own world, and you might quickly make it right." Her remark may be taken as a mere witticism, but she seems to be saying, as Iago might have taught her, that values are not absolute, only relative to the world that contains them. To own the world would be, as Shakespeare's Henry V tells the French princess, to be "the makers of manners." It is a bit of skeptical philosophy out of Desdemona's range.

Emilia's skepticism is the fruit of her protofeminism, in part

—something Desdemona has not shared. Quite beyond her is Emilia's response that if a woman is abused, "we have galls: and though we have some grace/Yet have we some revenge." Emilia asserts the humanity of women against the falsifying gender category created by men—

> Let husbands know
> Their wives have sense like them: they see, and smell
> And have their palates both for sweet and sour
> As husbands have,

and have the same appetites for sport bred of affection and the same frailty as men—and so challenges all conventions of character as well as of moral behavior. The skepticism of Emilia is not, of course, the same as her husband's in the end. For the truth of virtue (which Iago called "a fig") she will expose her husband's lies and die herself.

3

"Unaccommodated" Lear

In that dimly lit, unlocalized purgatory in which the characters in *King Lear* approach and address one another, nothing is so difficult as recognition. Their challenges to one another multiply the "Who's there?" with which *Hamlet* opens. Beyond any ordinary requirement of stage identification, they ask, continually, "Who are you?" or "Who is he?" and even demand, "What am I?"—as though they were struggling to see or to be seen through the mist of some primal indefiniteness. Their uncertainty is felt also by the reader or playgoer who may find himself unable to retain a clear sense of anyone in a play that has often been called incoherent. Disconnected moments accumulate as cruelty and suffering escalate and the action rolls forward like a barrel down a hill instead of progressing to a climax in the ordinary way. After the chief personage's preposterous single act of sentimental egotism that occurs right at the beginning, a force outside of the human actors seems to bring them to the absolute of disorder represented by the storm Lear goes out into at the end of the second act and that lashes him and his companions for five scenes. After this, it looks as though the playwright was unable to bring things to a stop. He permits the audience to expect from one moment to the next either the death of the chastised Lear and Cordelia or their survival (so allowing, structurally, for that "happy ending" provided in eighteenth-century productions), but arbitrarily, finally, he closes down all hope for the good as well as the bad.

The peculiar challenge to the stage of this great, mysterious work has always been acknowledged. Lear has no prehistory for the method actor to imagine. What kind of a ruler had he been? What kind of father? Or husband (his queen, the mother of his daughters, is never mentioned)? Others of the play's characters must make an initial impression that is contradicted later. Gloucester, who makes a very poor appearance at the start, is graduated with difficulty to the company of the worthy in the play. Not only the justly resentful Edmund but the drearily literal Cordelia prove to be something else than they first seem. Even Goneril and Regan seem florid rather than hypocritical at first. Also—the characters seem detached from one another rather than interacting. Particularly in certain scenes, like those on the storm-swept heath, they often seem not to hear what others say and speak past each other to the unlistening skies—the madness that overtakes Lear and the simulated madness of Poor Tom having added to the suspension of true interaction and the effect of disjunction between cause and effect. It is not always evident that what they say or do must lead to what happens next.

Nahum Tate's rewrite, which supplanted Shakespeare on the English stage from 1681 to 1838, is generally remembered because it eliminated the scene of Cordelia's death that made Dr. Johnson unable to read it again until he came to edit the play years after. But Tate also claimed, more significantly, that he had "found the whole . . . a heap of Jewels, unstrung, and unpolish'd; yet so dazzling in their Disorder, that [he] soon perceiv'd [he] had seiz'd a Treasure." So he provided a string of coherence—motivation for Lear's intemperate rejection of Cordelia at the beginning, for her stubborn resistance to his demand for avowals of love, for Edgar's cruel withholding of his identity from his own father—by inventing a love between Cordelia and Edgar which arises at the beginning and triumphs in the end. The Romantics defended the play as Shakespeare had written it—but only because it really belonged, they thought, to the literary reader and not in the *theater* at all. As Lamb wrote, "The Lear of Shakespeare cannot be acted. . . . The play is beyond all art as the tamperings with it show. . . . Tate has put his hook in the nostrils of this Leviathan—for Garrick and his followers, the showmen of the scene, to draw the mighty beast about more easily. . . . Lear is essentially impossible to be represented on a stage." The idea that it was a poem rather than a play— that there was no point seeking in it for dramatic logic—persisted. Even Bradley, writing at the start of the twentieth century, found it, as it had always been found, full of flagrant improbabilities, and "too huge for the stage." And so with later twentieth-century critics who rescued the play for appreciation only by seeking out its unifying patterns of verbal imagery, more perceptible to scrutinizing readers than to theater audiences.

Old-fashioned "character criticism" that treated dramatic characters as though they were flesh-and-blood persons with life-histories and consistent psychologies—persons whose behavior and destiny were largely determined by what they were—tended to construct a realist scenario to contain Shakespeare's baffling sequences. This has by no means been given up today, when the critic-as-analyst detects a primal drama hidden from view in the tensions between the loving yet cruelly demanding father and his three difficult girls. The case of Gloucester and his sons, the good Edgar no less than his envious sibling, Edmund, provokes a modern Freudian reading. Actors themselves strive to develop a variety of imagined selves to fill out, to rationalize the outlines of a fairy tale about the usual three daughters, two wicked, one good, and the incomprehensibly stupid, irrevocable decision of the royal father to cast out his favorite for her honesty. This is, probably, to repeat Tate's mistake. The play has been found to be best actable in modern times from the viewpoint of Beckett's *End Game,* with its denial that personality and events hang together in a world where explanation is generally absent, as Jan Kott suggested. Peter Brook expressed such a view in a notable absurdist rendition in 1962, an interpretation that has continued to infect productions to this day.

Of course, our minds — our ways of thinking of ourselves in a fashion that enables us to function confidently in life — abhor the vacuum of the unexplained. Absurdism will always seem repulsive. But we may go wrong to forget the story's ultimate folk-tale origins which lie deeper in tradition than any early written version. The play preserves the sense of a remote time, justifying the productions that evoke a sense of what Swinburne called the "elemental and primeval." *King Lear* retains the opacity of character and the obscurity of causes which reside in myth. The sources of human behavior are a mystery. The fairy-tale wickedness of Lear's two elder daughters and the goodness of the third need not be explained. Kent expresses the submission to bewilderment implied in the idea of an inscrutable heavenly determinism.

> It is the stars,
> The stars above us govern our conditions,
> Else one self mate and make could not beget
> Such different issues,

he says when he contemplates the unbelievable difference between Cordelia and her sisters. As Shakespeare dramatizes it, the story of Lear and his daughters is like that of the classical Oedipus (not Freud's) that devolves simply from the given — a plot imposed by destiny, which has no origin in personal individuality and prior experience and specific historic conditions. It is simply a conjuring of the hypothetical "What if . . . ?" that lies in the hidden folds of fate. "What if a man, the most powerful and respected, should do so foolish a thing as King Lear did? What then?" Equally inexplicable in the usual sense is the story of Gloucester and his sons. Edmund, of course, mocks the idea that any star that twinkled at his birth had anything to do with what he is and calls it an "admirable evasion of whoremaster man, to lay his goatish disposition on the charge of a star." But he offers no other theory. So the play forces one to reconsider the very idea of the connection between those easily named but immensely elusive entities we call plot and character in talking about plays, and, talking about real experience, distinguish as what we *do* and what we *are*.

For all its mythic remove, nevertheless, *King Lear* seems to have been prompted by immediate historic reality. The story could have been seen to have some application to the controversy King James was having with Parliament concerning the unification of "Great Britain"—England and Scotland under one rule for the first time since they had been separated remote centuries before. Unlike Lear, who cut his realm into pieces by scissoring the map, James wanted to put together again what had long been sundered. Shakespeare—or the printer of the earliest edition of the play, the First Quarto—followed the example of Shakespeare's source, the recently reprinted chronicle play of "King Leir," and titled the new play *The True Chronicle Historie of the Life and Death of King Lear and his three Daughters,* probably to stress its relation to a historical original sin; the play had a Christmas performance before the king in 1606 at a moment when the dispute over unification was at its height. It may be significant that the 1623 Folio, published at a time when the unification issue was no longer topical, retitles the play *The Tragedie of King Lear,* and it is placed between *Hamlet* and *Othello,* not with the histories in the collection.

Yet if a specific political reference might fade in importance, history in a larger sense remained central to the play in a way its mythic obscurities only reinforce. More than any other of Shakespeare's plays, *King Lear* reflects the way real life, as I have observed, seemed frighteningly baffling at the beginning of the seventeenth century. And the fact that the events of this history don't hang on any such string as Tate felt obliged to supply may express Shakespeare's vision of the social world he knew. One's life —like the progress of general events—often did not make a comprehensible story. The frequent collapse of the supply of a commodity like grain—due to inexplicable vagaries of nature—caused widespread famines, though the swings of the market could create sudden profits for some. A fortune made virtually overnight and prudent investments might make a rich man out of a modest farmer. But numberless yeoman and agricultural workers whose lives had once had an immemorial place in a particular village became persons with no definition at all. Such alterations disrupted many communities. The land was full of penniless wanderers, the desperate vagrants from the deserted villages who had lost a former identity without gaining another. These were the "poor, naked wretches" perceived by Lear when he has himself arrived at their condition—men and women who lived exposed to the weather like today's urban street persons, and whose original selfhood had become as reduced as their rags. More than any other play of Shakespeare's, this one exhibits the plight of the displaced poor about whom, like Lear himself, Shakespeare might have realized he had hitherto thought too little. Displacement, however, could overtake the greatest, as we see in the case of Lear himself. Even in the case of a king we are compelled to witness a process which peels off from the surface layer by layer of that confidence in being oneself which supports life. The play seems to reflect the general loss of confidence in the stability of an order in which each life has its determined shape.

It was under the new conditions of Elizabethan-Stuart society, I want to stress particularly, in considering this play, that the relation of generations became more fractious than before. Shakespeare's political sentiments may have been divided in the contest between the Crown and Parliament that was sharpening in Stuart times. Perhaps they were also divided when it came to the prevalent dissension between older and younger. Aspiring aristocratic sons jostling for position in an increasingly competitive political sphere, as well as yeoman or middle-class sons who yearned to convert the accumulations of their fathers into a higher style of life, were more ready than in earlier times to reject traditional restraints, to embrace a doctrine of personal revolution. In the Folio text of the play, Lear's Fool asks "whether a madman be a gentleman or a yeoman," and when Lear replies, "A king, a king," the Fool corrects him, "No, he's a yeoman that has a gentleman to his son; for he's a mad yeoman that sees his son a gentleman before him." Shakespeare's father was no madman, it should be noted. John Shakespeare was a yeoman who applied for and, perhaps with his son's assistance, was able to purchase a gentleman's coat of arms sometime around 1597 — and make his successful son a gentleman by doing so. But for some families, it was a wartime of the young against the old, of a younger generation whose mood is represented in poetic exaggeration by Lear's pragmatic though ferocious elder daughters and Gloucester's brilliant and angry son, Edmund, for whom we are pressed to have some temporary sympathy.

What has not sufficiently been noticed, however, is that even the loyal children of the play — Cordelia and Edgar — are engaged in a killing contest with their fathers. Cordelia, after all, who, unlike her sisters, upholds the principle of filial deference, begins everything by resisting her father's — as well as her sovereign's — will in denying him the flattery he demands. She is coldly legalistic when she says, "I love your majesty/According to my bond, no more nor less." She is inflexible in her refusal to yield to Lear's unstated appeal to her to indulge an old man's foolish craving for sentimental declarations. She shoves at him the truth that a daughter must grow into a woman who loves the father's ultimate rival, her husband, as much as or more than she loved her parent: "I shall never marry like my sisters/To love my father all." It is, of course, to rescue Lear and England from usurpers that she reappears in the fourth act at the head of the invading army of her husband's soldiers. But she has had to become a foreigner to do so. She tells her father that it is his business she goes about—echoing Christ himself—and denies that any "blown ambition" incites her. But she steps onto English soil in armor like an enemy of her own country, her ancestral domain, and casts her wicked rivals into the role of its defenders.

Then there is the case of Edgar. Disguised and transformed, he undertakes to watch over his rejecting parent. But he carries on a certain warfare of denial which seems his revenge against the father who was too easily turned against him, denying him any patrimony. When in the fourth act he leads Gloucester to a place the blind man imagines to be the cliff-edge at Dover, he is both kind and cruel. The ruse will defeat his father's aim of suicide but rob him of his will, and Edgar himself must say, defensively, "Why I do trifle thus with his despair/Is done to cure it." He will not disclose his identity to the father who has longed for a reunion with this wronged son, even though Gloucester hears something familiar in the voice of the rough peasant leading him by the hand in a reversal of the parent-child relation. He seems curiously reluctant to resume his old filial condition. In the trial mad Lear conducts in which universal lechery is castigated—Gloucester's own failing—Edgar still offers his father no personal comfort, and though he guards him and cares for him, refuses him, still, the joy of forgiving and being forgiven. Finally, he does not reveal himself until it is too late—when Gloucester's "flawed heart . . . burst smilingly."

The focus of the play is not only on the altered roles of parent and child but also on the general changeableness of social relations. This enforces the idea that the self, in general, is a condition readily altered. In Montaigne's essays, as I have noted particularly in discussing *Hamlet*, Shakespeare could have found a skepticism about the fixity of personal identity that the Frenchman's similar world gave rise to, being also a society in ferment and flux, a society in which generational conflict was intensified. Performed first in 1606, written, probably, in the previous year, *King Lear* gives strong evidence of the playwright's reading of Florio's translation published in London in 1603. It is claimed—though some of the correspondences are more of ideas than of words—that 23 passages from this book are directly echoed in the play, and that the play contains 116 words not previously used by Shakespeare which he could have picked up from Florio's Englishing. Even if some expressions shared with Florio might have come out of the general verbal climate of the moment, there are enough small verbal affinities to allow us to guess that he had read the book closely. Perhaps he had just returned to it in its printed accessibility after having first read it in manuscript, and again, as when writing *Hamlet,* its language stuck in his mind. But more than language probably caught his attention, and if he did not borrow from Montaigne, he was prepared to recognize the kinship of his own thoughts to this foreigner's.

As in *Othello,* deception plays a role in *King Lear,* also, in promoting skepticism about the human ability to perceive anything truly. Gloucester's "blindness" to the truth before he loses his physical sight is often seen, rightly enough, as comment upon the inadequacy of ordinary perception—literally of the senses, metaphorically of the mind. As Montaigne never tired of pointing out, our senses mislead us and so does reason, which depends on what the senses tell us about the world. Gloucester is deceived by Edmund just as Othello was by Iago—by means of manipulated appearances. Edmund operates on Gloucester like Iago making Othello "see" that Desdemona is a whore when he thinks he witnesses Cassio's boasting of his conquest and is shown the "evidence" of the fatal handkerchief. In a similar way, Edmund not only accuses his brother of plotting to kill their father but stages a false scene to confirm his accusation. He pretends to have been attacked and wounded by the would-be parricide. It is a case of "ocular proof" falsely provided, as it had been in Othello's case. By a double turn on the theme of deception—a ruse of impersonation which suggests that character is a merely transferable role —Edmund again attributes his own character to his brother. He claims to quote Edgar's assertion that he would manipulate the sense of whatever might be said by Edmund:

> If I would stand against thee, would the reposal
> Of any trust, virtue, or worth in thee
> Make thy words faithed? . . . I'd turn it all
> To thy suggestion, plot and damned practice.

Gloucester's attainment of insight comes, of course, after he is blinded at the end of the third act by Cornwall in that most gruesome literalization in which Cornwall grinds one eye of his victim under his heel, and plucks out the other with his "Out, vile jelly." It is then that Gloucester can say,

> I stumbled when I saw. Full oft 'tis seen
> Our means secure us and our mere defects
> Prove our commodities.

It is not generally observed that this is a statement of skeptic fideism. It is exactly in this way that Montaigne goes from the argument of man's weakness, the unreliability of his perceptions, to a reliance upon faith, maintaining that our weakness itself, when we acknowledge it, prepares us for a perception transcending ordinary human powers. Montaigne wrote, "The weaknesse of our judgement helps us more than our strength to compasse the same, and our blindnesse more than our clear-sighted eyes." And yet there is little sense that Gloucester's illumination has any real religious import. His illuminations are only peripeteia, the last—when Edgar reveals himself—making him happier than he can bear. It is an ironic further turn upon the theme of deception that Gloucester continues to be deceived by the good son who seems unable to give up his disguise even when it might seem possible and might give comfort to his blind father. And that Gloucester, when this is revealed to him at last, dies of the joy it gives him—as though true vision is more than can be endured by mortal man.

King Lear is the only one of Shakespeare's tragedies to use the motif of disguise—usually a device of comedy—and we are forced, almost against our will, to accept the dramatic convention that allows us to perceive true identity while a mere change of costume successfully obscures it in the stage world. But even in comedy the complete efficacy of stage disguise sometimes suggests a real alterity otherwise unacknowledged, or the force of magic or demonic possession which might change one from what one was or make one fall in love with—or hate—the wrong person. There is always a latent terror in comic transformation—or a warning. Our hold on the true self of the fugitive Kent or Edgar is weakened by a dramatic impersonation that plays a serious role in its own right, making us let go of our sense of ineradicable personality beneath appearances. The stranger who has unaccountably arrived on the scene becomes part of the drama in his new character. The unknown serving-man who attaches himself to Lear in the place of Kent, and Edgar's replacement, Tom o' Bedlam, bring into the play fictional pasts and maintain their disguises beyond necessity and with the barest excuse, as some critics have complained.

Edgar, particularly, as I have said, might have revealed himself earlier to his suffering, penitent father. But as the mad vagrant Tom he has become a new, though unlisted member of the *dramatis personae,* an inhabitant of the *Lear* netherworld in which forms dissolve. When Lear asks him, "What hast thou been?" he produces a thumbnail Theophrastan "character" that is a summary of a contemporary Elizabethan personality:

> A serving-man, proud in heart and mind, that curled my hair, wore gloves in my cap, served the lust of my mistress' heart and did the act of darkness with her; swore as many oaths as I spake words and broke them in the sweet face of heaven. One that slept in the contriving of lust and waked to do it. Wine loved I deeply, dice dearly; and, in woman, out-paramoured the Turk: false of heart, light of ear, bloody of hand; hog in sloth, fox in stealth, wolf in greediness, dog in madness, lion in prey. Let not the creaking of shoes, nor the rustling of silks, betray thy poor heart to woman. Keep thy foot out of brothels, thy hand out of plackets, thy pen from lenders' books, and defy the foul fiend. Still through the hawthorn blows the cold wind, says, suum, mun, nonny, Dauphin my boy, my boy, *cessez!* Let him trot by.

This fictional past self, who enacts serially the animal personalities of hog, fox, wolf, dog, or lion as needed, remembers a life indifferent to human essence in a court or household more vividly real, for a moment, than Lear's prehistoric one. Tom is a sort of ghost from the future who once knew more about Elizabethan great houses than we will ever learn from Edgar. His false self inserts a moment, along with others in the play, that reminds us that this placeless, mythic tale that derives from fairy tale is also, as I have claimed, Shakespeare's most bitter commentary on his own real times.

It is no accident that Poor Tom is an ambiguous impersonation, representing complex associations of Elizabethan ideas about witchcraft and possession as well as a glimpse of the social insecurity of the serving class. One of the most significant of contemporary references in the play is that to the fiends that torture him. Their delightful names—Smulkin, Obidicut, Hobbididence, Mahu, Modo, Flibbertigibbit, and others—Shakespeare seems to have picked up from a contemporary tract connected with a trial against healers professing to cast out devils, Samuel Harsnett's "Declaration of Egregious Impostures," published in 1603. Stephen Greenblatt has observed that Harsnett regards the cures achieved by the exorcisers as theatrical frauds of "designing clerical playwrights." Exorcism, like the possession it professed to cure, was a form of theater—and, therefore, inauthentic. From this idea it is a short step—though Greenblatt does not make it—to the idea that the theater in general is a kind of possession, a displacement of one's true self by an invader personality. Like Hamlet's pretended madness, Edgar's disguise and apparent madness are theatrical. Edgar's impersonations and simulated state of possession are a reminder of how alienable—rather than the reverse—is the core of self we call character.

Edgar's transformation into a starving, persecuted, homeless man represents the last reduction of the human. Shakespeare makes the metamorphosed Edgar, once a well-dressed upperservant, now a vagabond: "Poor Tom, that eats the swimming frog, the toad, the tadpole, the wall-newt and the water—; that in the fury of his heart, when the foul fiend rages, eats cow-dung for salads; swallows the old rat and the ditch-dog; drinks the green mantle of the standing pool; who is whipped from tithing to tithing [that is, from parish to parish, as the royal statute of 1589 enjoined] and stocked, punished and imprisoned—who hath had three suits to his back, six shirts to body." Even this reduction to the human minimum is a pretense, however, like the exhibition of painted sores and false mutilations by a beggar pretending to be a lunatic escaped from London's Bethlehem Hospital. The bedlam beggar's enacted misery forced charity from those not much better off in the poorest of farm or village. Edgar says,

> I will preserve myself, and am bethought
> To take the basest and most poorest shape
> That ever penury in contempt of man
> Brought near to beast. . . .
> The country gives me proof and precedent
> Of Bedlam beggars, who, with roaring voices,
> Strike in their numbed and mortified bare arms
> Pins, wooden pricks, nails, springs of rosemary;
> And with this horrible object, from low farms,
> Poor pelting villages, sheepcotes and mills,
> Sometimes with lunatic bans, sometimes with prayers,
> Enforce their charity.

A "Bedlam beggar" was a byword for fraud. In assuming this disguise of a disguise, Shakespeare is anticipating the postmodernist suggestion that there may be no irreducible residuum of identity. Edgar changes his identity several times in the play, even talking dialect as a West County yokel in the fourth act, and when he nearly—but not yet quite—is ready to revert to his original self, he portrays his discarded persona as a horned devil left on the crest of the cliff from which Gloucester believes he has tumbled. The new companion Gloucester finds beside him calls him "thou happy father" without, somehow, arousing recognition. Edgar's reluctant self-revelation—his recovery of his identity as his father's son, the once-privileged heir, is doubtfully worthwhile when it proves a shock of joy arrived too late to the blind Gloucester. To Edmund, Edgar is revealed only after he fights this brother to the death as a visored knight who says, "My name is lost."

But whether fraud or actor, victim of possession or authentic madman, the disguised Edgar becomes Lear's most absolute companion at the height of his suffering, his identity matched with that of the great man reduced to bare, forked animal. He emerges, in the Folio text, as the chief survivor and the successor to Lear's battered crown. It may be only the printer's desire to appeal to audience recollection of the stage success of mad Tom that accounts for his equal billing to Lear on the First Quarto title page, which promises not only the history of Lear and his daughters but "the unfortunate life of Edgar, sonne and heire to the Earle of Gloster, and his sullen and assumed humor of TOM of Bedlam." Yet Edgar, though he concludes the play with, "The oldest hath borne most; we that are young/ Shall never see so much, nor live so long," has shared Lear's ordeal more completely than anyone in the play. Even blinded Gloucester had not come to madness and nakedness. The embrace on the storm-swept heath of Lear and Edgar, both naked and shivering, represents their realized likeness and union.

To Edmund, Edgar finally identifies himself, resuming his lost original name—"My name is Edgar," like Hamlet saying "I am Hamlet the Dane." As he now destroys the former thief of his identity, he arrogates to himself the further designation, "thy father's son," the ineradicable biologic description Edmund has also had a right to claim. But at the end of the play, Edgar anticipates only a minimal futurity to follow upon the terrors of personal erasure he has known when he concludes the terrible history he has lived through with a mild injunction to a new generation: "Speak what we feel, not what we ought to say." As though Shakespeare had not been sure initially even of such recovery, Edgar's final words and the succession were first assigned, as the Quarto shows, to Albany. Kent, who has been invited also by Albany to share rule with Edgar, and who has served the dead king faithfully, too, though his transformations were never so spectacular, prepares for an ultimate withdrawal: "I have a journey, sir, shortly to go;/ My master calls me, I must not say no."

Kent is a representative of a nearly lost world of hierarchy—that fixed system of relation in nature and society many Elizabethans still believed in, however much it seemed a vanishing ideal. His devotion to Lear is the enduring relationship of a chief counselor to his royal master. In his change-over, he is still, at least, a loyal servant. But he has entered a world where order has fallen into disarray and his former dignity and title have lost significance; his original self seems irrecoverable and not merely hidden. As he enters into his disguise that is near nonbeing, he speaks to himself of having "razed [his] likeness." Lear asks the nondescript serving man who presents himself in Kent's place, "What art thou?" The answer is, "A man, sir"—without specification of rank or role. When Lear probes further with, "What dost thou profess?" he may mean, "What is your trade?" (by which one is socially defined). But Kent's "I do profess to be no less than I seem," suggests that he takes the king's question to mean simply, "How do you declare yourself?" He claims to be no less (maybe, no more) than the reduced humanity he exhibits, and simply offers a list of his qualifications for employment by a good master: "to serve him truly that will put me in trust, to love him that is honest, to converse with him that is wise and says little, to fear judgment, to fight when I cannot choose—and to eat no fish"—the last a joking play on *profess,* which can refer to religious affiliation, meaning that he is not a Roman Catholic. Still, once again, dissatisfied, Lear asks, "What art thou?" to which Kent says merely, "A very honest-hearted fellow, and as poor as the King"—honesty and poverty being negative qualities that unfit one for most roles in the society Lear inhabits. All these replies, in their Everyman generality, evidence the erasing Kent has suffered. "That which ordinary men are fit for I am qualified in"—no more. Yet even this reduction can go further when he is put in the stocks and protests at the indignity paid to one who is, at any rate, still the king's servant: "Why madam, if I were your father's dog/You should not use me so."

Along with this deliberately embraced anonymity on his own part, Kent is enraged to fury against Oswald, a contemporary type out of the same Elizabethan-Jacobean milieu to which Poor Tom once belonged as a "serving-man proud in heart and mind." Oswald says, "I know thee not," but Kent responds, "Fellow, I know thee," and proceeds to his profile: "A knave, a rascal, an eater of broken meats; a base, proud, shallow, beggarly, three-suited-hundred-pound, filthy, worsted-stocking knave, a lily-livered, action-taking knave, a whoreson, glass-gazing, super-serviceable, finical rogue; one trunk-inheriting slave, one that wouldst be a bawd in way of good service and art nothing but the composition of a knave, beggar, coward, pander and the son and heir of a mongrel bitch; one whom I will beat into clamorous whining if thou deniest the least syllable of thy addition." Usually passed over as simply abusive tirade, Kent's characterization seems to hold in scorn the "super-serviceable" upper servant limited by law to three suits and worsted stockings who eats leftovers from the table of his master and aspires to transformation by claiming to be a gentleman. He is a conniving menial, a self-fashioner of the new times. All he owns is no more than can be put into a single trunk, though the "hundred pounds" may mean, it has been suggested, that he has managed to purchase one of the knighthoods the king was selling for that price.

It is Lear himself whose questioning of his own and others' identity is most central to the play, though linked to the changes in Edgar, Kent, and the others. In the case of Lear himself we are compelled to witness a process that removes layer by layer the confidence in being oneself which sustains life. His loss of his own sense of self is connected with his loss of his sense of who others are. When she refused him a conventional show of daughterliness, he had willfully named Cordelia his "sometime daughter," declaring, "we/ Have no such daughter." And he will speak of Cordelia's reticence in the love-contest as having "like an engine wrenched my frame of nature/ From the fixed place." His donation of his own power and dignity to his other daughters proves as destructive of his sense of himself as of his view of them. After Cordelia is banished, and the kingdom is given over to her sisters, it will promptly be the turn of Goneril and Regan to lose identity for him as they become utterly undaughterly—so that he is driven to ask Goneril, "Are you our daughter?" He only half-pretends that, changed from himself, he cannot recognize Goneril: "Your name, fair gentlewoman?" He has not lost hope that Regan, at least, will treat him as he should be treated, so that he may be reconstituted:

> Thou shalt find
> That I'll resume the shape which thou dost think
> I have cast off forever.

But he approaches this now-favored daughter with the uncertainty that has already overtaken him. "Regan, I think you are. I know what reason/ I have to think so." His madness—or his wild humor (as in the case of Hamlet we are not sure which)—plays with the idea of misidentity of others and of himself: "By the marks of sovereignty, knowledge and reason, I should be false persuaded I had daughters."

But to his elder daughters he becomes, promptly, the "idle old man," just as they refer to Gloucester, like Kent an earl, as "the old man." And after Regan has denied him the superfluity of a single retainer, he declares, to the rain, wind, thunder, and fire he now thinks of as kinder than his daughters, "Here I stand your slave, a poor, infirm, weak and despised old man"—as though he has lost his name. As he enters the storm after Regan's denial, he cries out, "You see me here, you gods, a poor old man," and Regan, shutting the door behind him, remarks, "This house is little; the old man and's people / Cannot be well disposed." Cornwall reports that Gloucester "followed the old man forth."

Goneril has mockingly reproved him for exhibiting "these dispositions, which of late transport you / From what you rightly are" —for ceasing to "be himself," as we would say. She is quick to note the division of his qualities that once were united: "As you are old and reverend you should be wise"—an idea expressed also by the Fool, who says, "Thou shouldst not have been old till thou hadst been wise." Seizing the truth in Goneril's cruel words, Lear asks,

> Does any here know me? Why, this is not Lear.
> Does Lear walk thus, seek thus? Where are his eyes?
> Either his notion weakens, or his discernings are
> lethargied—Ha! sleeping or waking? Sure 'tis not so
> Who is it that can tell me who I am?

To this desperate appeal there is an answer, "Lear's shadow," which Lear himself utters in the Quarto but which is given to the Fool in the Folio. The revision suggests that Lear is still unready to realize the degree of his loss of selfhood, though it is perceived by others. But the Folio shows him beginning to perceive the division that has occurred, dividing his selfhood, for he replies to the Fool, agreeing, "I would learn that, for by the marks of sovereignty, knowledge and reason, I should be false persuaded I had daughters." Soon, he beats his head as he cries out, as though addressing someone else, "Oh, Lear, Lear, Lear!"

Like the assumed—or real—madness of Hamlet, Lear's is the representation of that self-alienation that he already suffers from before he seems literally mad. It is no mere verbal extravagance on Kent's part to say, in the very beginning, "Be Kent unmannerly / When Lear is mad." Only after the passing of that outer storm that also represents his madness are recognition as well as self-recognition fully recoverable. At the end of the fourth act he wakes from distraction and self-forgetfulness. Cordelia addresses him as subject as well as humble child. He kneels to her and begs her not to mock him. He still cannot recognize her any more than he can recognize himself and imagines them both as spirits in an afterlife, his of hell, hers of heaven, in the wonderful lines,

> You do me wrong to take me out o' the grave.
> Thou art a soul in bliss, but I am bound
> Upon a wheel of fire that mine own tears
> Do scald like molten lead.

She asks him, "Sir, do you know me?" He says, as he has said before, "I am a very foolish, fond old man." But then, at last, the sense of self coming back, he exclaims, "For, as I am a man, I think this lady / To be my child Cordelia." Lear's recovery of identity is linked with this recovery of the sense of who *she* is. "And so I am, I am," Cordelia responds, her rapture at his recognition and her *own* self-recognition expressed by the doubling of "I am," which occurs in the Folio and may be Shakespeare's change from the Quarto, in which she only says it once.

If there is a sense of purgation at the end of the play—as some claim—it is signified not just by the unsealing of Lear's blind eyes to love, his deaf ears to its silent language, but by his recovery of his lost integrity as king and man. This had been split since the fatal moment when he surrendered his power. Lear's partition of his kingdom is a fatal partition of self. Dividing his realm, donating his authority, Lear had resolved to "divest [himself] both of rule, / Interest of territory, cares of state." After Cordelia disappoints him, he decides to *in*vest his two eldest daughters and their spouses with his "power./Pre-eminence and all the large effects/ That troop with majesty," retaining "the name and all th' addition to a king," but leaving them "the sway,/Revenue, execution of the rest." Lear does not realize how dependent for meaning is his name—that is, his title—upon power. But as this splitting-off proceeds, even his title, with all that it connotes, drops away at crucial moments. When, to Lear's "Who am I, sir?" Oswald replies, "my lady's father," Lear's royalty has shriveled into the mean distinction of being father to Lady Goneril—an insult fully measured by loyal Kent. Kent's violence against Oswald has sometimes been taken to justify Goneril's intolerance of Lear's unruly followers. We may react too mildly to Oswald, the dignity of the English royal family having quite evaporated in our time. Still, Oswald is not wrong. Lear's royal identity has been "razed." In his indignation at Lear's rashness, Kent, himself, had exclaimed, "What wouldst thou do, old man?" though a moment earlier he has called him, "Royal Lear/Whom I have ever honoured as my king." His melancholy "fare thee well, King," as he goes off to banishment bids goodbye not only to his liege but to the king's own kingship. The truth-telling Fool is even more impudently truthful when, to Lear's "Dost thou call me a fool, boy?" he answers, "All thy other titles thou hast given away; that thou wast born with." Already, in the second act, Lear feels his hold on his royalty slipping. Beginning boldly, he ends timorously as he waits for an audience with Regan and her spouse. "The King would speak with Cornwall, the dear father/Would with his daughter speak, commands—tends—service." Regan makes no bones about it: "I pray you, father, being weak, seem so." She urges the elimination of his troop. As though to illustrate the propriety still observed by some, Gloucester promptly reappears to say, "The King is in high rage," and moments later Kent asks, "Where's the King?" Gloucester will continue to refer to Lear as "the King, my master." But Lear now runs "unbonnetted"—that is, hatless, and certainly crownless—in the storm. When his Fool asks him "whether a madman be a gentleman or a yeoman," Lear answers, "a king, a king," though he has already come to call himself "A poor, infirm, weak, and despised old man."

The relation of the private self of a king to his royal role was a much discussed topic in Shakespeare's day. A legal formulation of the king's "two bodies"—one political, one personal or "natural"—had emerged in English common law, as Shakespeare, with his interest in legal questions, might have been well aware. On the one hand, the idea that the royal personality had two parts, one immortal and one mortal, could be used to justify the theory of royal divine right that superceded the errors of the man, making the king an analogue of Christ in possessing both the attributes of deity and a mortal body. But the theory of the king's two bodies was also used to justify resistance to the king's personal will and, during the Puritan Revolution, rebellion and even regicide for the sake of the king's immortal character. During the time of Elizabeth and James I, the theory was a metaphoric legal device to protect the continuity of the Crown and prevent the splitting up of the nation. The queen had thought of giving or selling some of her property to one or another of her subjects, and her council had referred her to this doctrine in advising that her property, whether it came to her from her own ancestors or was a part of the royal estate she had come into, could not be given away by her. In 1608, the year the Quarto *King Lear* was published, James I wanted to raise money by selling off some of the royal lands and needed the reluctant approval of the Lord Treasurer to do so. But James, as I have mentioned, had also been urging Parliament to restore the ancient integrity of Great Britain by reuniting England and Scotland, and the doctrine of the king's two bodies here served him well. What belonged to the immortal body of his political kingship was inalienable from it, it could be argued; he was rightful ruler of the entire island, descended not only from a legitimate English Tudor line but also from eight generations of Scottish kings. He was entitled to the "two-fold balls and treble scepters" he carries in the visionary procession viewed by Macbeth in the play Shakespeare was to write immediately after this one. Not even the mythical Trojan Brute, ruler of an united kingdom three hundred years before Christ, had had the right to divide the country among *his* three heirs—scissoring up the map as Lear had.

It is the violation of this principle that shocks Kent in the first scene of *King Lear* as much, at least, as Lear's cruelty to Cordelia. In the earlier Quarto text that seems to represent Shakespeare's earliest version of the play, Kent merely urges "Reverse thy doom." The Folio text shows Kent making it more clear that Lear's error was political: Kent says, "Reserve thy state." Gloucester, in the next scene, registers the same shock as Kent, not merely at Cordelia's and Kent's banishment but because the king has "prescribed his power,/Confined to exhibition." *Exhibition* is generally taken to refer to that allowance of support and service Lear will now receive from his daughters. If the word as Shakespeare uses it has anything of the modern sense that was emerging in the seventeenth century, it may also suggest that Lear now retains only the empty *show* of royalty, including his title and the "addition," or "ceremonies" he formerly enjoyed. But having donated his land and his power to Goneril and Regan and their husbands, he loses even these, though this panoply of dignity had been the very mark of his inalienable royalty, of the immortal half of his double personality.

It is likely that the theory of the king's two bodies was a current idea familiar to Shakespeare when *King Lear* was presented at Whitehall before the king in 1606. One may recall that it is probably involved in Hamlet's riddling lines, "The body is with the

King, but the King is not with the body. The King is a thing—"
at which Guildenstern interjects, "A thing, my lord?" and Hamlet finishes, "Of nothing." The meaning is not clear, but Hamlet
may be saying that the immortal body of the Danish kingship is
not connected with this king, who is "nothing." This cannot be
true of Lear. Most of those occasions when he becomes simply "the
old man" may be seen as occasions when the "body politic" has
seemed separated from the "body natural" by his own foolishness
and the greed of others. The play allows for the interpretation of
the "two bodies" theory which maintains Lear's inalienable royalty.
He has lost his kingly role to usurpers but perhaps is always still
royal even if he, himself, temporarily forgets it. This would be so
though his enemies might invoke the "two bodies" doctrine to justify a seizure of the throne from the enfeebled mortal person. In the
fourth act, wandering at Dover, crowned with weeds instead of his
jeweled diadem, mad Lear meets Gloucester and Edgar and says,
"No, they cannot touch me for coining. I am the King himself"
(the right of coinage being a royal prerogative, a high crime if assumed by anyone else). Gloucester, who recognizes the royal voice
though he has lost his sight, asks, "Is't not the king?"—to which
Lear responds so famously, "Ay, every inch a king," asserting his
imperishable self despite all contrary appearance. He imagines, in
his delirium, a scene of vanished authority: "When I do stare, see
how the subject quakes." When Cordelia's gentleman approaches,
he demands, "I am a king, my masters, know you that?" It only
remains for Lear to wake from his madness and hear Cordelia say,
"How does my royal lord? How fares your majesty?"

But we must remember that she brings with her the de facto
power established by her military victory. Despite our sympathy
with Lear, our detestation of those who have stripped and reduced
him, the realpolitik of Goneril and Regan correctly exposes the
emptiness of social titles unconfirmed by true power. His loss of

title and authority would have had vivid meaning to Shakespeare's audience in a dynamic period of history when even royal selfhood was only another social selfhood that might crumble. Speaking of him simply as an "idle old man / That still would manage those authorities / That he hath given away," Lear's hateful daughters promptly identify his loss of effective royalty with a cruel accuracy. Lear did not quite realize what he had done. He had banished Kent for attempting, as he charged, to come "between our sentences and our power" without realizing that he had already thrown power away and left himself only helpless personal will or "sentences." The disguised Kent pretends not to recognize the king—as the king fails to recognize him—but offers him comfort when he tells him that he has "authority" in his countenance. Later on, though, Lear himself comes to deprecate the meaning of such an appearance when he sees that the image of authority is a farmer's dog barking at a beggar: "A dog's obeyed in office."

No reduction, certainly, is more striking than Lear's fall from being the most potent and exalted of mankind to the status of a "mere" man. But the king really shares a common problem that might concern anyone in the playhouse audience. To what extent is one's identity detachable from what one can do and own in the world, and to what extent is it defined by these realities? The falsity of the idea Lear acted upon—that he might continue to be a ruler without the authority to rule—would have had a general application when all traditional ranks or titles were becoming merely ornamental unless sustained by wealth and political power. The stripping of royal selfhood from Lear is only the most extreme illustration of the erosion of identity inflicted by the loss of social role. For what are we without the roles that sustain us in life? It may be argued that we are nothing, a word that reverberates in the play, the word we have already heard in Hamlet's remark to Guildenstern that the king is "a thing of nothing." Edgar, in assuming the disguise that means, for a while, a surrender of his self as an earl's son and heir, will say "Edgar I nothing am." The Fool equates Lear with himself and offers Kent the same identity change as he holds his coxcomb out to him as a costume befitting the fool Kent has become. But he goes further to deny Lear even this last selfhood: "I had rather be any kind o' thing than a fool, and yet I would not be thee, nuncle. Thou hast pared thy wit o' both sides and left nothing i' the middle. . . . Now thou art an O without a figure; I am better than thou art now. I am a fool, thou art nothing."

This possibility of reduction to nothing had already been invoked by Cordelia when, in response to her father's demand, "What can you say to draw a third more opulent than your sisters?" answers, "Nothing, my lord." His incredulous repetition, "Nothing?" is met by her own repeated "Nothing." Lear's platitude, "Nothing will come of nothing," may suggest more than the warning that Cordelia will receive no portion. His disinheritance and rejection of Cordelia simply completes what she already seems to admit. She is a royal princess banished and undowered—and so, as a social being, nothing. His "thy truth then be thy dower" is ironical. The king tells her suitors that he will give her "nothing," so stripping her of her identity as his daughter and heir and dooming her to be "with our displeasure piece'd,/And nothing more"— his displeasure, that is, being all that is added, like a patch, to a self in rags. The king of France repairs her torn and reduced garment of self in making her his queen, but she has lost the connections of child to a royal father that made up her original self.

We may, perhaps, see in Cordelia's dependence on an endowment of selfhood from father or husband a particular nullity deriving from her femininity. She resembles Ophelia, who is nothing when Hamlet withdraws his love. "I think nothing, my lord," Ophelia tells him when they are watching the "Mousetrap" play together and he asks if she is thinking of "country matters." Some feminist critics see a reference to the fact that "nothing" was Eliza-bethan slang for the female genitals when Hamlet goes on to say, "That's a fair thought to lie between a maid's legs," and, when she asks, "What is, my lord?" answers "No-thing." That women lack what men have — the penis — is, however, one might also say, a way of saying that women, even more than men, are creatures whom others must supply with being.

Or, to put the matter differently, Cordelia's inexpressible and sacred spirit is denied, and Lear's "ex nihilo nihil fit" hints at the materialism of that Renaissance skepticism which denied even the miracle of God's creation of the world out of nothing. Lear's "Nothing will come of nothing" is a statement that occurs twice in the play — the second time when, in reply to the Fool's ques-tion, "Can you make no use of nothing, nuncle?" Lear answers, "Why no, boy; nothing can be made of nothing." It resonates with the religious and philosophical controversies of Shakespeare's day. Raleigh's friend, Thomas Harriot, who was suspected of atheism, was thought to have subscribed to the "ex nihilo nihil fit" idea, for when he died of a cancer that had begun as a small spot on his nose, a contemporary observed, "a nihilum killed him at last." The doctrine that God had created the universe out of no prior stuff had been formulated at the Fourth Lateran Council in 1215 and has always been a theological prop of the idea (to be reaffirmed by the Vatican in 1870) that all that exists is the expression of divine will. It was continually invoked in Shakespeare's time by many writers; its denial by Lucretius and Sextus Empiricus, as well as by Re-naissance Pyrrhonists, was called by Calvin a "filthie errour." Even Montaigne seems to have found intolerable the skeptic insinuation that "because nothing is made of nothing, God was not able to frame the world without matter." The creation of the world was one of those sacred mysteries beyond our understanding. Shakespeare was well aware of the orthodox idea of creation out of nothing as the supreme paradox; Romeo mentions "anything of nothing first create" as an idea—like love—that is an incomprehensible contradiction. Whatever Shakespeare personally believed is, as usual, uncertain. He must have understood, in any case, what skepticism is implied by Lear's utterance. *Nothing* can represent in *King Lear* also that emptiness, that absence which, for the ultimate skeptic, stands behind the scrim of appearances. Lear enacts, in his mad mockery, the objective study of the seventeenth-century scientist skeptical about immaterial essences or souls when he demands, "Then let them anatomize Regan; see what breeds about her heart. Is there any cause in nature that makes these hard hearts?" Or *nothing* can represent, less nihilistically, the way the truth, or whatever really is, *is* there, but is unknowable.

Cordelia's own "nothing" in reply to Lear's "What can you say to draw / A third more opulent than your sisters?" is also a commentary on the uses of rhetoric. The fulsome speeches of Goneril and Regan are not patently false; true affection—as in contemporary love sonnets, including Shakespeare's—often expressed itself by means of hyperbole, language that implies its own inadequacy but reinforces its message by obvious exaggeration. Shakespeare could use hyperbole as major mode of affirmation in his plays: we have seen it to be a figure resorted to by Othello when he is most sincere. But the love and duty Goneril's and Regan's speeches to their father purport to represent is a vacancy. The hyperbolic gesture they make is insincere, exposed by the cruel, self-revealing bluntness they later employ. Cordelia has nothing to offer in the place of her sisters' empty conventional avowals without resorting to language they have debased. Her "nothing" is a despairing renunciation of *all* language as inadequate to express the truth. Lear's insistence that his youngest, dearest daughter must articulate her devotion if it truly exists is a challenge to the unspoken, unexhibited self. Her stubborn silence is a threat to any conviction we might have of that self's persistence. The collapse of language that she represents may suggest the surrender of all trust in the terms that express love or any other ideal conception—and perhaps skepticism concerning the reality of what they make reference to.

Cornwall's comment about the disguised Kent, "He cannot flatter, he," brings us back to Cordelia's refusal to flatter. Along with Cordelia, Kent becomes the representative of plain language, even of silence, paradoxically more clearly so in his disguised pose of a rough serving-man. He expresses the same opposition she has shown to that inflated rhetoric practiced in courts Lear had demanded and Goneril and Regan had supplied. Kent has qualified himself to Lear with the declaration that he can "deliver a plain message bluntly," and he tells Cornwall, "'tis my occupation to be plain." He is even laconic, except for his outburst of rough outspeaking against Oswald. But this renunciation of show in speech—even of speech altogether—can be suspect. It may, after all, be just another disguise—as even Cordelia's reticence disguised her unexpressed love. Cornwall will be right to imagine that there is something undisclosed in the language of the man he does not recognize—and like an astute literary critic, he makes a comment about it as though critiquing the "plain style" advocated by the scientists of the Royal Society or the plainness espoused by Puritans distrustful of fancy dress and richly decorated churches. He points out that though it pretends frankness, it may itself be a form of insincerity.

> This is some fellow
> Who, having been praised for bluntness, doth affect
> A saucy roughness and constrains the garb
> Quite from his nature. He cannot flatter, he;

An honest mind and plain, he must speak truth;
An they will take it, so; if not, he's plain.
These kind of knaves I know, which in this plainness
Harbour more craft and more corrupter ends
Than twenty silly-ducking observants
That stretch their duties nicely.

Because the utterly wicked Cornwall is the speaker of these lines, we might be tempted wrongly to ignore their strength—and, after all, it is true that Kent is hiding his identity. Just as Edgar's role as a naked beggar is made suspect by his Tom o' Bedlam character as an impersonator, so Kent's honest ruffian impersonation—another conventional theatrical type—must be felt to be a box with a false bottom. "I do profess to be no less than I seem" is a mystification, suggesting merely, that, minimal as his outer self is, what you see is what you have. Kent may be deemed to be ultimately honest—in the sense of honorable.

But we remember that the attribute of "honest" he claims is the attribute Iago appropriated. When the villain of the earlier play calls Othello's style of speech "bombast circumstance," we tend to reject this characterization. Othello is not someone who *lies!* Iago's honesty is a mode of pretense that achieves its results by seeming precisely what it is *not*—plain speaking opposed to the *pretentious.* And yet—Othello's heroic music *is* a style of inflation. It is, thus, even allied to the meretricious and banal style of "silly-ducking observants" that Goneril and Regan employ in their declarations of devotion to Lear. And just as surprisingly, perhaps, Iago's ultimate *silence* is a rhetorical stance that we can rediscover in Cordelia. Is not her response of "Nothing" to Lear's importunateness a turn upon the cornered villain's embrace of silence when he says, "Demand me nothing. What you know, you know. From this time forth I never will speak word"? In *King Lear,* Shakespeare seems to move beyond *Othello* in his distrust of his own art of expression, and seems to suggest that *all* speech is suspect, even the rhetoric of silence.

Iago's true analogue in the play, is, however, neither Kent nor Cordelia but Edmund. Edmund shares Iago's skepticism about all ideal conceptions, about love and virtue, about the ordained hierarchy of nature and society. He expresses even more overtly than Iago the philosophic denial of these in the most famous of his speeches,

> Thou, Nature, art my goddess; to thy law
> My services are bound. Wherefore should I
> Stand in the plague of custom, and permit
> The curiosity of nations to deprive me?
> For that I am some twelve or fourteen moonshines
> Lag of a brother? Why bastard? Wherefore base?
> When my dimensions are as well compact,
> My mind as generous and my shape as true
> As honest madam's issue? Why brand they us
> With base? With baseness, bastardy? Base, base?
> Who in the lusty stealth of nature take
> More composition and fierce quality
> Than doth within a dull stale tired bed
> Go to the creating of a whole tribe of fops
> Got 'tween a sleep and wake. Well, then,
> Legitimate Edgar, I must have your land.
> Our father's love is to the bastard Edmund
> As to the legitimate. Fine word "legitimate"!
> Well, my legitimate, if this letter speed
> And my invention thrive, Edmund the base
> Shall top the legitimate. I grow, I prosper:
> Now gods, stand up for bastards!

This extraordinary soliloquy, like Cornwall's analysis of Kent, is not diminished in strength by the fact that it is spoken by a man who will prove a villain. Edmund's intelligence and skepticism link him for a moment not only with Iago but with Hamlet, until his perfidy and brutal cruelty destroy such comparison and relegate him to the moral ("base," or bottom) category he rejects. He, like Hamlet, resists conventional confinement to type, and at the end comes to fulfill a type assigned even as Hamlet, however much he differs from an Edmund, must finally be the destined Revenger. There is also his obvious vigor and will, beside which his dull father does not look good at all as the play proceeds. "Let me," Edmund says, "if not by birth, have lands by wit"—and before we know what this means we are inclined, out of our own distaste for arbitrary privilege and our modern valuation of the ideal of freedom, to sympathize with him. Here, at the opening of the play's second scene, his villainy is just beginning to be apparent in the soliloquy's last lines, which explain the purpose of the letter he holds in his hand.

Edmund is a skeptic philosopher. His Goddess Nature is not the force that keeps all creation in its eternal design according to the dominant view of writers like Richard Hooker, whose *Of the Laws of Ecclesiatical Politie,* published in 1597, had elaborated for numerous readers the old idea of universal law. By rejecting the idea of a social and natural order that subdues him to his parent and makes him inferior to his legitimate brother, Edmund rejects, in effect, the tradition that sets each person in his "natural" place in society and restrains our illegitimate—that is, unlawful—impulses. Such a "natural" governance is still invoked by Gloucester, who, accepting Edmund's lies about his brother, not only calls the slanderer his "loyal and natural boy" but, when he is blinded, longs for Edmund to "enkindle all the sparks of nature / To quit this horrid act." Gloucester's usage is exactly like that of Lear when he hopes, in his delusion, that Regan will perform "the offices of nature, bond of childhood" already cast off by Goneril. When Gloucester speaks of Cornwall's and Regan's "unnatural dealing" with Lear, even Edmund, playing his part, chimes in to proclaim it "most savage and unnatural." Supporting Cornwall's assault upon Gloucester, Edmund hypocritically declares himself distressed that "nature thus gives way to loyalty." In all these examples, the older sense of *nature* is called upon by a deluded or enfeebled—or (in the last instance) dishonest—spokesman. Edmund's true view of nature is disclosed only in his soliloquy.

In Edmund's status as merely a "natural"—that is, illegitimate—son, there is the implied pun on the thought that he is a precivilized man, a natural man of the kind Europeans had just begun to hear about in explorers' tales in Shakespeare's day. The "savage" natural offers a skeptic critique of "civilized" ideas. Montaigne, who had read such accounts, wrote about the inhabitants of the New World in "Of the Canniballes," the essay which Shakespeare drew upon directly in writing *The Tempest:*

> They are even savage, as we call those fruits wilde, which nature of her selfe, and of her ordinarie progresse hath produced: whereas indeed they are those which our selves have altered by our artificiall devices, and diverted from their common order, we should rather terme savage. In those are the true and most profitable vertues, and naturall properties, most lively and vigorous, which in these we have bastardized, applying them to the pleasure of our corrupted taste. And if notwithstanding, in divers fruits of those countries that were never tilled, we shall finde, that in respect of ours they are most excellent, and as delicate unto our taste; there is no reason, art should gaine the point of honour of our great and puissant mother Nature.

When Coleridge came to say, "Edmund has stood before us in the united strength and beauty of earliest manhood," he seems to have suggested not merely Edmund's youth but such a Romantic view of the youth of mankind.

In a related punning suggestion, Edmund, as a "natural" son, is the offspring of "natural"—that is, lawless—passion, and all the better for it, he convincingly asserts. Shakespeare lets us feel Edmund's attractive physicality, which is commented on by Kent when he first sets eyes on him in the opening scene. His father had admitted, "there was good sport at his making," and Kent has conceded, "I cannot wish the fault undone, the issue of it being so proper." He is superior to the issue of a "dull stale tired bed"—perhaps Edgar. One can understand his sexual allure, later acting so powerfully on Goneril and Regan. He himself looks back on his conquests of these two with a melancholy satisfaction. "Yet Edmund was beloved," he says. Still, sexuality is viewed ambiguously in the play. Lear, himself, offers an *ironic* naturalistic defense of lust in his mad speech as royal judge in the fourth act:

Adultery?
Thou shalt not die—die for adultery? No!
The wren goes to 't, and the small gilded fly
Does lecher in my sight. Let copulation thrive,
For Gloucester's bastard son was kinder to his father
Than were my daughters got 'tween lawful sheets.

Of course, Gloucester has been deceived and Lear is wrong; it is the illegitimate son, not the legitimate, who has proved unkind. But the argument is made that sexuality unrestrained is the rule of nature.

The often-noted prevalence of animal imagery in the play has been remarked upon without account being taken of how two-sided it is. Lear, in his bitter rage and madness, removes the dis-

"Unaccommodated" Lear   171

tinction between man and the rest of animal nature ranked beneath in the chain of being. "Man's life is as cheap as beast's," he says. Edmund's own character as a "lower" animal is manifested as the brute animal savagery Albany sees in him, and also in Regan and Goneril, whom he calls "tigers not daughters," who prompt the remark, "Humanity must perforce prey on itself / Like monsters of the deep." But the skeptic Edmund might be supposed to embrace—without fear—the view that Hamlet's "paragon of animals" is undistinguished from all the rest. Montaigne sometimes deprecates man by comparing him to the meanest of other animals: "wretched weake and miserable man: whom if you consider well, what is he, but a crawling and ever-moving Ant's nest?" He argues for many pages, in the "Apologie of Raymond Sebond," the actual superiority of other animals to ourselves, giving instance after instance. Animal nature, Montaigne insists in his essay "Of Phisiognomy," is superior to human nature, despite the reason we pride ourselves on uniquely possessing "a singular testimonie of mans infermitie: and that this reason we so manage at our pleasure, ever finding some diversitie and noveltie, leaveth unto us no maner of apparant tracke of nature. Wherewith men have done, as perfumers do with oyle, they have adulterated her, with so many argumentations, and sofisticated her with so diverse farre-fetcht discourses, that she is become variable and peculiar to every man, and hath lost her proper, constant and universall visage: whereof we must seeke for a testimony of beasts, not subject to favor or corruption, nor to diversity of opinions."

The Nature whom Edmund addresses in his early soliloquy is a proto-Romantic goddess of a new freedom from what he calls "the plague of custom," and here he may, again, reflect Shakespeare's reading of Montaigne, who repeatedly contrasts nature and custom in favor of the former. Montaigne's view of custom could have been one of the most provocative of the ideas discovered by the first readers of Florio's translation, with its dedicatory verse by Daniel praising the writer who had

> made such bold sallies out upon
> *Custome,* the mightie tyrant of the earth,
> In whose Seraglio of subjection
> We all seeme bred-up, from our tender birth.

In his essay "Of Custome," Montaigne, though arguing against rash innovation, calls his subject *"a violent and deceiving schoole-mistris"* who establishes her authority over us "upon every occasion to force the rules of Nature." In a celebration of the sensuous life in "Upon Some Verses of Virgil," Montaigne declares: "The wisdome and reach of my lesson, is all in truth, in liberty, in essence: Disdaining in the catalogue of my true duties, these easie, faint, ordinary and provincial rules. . . . Among nations, where lawes of seemlinesse are more rare and slack, the primitive lawes of common reason are better observed: The innumerable multitude of so manifold duties, stifling, languishing and dispersing our care." Custom regulates the relation of higher and lower, king and commoner, father and child. But Edmund's ambition is justified by a theory of revolutionary overthrow of the whole social system, as well as by nature conceived as lawless force. It is by invoking an anarchic nature and by ignoring the rule of custom that Edmund justifies his plot against brother and father.

Above all, he protests, in his "Thou, Nature" soliloquy, against the fact that the "curiosity [that is, the fussiness] of nations" will "deprive" him—and uses the word *deprive* with no designation of what he is deprived *of.* What he describes is a general condition of deprivation, a state of nonhaving. Being illegitimate, Edmund lacks even the legal title of son, as well as the noble rank which is his father's and will be inherited by Edgar, Gloucester's "son by order of law." Edmund is the identity-less man of force without social application. He is known by what he is not—he is *not* legitimate. In both the Quarto and Folio editions his entrances and speeches are most often tagged with the oppressive title of Bastard instead of with his proper name. He desires, in his justified resentment of this way he is seen, to seize new identity, first Edgar's, then Gloucester's, appropriating his brother's favored status and his inheritance as the elder, and then his father's title even before the old Earl dies. Kent's question, "Is not this your son, my lord?" at the opening of the play, poses the question of identity even before Lear appears and reminds one of the opening line of *Hamlet*, "Who's there?" It is answered with the wry assent to the incomplete identity this father gives his unacknowledged child. "I have so often blushed to acknowledge him that now I am brazed to it," he says, and goes on to explain that he also has another, legitimate, son, who is no dearer. At this earliest moment of our encounter with him, Edmund seems acquiescent; he tells his father's amiable friend that he will apply himself to deserve interest. But when we are alone with him in the next scene we discover that he rages with the sense of his incompleteness. We cannot help approving his desire to be more than the "nothing" to which his illegitimacy consigns him. It is not surprising that Coleridge, with both admiration and fear, compared Edmund to Napoleon. Shakespeare, said Coleridge, "had read nature too heedfully not to know, that courage, intellect, and strength of character, are the most impressive forms of power, and that to power in itself, without any reference to any moral end, an inevitable admiration and complacency appertains, whether it be displayed in the conquests of a Buonaparte or Tamerlane, or in the foam and the thunder of a cataract."

Edmund will, of course, soon show the most devastating illustration possible of a villainy that, like Iago's, exceeds credibility. But as though feeling some lingering pity for his creature, Shakespeare gives him a different ending from that of Iago, who declares simply that they will get nothing from him when he is finally charged with his crimes. Iago, who has had no motive comparable to Edmund's sense of inequity, expresses no regrets. But Edmund is seized by a futile spasm of compunction that makes him want to make some reparation and save Cordelia before he dies. "I pant for life," he says, "Some good I mean to do,/ Despite of mine own nature." He pants, of course, because he is taking his last breaths, but he also pants for the alternate life—and self—that has been denied him. He would have been king if his plans had succeeded, marrying one of Lear's daughters after killing Lear. But he might have been a better man if he had not been, inescapably, Edmund the Bastard. It is his younger brother Edgar who will succeed to the throne of Britain, gaining the throne by desert rather than lineal descent, for all three of Lear's daughters are dead. In their last duel Edgar and Edmund look like twins in their armor. Starting from social nonbeing, Edmund's attempt to acquire identity is an effort to describe a reverse arc across the descending curve of Lear's and Edgar's degradation. But they recover their lost selves, while his ascent into a fuller selfhood does not take place.

The suspicion, which permeates the play, that the social order is arbitrary and dishonest, gives a justification to Edmund's subversive desire to overturn those relations traditionally called "natural" and make the "base" replace the elevated. Edmund could argue that displacement and reversal are *already* manifest in a world that pays lip service to Hooker's order. Such a view is represented in Lear's denunciation of "the rascal beadle . . . [who] dost lash that whore [though he] hotly lusts to use her in that kind/ For which [he] whipp'st her" and the "usurer [who] hangs the cozener." Only social advantage distinguishes the justice from the thief he rails at: "Change places and handy-dandy, which is the justice, which is the thief?" Lear's Fool, who tells him, "thou mad'st thy daughters thy mothers. . . . Then they for sudden joy did weep,/ And I for sorrow sung," continues to refer to such reversals as "The codpiece that will house/ Before the head has any"—that is, the fornicator who satisfies his lust before he can take care of a family—and offers prophecy on the stormy heath that indicts a society in which all do the opposite of what they are supposed to:

> When priests are more in word than matter,
> When brewers mar their malt with water,
> When nobles are their tailors' tutors,
> No heretics burned but wenches' suitors.

Gloucester's anticipation of a time when "love cools, friendship falls off, brothers divide: in cities, mutinies; in countries, discord; in palaces, treason; and the bond cracked 'twixt son and father" is proved dismally accurate, even though it is based on superstition about the effect of eclipses.

Reflecting the Elizabethan-Jacobean generational conflict I referred to earlier, Edmund slanderously attributes to Edgar what could be his own views. He claims that his brother has urged that "sons at perfect age and fathers declined, the father should be as ward to the son and the son manage his revenue." Edmund/Edgar, in saying this, is like one of those young bloods Shakespeare probably knew who were eagerly seeking argument for rebellion against stingy fathers. Here too, Montaigne's ideas may have played a part in Shakespeare's thinking. In "Of the Affection of Fathers to Their Children" Montaigne is concerned with the abuses of parental authority, whether through tyranny or foolish indulgence, which Lear and Gloucester illustrate. But also with the dangers of unbridled greed and ambition which Goneril and Regan and Edmund illustrate as they reject the ancient deference to patriarchy and all authority. Montaigne describes in this essay the results of paternal selfishness which denies grown children their proper state: "It is meere injustice to see an old, crazed, sinnow-shronken, and nigh dead father sitting alone in a Chimny-corner, to enjoy so many goods as would suffice for the preferment and entertainment of many children, and in the meane while, for want of meanes, to suffer them to lose their best dayes and yeares, without thrusting them into publike service and knowledge of men; whereby they are often cast into dispaire, to seeke, by some way how unlawfull soever to provide for their necessaries." This viewpoint, an overturning of the hierarchical deference of youth to age and the ancient principle that age may hold on to all to the last, may have contributed to Shakespeare's complex portrait of Edmund. It is expressed in the letter Edmund composes and hands to his father as Edgar's: "This policy, and reverence of age, makes the world bitter to the best of our times, keeps our fortunes from us till our oldness cannot relish them. I begin to find an idle and fond bondage in the oppression of aged tyranny, who sways not as it hath power, but as it is suffered." Of course, Edmund's illegitimacy, and not his father's senile selfishness, is the cause of the neglect he has suffered. But the views Edmund attributes to Edgar—views that scandalize Gloucester, as Edmund intends—serve to illustrate seriously the resentment of any son denied while his father keeps a miserly hold on his wealth. Edmund's own criminality even might claim the explanation Montaigne offers in his examples of "yong-men of good houses" driven to theft and other crime by a parent's mean denial.

Lear calls upon the same goddess Nature as Edmund when he curses Goneril with sterility or the bearing of a "child of spleen" so that she may know what he feels as a result of her cruelty. In his despair on the heath, Lear becomes—more than the utterly sane Edmund—the spokesman of a cosmic convulsion in which the forces of nature are invited to riot, and to destroy the ordered cosmos. Lear's own frenzy, as well as the storm that obscures all landmarks, already illustrates the convulsions human and physical nature are capable of. He asks thunder to "strike flat the thick rotundity o' the world, / Crack nature's moulds, all germens spill at once." Cordelia prays for a cure of the "breach in [the] abused nature" of her "child-changed" father, but the self-alienation of his madness is more than mere breakdown induced by his suffering. The evil of others (like Iago's influence on Othello, which also produced a kind of madness) and (again, as in the case of Othello) his own folly have produced a surrender of what he has been. But they have also produced a loss of confidence in the order of the world, and as Othello said, "chaos is come again."

Is this chaos ever really dispelled and order restored? Is there in this play any confidence in the ultimately unshakeable order of things? Robert B. Heilman wrote more than a half-century ago that *Lear* "affirms the pre-eminence of order; the paradox of tragedy is that order comes out of a world wracked by disorder, that chaos proves order. There cannot be a breach in nature unless there is a nature." But order seems hardly evident even at the outset of the play, which never looks back at any kind of better state. And order is only feebly recovered. Even in the wonderful recognition scene at the end of the fourth act, the king's original majesty is not restored on unmodified terms, as he continues to call himself "a foolish, fond old man" and kneels to the daughter who has tried to kneel to him. When they are captives he dreams of their prison life outside of life, and says: "When thou dost ask me blessing I'll kneel down / And ask of thee forgiveness." Handy-dandy prevails. At the end there is Edgar's minimal "The weight of this sad time we must obey; / Speak what we feel, not what we ought to say." What does this mean? If Goneril and Regan should not have spoken their obligatory words of hypocritical flattery to Lear, would it have been better if they expressed their true greediness and opportunism?

Lear also, like Edmund, might be said to be acquainted with Montaigne. His decision to divide his kingdom is based on the same reasoning as Edmund's argument for wresting power from his enfeebled father. Montaigne wrote approvingly of the Emperor Charles V, who "resigned his meanes, his greatnesse and Kingdome to his Sonne, at what time he found his former undaunted resolution to decay, and force to conduct his affairs, to droope in himselfe, together with the glory he had thereby acquired." Like Charles V, Lear acknowledges weakness and age and the need to hand power on to the young. It has been argued that Lear is not as feeble as he wants to appear; doesn't he go hunting with his knights? Acting interpretations have varied between those, like John Gielgud's, that portrayed a vigorous monarch, and those that give legitimacy to his claim of weakness (in Deborah Warner's 1990 National Theatre Production, Brian Cox appeared, in the opening scene, in a wheelchair). Shakespeare appears to have felt that Lear's sense of encroaching agedness had not been made clear enough in the Quarto, where Lear says, merely, that he has decided "to shake all cares and business of our state/Confirming them on younger years." In the Folio (which, perhaps, no longer directs itself to James, who liked hunting) he rewrote:

> To shake all cares and business from our age,
> Conferring them on younger strengths, while we
> Unburdened crawl toward death.

Montaigne had written: "The worthiest action, that ever the Emperour *Charles* the fifth performed was this, in imitation of some ancients of his quality, that he had the discretion to know, that reason commanded us, to strip or shift ourselves when our cloathes trouble and are to heavy for us, and that it is high time to goe to bed, when our legs faile us."

If Shakespeare's Lear can be said to have a clear reason for his decision to relinquish his throne, it may be that this one is most significant, though it has seldom been taken seriously by critics. Such a rational explanation is the *only* motive he declares, though it is never offered in Shakespeare's immediate dramatic source, the anonymous chronicle play of *King Leir*. Leir gives up his throne to his daughters because his wife has just died and because he wishes to prepare himself religiously for his own death. He institutes the "love-test" of Cordelia and her sisters because he wishes her to renounce — out of completest love for him — a marriage that will take her from his side. These are motives never heard of in Shakespeare's play. It would seem, however, that the idea of such a voluntary surrender of all that had once defined a great man provoked Shakespeare's imagination. However motivated, Lear's self-divestment was a violation of order that would serve to initiate a process in which the whole universe would eventually collaborate.

Lear's journey to death — the final surrender of identity, as Hamlet realized — is dramatized even more profoundly than Edmund's struggle to justify his "natural" character by the illegitimate acquisition of identity. It is a denudation that climaxes in the literal nudity he comes to share with "the naked fellow," Tom o' Bedlam. A recent production at the Royal National Theatre in which Ian Holm as Lear and Paul Rhys as Edgar embrace each other in entire nakedness was true, I think, to the use the play makes of the theme, more true than the older stage tradition which allowed Kent and the Fool to restrain Lear from tearing off his clothes, and better than the modern style of showing him still clothed though only in rags or an undershirt. Lear has reached a final state in which he is like an animal exposed in its own skin to the weather in the storm over the shelterless heath. The process has a metaphoric meaning — perhaps several metaphoric meanings. It can be claimed that he has shed superfluous and constricting coverings, self-deception and vanity. Nakedness suggests not merely a casting off of corruption and pride but a cleansing from the essential self of every superfluity — and a return to some primal innocence. The need to cover ourselves — like Adam and Eve after the Fall —

may be the mark of our fallen nature. In Titian's *Sacred and Profane Love,* Sacred Love is naked, Panovsky told us; Profane Love has her clothes on.

But has Lear, in his reduction to the naked self, attained a higher state? Nakedness in its opposition to clothing has alternate traditional senses. Lear's denuding is both a return to a prelapsarian condition and a reduction of the human. It may be merely pitiful. Clothing may stand for the seemly vesture of the creature who is better than all other animals because of his self-awareness and moral consciousness. Lear says at the beginning that he is determined to "divest"—literally unclothe—himself of "rule, interest of territory, cares of state," and to "invest" (thus clothe) others with these. He will "unburdened crawl toward death," he says, echoing the passage I have quoted from Montaigne's praise of Charles V, which makes more conspicuous the metaphor of unclothing by referring to the coming of a time "to strip or shift our selves when our cloathes trouble and are to heavy for us."

But Lear chooses the wrong legatees and does not take the precaution Montaigne urged—to make his gifts revocable. It is Lear who will be a naked pauper, finally, when he is joined in brotherhood to Poor Tom crying constantly that he is "a-cold." Equally irreversible are his pauperizations of others, though he will come to regret them. Having stripped Kent of his original identity, Lear fails to recognize him as a mere serving-man forced to wear the stocks that are called "cruel garters" in mockery of his lost costume of dignity. Cordelia will be driven out naked into the world. Her stubbornness will "dismantle" (divest, again) those "many folds of favor" she once enjoyed, as though tearing off her fine gown and cloak (or "mantle") and every stitch beneath them before she is pushed out the door. Lear does not realize, of course, that it is he himself, rather than Cordelia, who will be impoverished as well as denuded of selfhood to the point of nakedness, while Cordelia, who seems to the king of France "rich being poor," will be swept off to regal affluence as a queen destined to return clothed in the more-than-clothing of armor and power. But Lear has uncovered himself to punishment, as his Fool notes when he compares the king to a child preparing to be whipped on the buttocks; he gives the rod to his daughters and "putt'st down [his] own breeches." The fool tells him that even a snail keeps its shell, its "house" to "put's head in, not to give it away to his daughters."

Lear's stripping has suggested a process that is corrective of social inequality. He becomes the equal of the poorest. In the midst of the storm, he turns to observe the "houseless poverty" of the Fool and Edgar and to think—for the first time in his life—of all who must live exposed to the wind and the rain. He asks,

> How shall your houseless heads and unfed sides,
> Your looped and windowed raggedness, defend you
> From seasons such as these?

and he chides the rich, "Take physic, pomp . . ./ That thou mayst shake the superflux to them." The extravagance of the rich person's costume was an exhibition of the "superflux" of wealth and also metaphor for the privileges wealth enjoyed which concealed the body of vice while poverty, like a beggar's tatters, exposed the wearer's faults. In the storm, Lear calls for the revelation of hidden truth, crimes that "under covert and convenient seeming practice on a man's life." He cries out, "Through tattered clothes great vices do appear;/ Robes and furred gowns hide all."

The metaphor of clothes, so important in *King Lear,* was social metaphor ready to Shakespeare's hand. Dress represented social identity in times when those who had money could buy the luxurious imported satins and piled velvets, the laces, embroideries of gold and silver thread and pearls and precious stones in exquisite elaboration that made up the peacock costumes of lord and lady.

Mad Lear ironically mocks Poor Tom's rags as though he were a style-watcher at court: "I do not like the fashion of your garments. You will say they are Persian attire, but let them be changed"; Persian silks had come into vogue as a result, it is thought, of the visit of a Persian embassy. And those who aspired to rise higher, and could afford it—the newly mobile of society—imitated the older nobility by dressing in the same grandeur. If one could afford fine clothes one might really acquire a new self. Change of costume, the work of a tailor, rather than any interior development, signified the changeableness of selfhoods that could be put on, proclaiming the new man, or exchanged for something else. Those who might wear on their backs the worth of a yeoman's freehold had become "their tailor's tutors," as the Fool says in his prophecy. The fool can also chant, "Have more than thou showest," but an interior and unexpressed personal truth—a truth of unexpended wealth—was hardly to be believed in. Even if a restrained taste inspires Polonius to advise Laertes that his dress should be "rich not gaudy," he adds the observation that "apparel oft proclaims the man"—which may mean not that it discloses the inner person but that it *makes* the man what it announces.

Attempting to conserve vanishing distinctions, the state tried to keep the lower ranks from emulating such metamorphoses. A proclamation by the mayor of London complained, in 1572, "Of late tyme servauntes and apprentices within this cytty ar by indulgence and lack of convenient severytie growne to grete disorder in excess of Apparrell and fasshions therof uncomly for ther caulinges." "Sumptuary" ordinances, designed to control the new rage for dressing out of one's class, restricted costumes made of expensive imported fabrics. Observing the same attempt in France to keep such literal self-fashioning in bounds, Montaigne commented, "To let none but Princes eat dainties, or weare velvets, and clothes of Tissew, and interdict the people to doe it, what is it but to give reputation unto those things, and to encrease their longing to use them?"

Shakespeare takes note of the phenomenon in *King Lear*. Kent describes the upstart steward, Oswald, as a "three-suited . . . worsted-stocking knave"—someone, that is, limited by the ordinances to three suits a year and plain woolen stockings instead of silk. Oswald, however, has aspirations just the same, and is something of a fop, and Kent says to him, "nature disclaims in thee—a tailor made thee." Tom o' Bedlam, who also once owned three suits—the wardrobe of a servingman, though "proud in heart and mind"—must have been someone similar before he lost employment or went mad, and become a ragged beggar. Now he is one of those "poor naked wretches" whose loss of all identity is represented by his utter lack of clothing of any kind.

The stage tradition that first presents Lear in scarlet, ermine-trimmed robes—or some equivalent costume of grandeur—and brings him finally to rags through which one sees his naked body provides a more than literal representation of his history. In his progress toward nakedness he loses much that had made him himself, that had constituted his relationship to family and realm, his social selfhood. He begins to realize his loss of his figurative clothing of self when he loses his token retinue of knights. Goneril argues that he does not "need" twenty or ten or five of his train. "What need one?" asks Regan. And Lear cries,

Oh, reason not the need! Our basest beggars
Are in the poorest thing superfluous;
Allow not nature more than nature needs,
Man's life is cheap as beast's. Thou art a lady;
If only to go warm were gorgeous,
Why, nature needs not what thou gorgeous wear'st,
Which scarcely keeps thee warm. But for true need—

and he breaks off, unable to explain that the need he speaks of is not merely of "nature"—a need like the bodily requirement of covering against the cold—but rather a figurative clothing for the naked self. Lear recognizes the social symbolism of a fine lady's dress when he reminds Goneril of the meaning of her "gorgeous" appearance. But "true need" is still something else than vanity's lust for display—it is the need for a necessary *outerness* clothing one in social being. When Lear kneels to Regan begging "raiment, bed and food," he presents himself both as the humbled beggar he later becomes and as a great man who has already lost his greatness. When she harshly tells him, "being weak, seem so," Regan insists on a correspondence between appearance and reality—and he is brought to acknowledge this principle when he tears off his clothes.

Lear's folly first matched him with his motley-costumed Fool. But as he tears off his clothes, he identifies himself with a madman out of Bethlehem Hospital who is not only naked but pursued by fiends tempting him to suicide. Remarking Tom's wretchedness, he is himself mad. He says, "Nothing could have subdued nature / To such a lowness but his unkind daughters." In the thematic climax of the play, he cries to Tom, "Why, thou wert better in a grave than to answer with thy uncovered body this extremity of the skies. Is man no more than this? Consider him well. Thou ow'st the worm no silk, the beast no hide, the sheep no wool, the cat no perfume. Ha? Here's three on's us are sophisticated; thou art the thing itself. Unaccommodated man is no more but such a poor, bare, forked animal as thou art. Off, off, you lendings: come, unbutton here." This famous speech is closely linked to Montaigne's discussion in the "Apologie of Raymond Sebond" in which, in his general deprecation of human presumption, he points out that "man . . . is the onely forsaken and out-cast creature, naked on the bare earth . . . having nothing to cover and arme himself, withal but the spoile of others; whereas Nature hath clad and mantled all other creatures, some with huskes . . . with wool . . . with hides . . . and with silke." The thought is repeated in another passage in which he says, "We may be excused for borrowing those which nature had therein favored more than us." (Shakespeare's *lendings* is generally glossed as borrowed clothes.)

"Unaccommodated" man is inferior to all other species in his nakedness. And the bare, forked animal is Shakespeare's final image of the pitiful condition of man stripped of the covering of social selfhood. To that nakedness Lear has come as he asks for help to "unbutton here," the gesture repeated when he dies. Montaigne had confessed in his essay "Of the Use of Apparell" that though he himself could "not endure to goe unbuttoned or untrussed," the plain "husbandmen" who were his country neighbors would have felt themselves "as fettered and handbound, with going so." Responding, as he does elsewhere, to explorers' reports of travels to far parts of the globe, he ponders "the fashion of these late discovered Nations to go naked," wondering whether nakedness is not "an originall manner of mankind." So Shakespeare, one can imagine, might have wondered, reflecting, metaphorically, on the significance of the clothes of "civilized" men and women. In his extremity, Lear would "unbutton," discard the clothing of self. Only shortly before his death does he find himself finally clothed again in the "fresh garments" Cordelia provides, garments he says, at first, that he cannot remember, as he cannot remember what they signify. Then, he becomes once more, for a moment, both father and king. Yet with Cordelia's death, this recovery is rescinded, and his almost-last words are "Pray you undo this button."

A considerable tradition of interpretation of the play argues that in death Lear achieves a Christian redemption. If so, the close of this play recovers an element of belief to a greater degree than *Hamlet* or *Othello*. Lear has surrendered pride and come to understand the suffering of others, the poor and unfortunate to whom he had never previously paid attention. He has acknowledged his sin against those most loyal to him, and now is united in perfect love with Cordelia, who dies for love of him at the hands of savage Evil. As he holds her dead body in his arms he even resembles, sexes reversed, the Pietà image of Mary holding the body of the dead Christ on her knees, so familiar in centuries of religious painting. There is, to support this view, the remark of the anonymous "gentleman" in the fourth act who says that Cordelia "redeems nature from the general curse."

But Shakespeare's reference to conventional religious concepts is indirect if present at all. Edmund's contempt for Gloucester's credulity may be also a putting-down of the religious idea of divine predestination when he observes, with intelligent scorn, "I should have been that I am had the maidenliest star in the firmament twinkled on my bastardizing." Shakespeare may have shared Edmund's skeptic rejection of Gloucester's fear that eclipses were an ominous portent. A modern voice—and not a negligible one— is Edmund's when he says, "This is the excellent foppery of the world, that when we are sick in fortune, often the surfeits of our own behaviour, we make guilty of our disasters the sun, the moon and the stars, as if we were villains on necessity, fools by heavenly compulsion, knaves, thieves and treachers by spherical predominance; drunkards, liars and adulterers by an enforced obedience of planetary influence; and all that we are evil in by a divine thrusting on." His "necessity," "heavenly compulsion," and "divine thrusting on" sound like references to religious predestinarianism—in which Shakespeare could have disbelieved without being an atheist.

It is possible, as I have said, that the Quarto title was meant to point up a current significance of the story as an ancient historic instance of national partitioning. But I want to suggest as well that Shakespeare might have really responded strongly to the endless "and then . . . and then" of chronicle story, and shaped it into tragic roundedness with difficulty in writing this play. In chronicle history, events never conclude. In Holinshed, Hamlet lives on to reign in the place of his uncle, and to meet new enemies who finally destroy him, and Macbeth reigns for a long time before being overtaken by the party of Macduff and Malcolm. After the insurrection led by the husbands of his wicked daughters, Leir escapes to France and then, with Cordeilla's help, returns to regain his throne, in the twelfth-century *Historia Regum Brittaniae* of Geoffrey of Monmouth, which Shakespeare could have read. When Geoffrey's Leir dies, finally, Cordeilla succeeds him. But there is more. The sons of her sisters make a new rebellion and imprison their aunt until she commits suicide. And after *that,* the two brothers quarrel, there is civil war, and one brother is killed and, for a long period, the other reigns peacefully. But even the older play that was Shakespeare's direct model kept the ending open. After Leir's successful return, Cordelia's sisters and their husbands flee into banishment, but no bodies litter the stage as in the terrible tableau that terminates Shakespeare's play. Anything may still happen.

Shakespeare, of course, shuts things down at last with the deaths of nearly everyone—Lear and his three daughters, Cornwall, even Lear's Fool, and Edmund as well as Gloucester. But the end is not apocalyptic. Gloucester exclaims, when, now blind, he recognizes Lear in his maddened state, "O ruined piece of nature, this great world/ Shall so wear out to naught"—another vision of ultimate nothingness, the end of time without revelation. Cordelia returns, her forces seem to win but then are defeated, and then she and Lear are prisoners, while Gloucester has died in Edgar's arms. But Edgar kills Edmund in single combat, and Regan is poisoned by Goneril, who kills herself in turn, and we expect that Cordelia may even be rescued by the order of a repentant Edmund. But the happy ending almost reached does not come about, after all. Events seesaw. "Is this the promised end?" Kent asks. "Or image of that horror?" Edgar adds, as they both see Lear enter with dead Cordelia in his arms. There is a moment of hope or delusion that Cordelia is still alive before Lear dies—before the unmeaning endlessness of chronicle time resumes.

One of the most notable changeovers from the story Shakespeare found in the old play that was his source is his alteration of its Christian setting. *King Leir,* set in a Christian Britain, is actually anachronistic: the Lear of old legend is supposed to have reigned over Britain six hundred years before Christ. But the "gods" referred to by Shakespeare are clearly pagan and plural except, doubtfully, for the one time Lear tells Cordelia that he and she will become "Gods spies." The usual editorial change to "God's spies" may suppress another reference to the multiple gods of pagan faiths. But more important, these "gods" do not inspire the same faith in all who refer to them. Lear banishes Cordelia in the name of Apollo and Jupiter, while Kent comforts her with the prayer, "the gods to their dear shelter take thee." Edgar says, "The gods are just," but to his father are given the unforgettable contrary lines, "As flies to wanton boys are we to the gods,/They kill us for their sport." Cordelia, coming at last upon the broken, sleeping Lear, appeals to the "kind gods" to cure his madness. But their own loving reconciliation before death does not look toward the heavenly afterlife religion promises. In his madness Lear had had a vision of himself in hell, "on a wheel of fire," and of Cordelia in heaven—but when he dies at last it is only the condition of recovered selfhood and sanity that can replace despair and confusion in a purely secular way. Lear's last dream of happiness is of an impossible utopia in prison, when, withdrawn from the human world of "court news .../Who loses, and who wins, who's in, who's out," father and child will "wear out/In a walled prison pacts and sects of great ones" and "sing like birds i' the cage" and, he says, "take upon's the mystery of things." A stoic acceptance of the mystery of our arrival and departure is the burden of Edgar's famous remark to Gloucester,

> Men must endure
> Their going hence even as their coming hither.
> Ripeness is all.

The mysteries of all things in the world, and of human fates, become what to the skeptic mind they must remain, mere speculations for philosophic reflection. Lear imagines a time when, *like* spies of the mocking gods, he and Cordelia will observe the others who, as Montaigne, observed, "know nothing themselves, and yet will take upon them to governe the world and know all."

4

Macbeth's Deeds

Like King Lear, *Macbeth* has its ultimate source in myth, and it retains the universality as well as the obliquity of myth; it tells the old story of a man misled by riddling prophecy. It shows, like many folk tales, the fatality of such confident anticipation of what will happen. The hero will know more than he should about the future—yet not enough. It does not matter who he is or when or where he lives. His particular personality and condition are unimportant. However he might resolve to let fate simply have its way without his stir, he will be destroyed by his foreknowledge or his illusion of foreknowledge, and the act he dreads to do will be the product of his will after all. Such a hero may even be one of those persons described in folk tales who would like to evade a prediction, suspecting, as Macbeth does, that what it might entail is something to make his hair stand on end.

Before his murder of Duncan, Macbeth resembles Hamlet in his resistance to an anticipation of bloody murder. He is more prompt than Hamlet to submit to the progress of events that seem somehow dictated. But he also seems to want things to happen of themselves and not because of the ambition his deed implies. He suffers more acutely, in his way, from Hamlet's division between idea and act in the illusion that the act need have no relation to his will. And once the prophecy that he will be king is realized, he is unprepared to accept the fact that his deeds are his own, committed by him, and inseparable from him, and that he must now embrace further deeds and developments. He does not, till the very end, understand that trust in one's anticipations is perilous, especially when they are fulfilled, as we learn from the fairy tales that warn us not to hope too much that our wishes will come true—for they may. Prophecy promotes a blindness to the incalculable that may unfold after the enactment of what has been conceived. Too often, the promised futurity comes to pass in a way the prophecy obscured. Macbeth overlooks—only to remind himself of it later—that others' futures are guaranteed as well as his own, like the promise to Banquo that his descendants will rule Scotland in time to come. And once Banquo is disposed of and more murder follows, the witches' prophecy leads Macbeth to believe in his invulnerability. He should have placed no trust in a security against all but an enemy not of woman born and in the reassuring impossibility of defeat said to be as inconceivable as the relocation of a whole forest. That human deeds are ambiguous in their outcome is the meaning of the witches' first utterances that precede the opening of the human action in the play: descending upon a field of futile human contest they agree to meet "when the hurly-burly's done, / When the battle's lost, and won," and opposed truths converge.

In Shakespeare's time a general appetite for magical forecasting was probably promoted by the fact I find myself again referring to—that social and economic instability made for unprecedented opportunities and insecurities. Believers in their own good luck were likely to be driven by ambitious expectations of what was really unpredictable, tormented by the desire to know the outcomes of the events they were living through each day, their minds reaching feverishly forward toward the future even when they did not resort to necromancy. The anticipation of their own ends was so intense for certain men as to strip of moral importance all the steps by which accomplishment might come about, or the further consequences of it. Nothing counted but the attainment. Such a "Machiavel" had been Richard III as Shakespeare depicted him in his earlier history play. Macbeth, the usurping murderer prompted by prophecy, is often compared to Richard, but the comparison is not very close. Richard needed no promise of witches to arouse his hopes, and his character as a man of diseased ambitiousness and cheerful ruthlessness is not duplicated in Macbeth, in whom ambition is oddly invisible and depression more apparent than cheer. But the Machiavel's subordination of means and sequels to some conceivable or inconceivable goal is not unlike Macbeth's condition of mind.

Shakespeare had always been fascinated by the power struggles that had dominated English public events since the fourteenth century and the way that lust for futurity we call ambition played a part in them. He had written his series of eight history plays as commentaries on the role of ambition in the evolution of the modern state. In *Richard II* he had dramatized the fifteenth-century takeover of the English throne by the ambitious and able Henry Bolingbroke. *Henry V* continues a history that reflected the ambiguous politics of Elizabeth's reign. Written in 1599, the play alludes directly to Elizabeth's favorite, the popular, ambitious Earl of Essex, who was expected to return from Ireland "bringing rebellion broached on his sword" after putting down the revolt of the rebel Tyrone; Essex had become the bright hope of a faction that saw him worthy to replace Elizabeth herself. He was probably identified ambiguously by his supporters not only with the glamorous hero of Agincourt who had put down the Lollard rebellion in his time but also with Henry V's father, the Bolingbroke who had seized the crown from the weak but legitimate Richard. Shakespeare's patron, the earl of South-hampton, was one of Essex's admirers. How Shakespeare himself felt about Essex is not certain, but as though anticipating the outcome of usurpation, the epilogue of *Henry V* warns that the crown appropriated illegitimately by Henry IV was bound to pass from Lancastrian hands. All Harry's brilliant conquests would be lost, history showed, and conflict would take over the realm soon after his death. As it turned out, Essex's Irish foray proved a fiasco, and hardly two years after he had fought against rebels in her defense he became himself a rebel who hoped to seize the throne from the queen who had once adored him. His followers revived *Richard II* at the Globe, suggesting an analogy Elizabeth also seems to have recognized when she remarked, "I am Richard II, know you not that?" Essex, condemned for treason, paid with his life for the inaccuracy of the parallel.

Shakespeare's tragedies, from *Julius Caesar* on, had, with the exception of *Othello,* dealt with the intersection of ambition and the political issue of the succession of rule. But for all its mythic design, *Macbeth* makes more direct reference to contemporary events than *Hamlet,* and even than *Macbeth*'s immediate predecessor, *King Lear,* deeply involved with Elizabethan social conditions as that equally mythic play is. As Elizabeth grew old still childless, and refused to name an heir, a resumption of the endless back-and-forth of dynastic wars, as in pre-Tudor times, was feared. Then, in 1603, she died, and her successor was the son of that dangerous claimant, the Scottish Stuart queen she had had to execute. James, whose own *True Law of Free Monarchies* (1598) enunciated the doctrine that only God could depose a rightful king, had cause for anxiety equal to his predecessor's. It was not clear that rule could always be handed on by means of traditional continuities like legitimate descent, or whether only will and power really mattered. His previous reign as king of Scotland had been beset with dangers and alarms since the moment in his childhood when he assumed the throne from his beheaded mother. James even believed that a group of witches had caused a storm to threaten his ship when he sailed home to Scotland with his Danish bride in 1589. One of the condemned in the trial of these witches was burned at the stake as an agent not only of Satan but of James's human enemy, the earl of Bothwell. In 1600 James barely escaped murder by a member of his own court, the earl of Gowrie, during a visit to the earl's house in Perth. Eighteen months after James's English coronation, Shakespeare's company, recently come under the king's patronage, put on a play called *The Tragedy of Gowrie*—perhaps as a warning to conspirators—and almost immediately, Shakespeare found, in his favorite historical sourcebook, Holinshed's *Chronicles,* a story of eleventh-century Scottish king-murder bound to be interesting to James because of the presence of Banquo, whom James claimed as his ancestor. After the death of the historic Macbeth, a son of Banquo's son, Fleance, had gained the Scottish throne. James's descent from a line of succeeding Scottish Stuarts would be displayed in the apparitional procession shown to Macbeth in the fourth act of the play Shakespeare wrote.

Macbeth would also interest James for its prophesying witches who amused themselves by such capers as tossing a ship at sea—just as those he had accused in his Scottish court had supposedly done; the witch who boasts in the third scene of sailing after her victim in a sieve and "like a rat without a tail" even duplicates picturesque details brought forth by the prosecution. But one feature of the Macbeth story as Shakespeare rendered it could have caught the royal attention sharply. The historic Duncan had been ambushed out of doors, not knifed to death by Macbeth in his own castle. Shakespeare made the reference to James inescapable by depicting the fiendish inhospitality that had so recently threatened the king when he had visited Gowrie. ("What, in our house?" Lady

Macbeth responds, with the consternation of an embarrassed hostess, when Duncan's murder is discovered.) Another ancient Scottish monarch whose reign is chronicled by Holinshed, a certain King Duff, *had* been murdered on a visit to one of his thanes—and there is some evidence that Shakespeare took a look at this instance too. But the death of King Duff, often cited by scholars as the source of Shakespeare's alteration of the Macbeth story, would hardly have come to the minds of members of Shakespeare's audience as readily as Gowrie's notorious attempt on James. The Guy Fawkes conspiracy to blow up Parliament and kill the king at the same time was only a few months old. The heads of the executed conspirators grimaced from the top of the London Bridge tower when Shakespeare undertook to write his play.

It is significant that *Macbeth,* which deals directly with conspiracy and insurrection, is Shakespeare's play in which witches are among the visible actors. It was a time when the saying in the book of Samuel—"For rebellion is as the sinne of witchcraft"—was in every mouth. The spells of witchcraft, which threatened the natural order of things, were associated with disturbances of the political order. The Earl of Gowrie had been found to possess a bag full of necromantic notes, and the trial of the Scottish witches had been, essentially, a prosecution of conspiracy, as I have noted; James himself attended the trial at which he was their chief accuser. Priding himself on his scholarly abilities, he wrote his *Demonologie,* designed to answer contemporary skeptics like Reginald Scott, whose *Discovereie of Witchcraft* (1584) had attacked belief in the powers of witches. The royal author's little treatise, published in 1597, was reprinted in England after he became England's king, and it was probably read by Shakespeare. Whether or not Shakespeare shared James's views, he permits us to think that the witches in his play may be responsible for having at least promoted Macbeth's resolution to murder. The Marxist critic Terry Eagleton has called Shakespeare's witches the revolutionary heroines of the play. "It is they," he says, "who by releasing ambitious thoughts in Macbeth expose a reverence for hierarchical social order for what it is, as the pious self-deception of a society based on routine oppression and incessant warfare." Heroines or not, Macbeth's witches are overturners of all rule and order. Everything they have to do with is convertible to its opposite. "Fair is foul, and foul is fair," they say—a statement that skeptically obliterates distinctions either of the weather or of social value.

In Shakespeare's England, the belief that witches or sorcerers could know the future unknowable to the rest of mankind was part of their special fearsomeness. As personal futurity became more unpredictable than it had ever been, it seemed as though one could gaze into the shuttered future only with the aid of God's great enemy—such knowledge being, then, a cursed thing. The sense of menace in the ambiguous power of the necromancer who offered a forecast of events is reflected in the horror felt by Queen Elizabeth herself. Her first Parliament debated a bill to punish prophecy, and it was passed in her second Parliament. An act passed in 1581 was directed against "divers persons wickedly disposed who not only wished her majesty's death, but also by divers means practiced and sought to know how long her highness should live, and who should reign after her decease, and what changes and alterations should thereby happen." Prophecy by witchcraft was traditionally associated with plots to seize the throne. It could encourage rebellion by assuring success, or stimulate attempts at assassination by predicting the ruler's death. The Yorkshire uprising of 1549 had been blamed on the promise of success the rebels had received from "fantasticall prophecie," as Holinshed records. Predictions of an army's defeat might encourage going over to the enemy, even though it might eventually turn out that the prediction was false; Montaigne had pointed out that Francis I's lieutenant general had been so frightened by a prediction that the Emperor Charles V would defeat Francis's forces that he "revolted, and became a turncote on the Emperor's side, to his intolerable losse and destruction, notwithstanding all the constellations then reigning." When at the end of the play Macbeth's severed head is carried high at the end of Macduff's lance (exactly as Macbeth had carried the rebel Macdonald's head from the field of battle and placed it on Duncan's battlements before the play begins), there is a grim reminder to the audience of a traditional mockery of criminal aspiration to mount above all, an aspiration often aroused by prophecy. In the thirteenth century, a witch told the rebel Welsh chieftain Llewellyn that he would gain high place, and after his execution his mockingly crowned head was borne uplifted above the throng through London and set up on the Tower in fulfillment of just such a misleadng promise of elevation as Macbeth receives. Boiled and tarred for preservation, the severed heads of the Gunpowder conspirators had been stuck up on the Bridge tower in the same mockery of their expectations.

Prophecy was felt to be not only unnatural to man but a rhetorical perversion, because it was characteristically double-dealing, like the prophecies of ancient oracles. It corresponded in its deceptive nature with the conniving subversiveness it served. But it might also be felt to be a rhetorical strategy of justified rebellion compelled to express itself in muffled language—a lie justified by its end, like the "equivocation" justified by the defendants in the Gunpowder Plot. It is not clear whether the witches' evasive prophecy to Macbeth serves some necessary end. Although his career must have had an admonitory function as Shakespeare presented it, we should also account for the impression the play sometimes gives that his criminal deeds had been historically inevitable.

We can glimpse some buried suggestion that Macbeth is the man of Machiavellian subterfuge and force appearing at a time when these attributes are called for—and that the combination can be a necessary strategy for progressive ends. The Machiavellian element in Macbeth's character can remind one of the theory of the author of *The Prince* that the stable state can be created only by calculated force and strategy that subordinates moral restraint to desirable ends. Shakespeare would have found basis for such a view of Macbeth in Holinshed. In the chronicle, a Scotland divided by civil war is actually set into order by Duncan's murderer, who governs for many peaceful years before fear of betrayal causes him to contrive the death of Banquo. Shakespeare suppresses this post facto validation of the putsch that brought Macbeth to power; he makes Macbeth's reign an explosive train of further murders and social degeneration. These are changes that erase offense to a king who might identify himself with Duncan and any would-be assassin with Macbeth—and forbid the invitation to insurrection that had been found in *Richard II*. Denied also is any specific provocation of Macbeth's defection. Shakespeare does not explain Macbeth's grievance, about which one hears only in Holinshed—that he had been entitled to election to the throne by Scottish rules and had been bypassed by Duncan's arbitrary appointment of Malcolm as his successor. In the play we are unprepared to hear him exclaim, "That is a step / On which I must fall down, or else o'erleap."

But there were always reasons for thinking that under some circumstances a strong usurper was better than a weak legitimate incumbent. In *King Lear,* as I have argued, Shakespeare had recently shown the emptiness of title without power. Holinshed's Duncan is described by the rebel warrior Macdonald as a "fainthearted milksop, more meet to gouerne a sort of idle monks in some cloister than to haue the rule of such valiant and hardie men of warre as the Scots." Even Macbeth and Banquo, who come to the king's rescue, complained, Holinshed relates, about "the kings softnes, and ouermuch slacknesse in punishing offenders," and when they decide to plot his murder they become indistinguishable from the fierce warrior thanes who had threatened Duncan earlier. The chronicler compares Duncan with his cousin Macbeth:

> Duncane was so soft and gentle of nature, that the people wished the inclinations and maners of these two cousins to haue beene so tempered and interchangeablie bestowed betwixt them, that where the one had too muche of clemencie, and the other of crueltie, the meane vertue betwixt these two extremities might haue reigned by indifferent partition in them both. . . . The beginning of Duncans reigne was very quiet and peaceable, without anie notable trouble; but after it was perceiued how negligent he was in punishing offenders, manie misruled persons tooke occasion thereof to trouble the peace and quiet state of the common-wealth, by seditious commotions.

In Shakespeare's play, we know nothing about Duncan's earlier years; we simply come upon him dangerously embattled against a foreign enemy and rebels who have organized themselves against him, though the history of their enmity is denied us. To show us his character, Shakespeare allows us to see Duncan in one exquisite moment when, as he approaches Macbeth's castle, he seems responsive to the harmony of nature, generous and affectionate to his fellow-man—almost a man of a different culture from the primitive world surrounding him. His language distinguishes itself by its studied Renaissance grace:

> This castle hath a pleasant seat; the air
> Nimbly and sweetly recommends itself
> Unto our gentle senses.

Yet it could not be more inappropriately applied to the house of death he is entering. Duncan's blind trustfulness and mildness may be meant by Shakespeare to account for the internal unrest of his realm and the threat of invasion by a foreign enemy—conditions which might make his replacement seem as inevitable as Richard II's, after all.

Shakespeare also goes some way to sanitize James's ancestor, Banquo, detaching him from Macbeth's plot to kill the king, though in Holinshed he is plainly Macbeth's collaborator in the murder of Duncan. But the erasure of this complicity is not complete. Shakespeare lets us know that Banquo is tempted to follow Macbeth's course when he says to Fleance on the night of the murder,

> Merciful powers,
> Restrain in me the cursèd thoughts that nature
> Gives way to in repose.

Banquo, too, after all, has received a thrilling promise of futurity from the witches, and it, too, depends for its fulfillment on the removal of Duncan and, eventually, of Macbeth himself, as Macbeth later realizes. Whether or not he is prepared to assist its fulfillment, Banquo is the only one besides Macbeth who knows about the prophecy. He correctly suspects that Macbeth played "most foully" for the crown. But he does nothing to block his election at Scone.

As one goes back and forth among shifting impressions, one sees that Shakespeare has allowed conflicted views of the uses of ambition to be felt. Macbeth is not entirely the conventional political criminal driven by sinful lust for power. But neither is he a justified rebel, though some potential for that role vibrates in the play at moments. The puzzle of Macbeth's cruel treachery begins with our impression that up until the time the play begins, his prowess and devotion have been exercised against traitors who have menaced Duncan. Yet they are his forerunners. Macbeth resembles them in heroic resolution as much as in a capacity for betrayal, and his own end, as I have noted, is anticipated by Macdonald's final beheading. As though hinting something to us, the report of the "bleeding captain" shows Macbeth and Macdonald as twins embracing on the battlefield as they struggle against one another, "as two spent swimmers that do cling together/And choke their art." The "merciless Macdonald" is ambiguously described as having been locked in equal combat with Macbeth, "Fortune on his damned quarrel smiling," before he had been cut down. The rebel Cawdor is described by Ross as having been

> confronted [by Macbeth] with self-
>   comparisons,
> Point against point, rebellious arm 'gainst arm,
> Curbing his lavish spirit.

There is also Malcolm's homage to Cawdor's bearing at his execution; he had died

> As one that had been studied in his death,
> To throw away the dearest thing he owed
> As 'twere a careless trifle.

Macbeth, now called by Duncan "my worthy Cawdor," is given the title just removed from this hero of a bad cause and inherits, perhaps, a little of his dubious glamour. He also inherits a traitor's role that illustrates the instability of apparent character. When Malcolm reports how Cawdor met his death, Duncan exclaims, in bafflement,

>   There's no art
> To find the mind's construction in the face.
> He was a gentleman on whom I built
> An absolute trust.

At this moment, Macbeth, the traitor-in-the making, enters and is greeted by the trusting Duncan with, "O worthiest cousin . . ." Most commentators read this as an ironic reminder to the theater audience that knows what is soon to happen. But Macbeth has risked his life for king and kinsman and *is* worthy. As I have suggested, the complex political issue of rebellion—which could be valued either negatively or positively in certain historical circumstances—permits us to see various possibilities inherent in Duncan's displacement.

In any case, Macbeth's soldier courage, like Macdonald's or Cawdor's, has an independent value, like the courage of Fortinbras, who, we remember, was so envied by Hamlet for his readiness to fight bravely for a straw. Here again, Shakespeare seems to invoke an older, Homeric view that martial belligerence is a virtue disconnected from the occasion or allegiance it serves. We can recall Othello's sad farewell to "the plumed troops and the big wars." These "make ambition virtue," he said. And it is Macbeth's military valor that makes an epic "virtue" of his ambition. Though the bloodletting of Duncan makes him shake as though he has never cut anyone's throat before, his sword had "smoked with bloody execution" as he "carved out his passage" on the battlefield and did not pause until he had "unseamed" Macdonald "from nave to th' chaps"—much as Pyrrhus had "minced" the limbs of Priam, as described in the Player's recital to Hamlet. Macbeth had been called "Valour's minion" as though he had been the favorite of a deified abstraction, and "Bellona's bridegroom," as though he had mated with the goddess of war. The murder of Duncan is no act of battlefield valor, of course; it is a perfidious assassination of his unsuspecting victim done secretly behind doors, a covert act that is the reverse of honorable. But Macbeth's assurance to his wife that he dares to do the murder they have planned, dares to do what "becomes a man," will be a declaration of that same readiness to shed blood for which he had once been praised in the report of the "bleeding captain." Though he does not prove quite so ready after all—and it is the very bloodiness of his murder of Duncan that afterward horrifies him—he does the deed. And afterward, he will not fear the bloody work of others' swords. As he hears of the English army massed to confront him near the end, he declares to Seyton, "I'll fight till from my bones my flesh be hacked." He is still "Bellona's bridegroom." As he prepared to order the murder of Banquo, he saw himself as the man who collaborated with Fate to bring about his ascent to the throne and called upon Fate as if asking his Olympian sponsor to take his part: "Come Fate into the list,/And champion me to th' utterance." Now he cries, "They have tied me to a stake; I cannot fly,/But, bear-like, I must fight the course," and encounters his foretold destiny:

> I will not yield
> To kiss the ground before young Malcolm's feet
> And to be baited with the rabble's curse.
> Though Birnam Wood be come to Dunsinane
> And thou opposed being of no woman born,
> Yet I will try the last. Before my body,
> I throw my warlike shield. Lay on Macduff,
> And damned be him that first cries, "Hold, enough!"

—a final utterance that might have served Leonidas at Thermopylae before *his* head was cut off by order of the triumphant Xerxes, though the last word about Macbeth is that his bloodthirstiness has made him, simply, a "dead butcher."

Satanic heroism at best—but who is available to replace Shakespeare's most dubious hero? Rebels, again, though rebels acting in the name of legitimacy. There is even a doubt of the value of this legitimacy, a doubt uneasily removed after Malcolm withdraws the damning self-characterization by which he tests Macduff's loyalty. Macduff's "the truest issue of [Scotland's] throne/ By his own interdiction stands accursed" suggests that lineal claim is not enough. Malcolm, like Banquo, Ross, and Macduff, his comrades in the party of order, remains a dubious upholder of the right. One is reminded that the murderous Richard III had been replaced by Queen Elizabeth's grandfather, Henry Tudor, a man of tenacious Machiavellian will whose claims to the crown were not impeccable.

The political ambiguity I have identified in *Macbeth* goes some way to explain Shakespeare's presentation of his hero/villain, making it difficult to relate the murderer to the man we first encounter as a loyal thane, then observe as someone of sensitive imagination who shudders at bloodshed yet still murders, and then murders and murders again. This mutability of personality has some rooting, perhaps, in the Machiavellian principle of opportunistic self-making. Thinking only politically, Machiavelli had offered a recipe for contemporary ambitiousness that deprecated essences in favor of appearances. For all the differences between them, Machiavelli's skepticism met Montaigne's on a common doubt about the concept of character. Machiavelli had said in *The Prince*, "let not the Prince fear to incur blame for those vices without which he cannot easily preserve his States; for if one considers everything carefully, one will find something which *seems* to be virtue, and to follow it would be ruin; and something else which *seems* to be vice, but ultimately security and prosperity come of it." Appearances might be, for the Prince himself, all that practically counted, but the Prince "need not be a slave to them either; he need not have all the good qualities . . . but should certainly appear to have them. I would even go so far as to say that if he has these qualities and always behaves accordingly he will find them ruinous; if he only appears to have them they will render him service. He should appear to be compassionate, faithful to his word, guileless, and devout. And indeed he should be. But his disposition should be such that, if he needs to be the opposite, he knows how. . . . He should have a flexible disposition, varying as fortune and circumstances dictate."

But this condition also transcends the political-historical issue out of which it arises. In the contradictions of power politics Shakespeare found the more general subject he had also found in Montaigne. The practical problem of the proper function of the ambitious man—the subject of the history plays—is still present in *Macbeth,* even given a new complexity so that ambition itself is no longer so clearly distinguishable as a consistent trait in this strange protagonist. But what makes this last of his major tragedies more intolerably tragic is the doubt that even a stereotype of human flexibility like the "Machiavel" cannot be taken as a true representation of what we are. When Duncan says concerning the traitor Cawdor that "there's no art to find the mind's construction in the face," his bafflement seems to pay tribute to Machiavellian dissembling but more profoundly suggests that a constant human essence—Hamlet's "that within which passeth show"—is unavailable.

Shakespeare offers a version of the Macbeth story more disturbing to our deepest sense of the quality of being human by throwing out the logic that gives us assurance that we understand why we act as we do. The presence of witchcraft's riddling prophecy —which seems to reveal the inaccessible truth but really misleads —is a way of exposing the human delusion that one *can* understand what will happen and who we are. The mythic obliquity remains. The play invites a glance at the void over one's shoulder, challenging skeptically those conventions that govern our negotiations with reality—those fictions without which we cannot live. I am reminded, as I have been before, of Montaigne's insistent denial of the constancy—even the reality—of human character. Such a view is illustrated by Macbeth's unclear sense of purpose which seems, as Montaigne would say, transported by the wind of occasion without his prior design.

Turning the play about another way to look at some of Shakespeare's changes from the original Macbeth story he found in Holinshed, I want to observe now that they demonstrate the same indifference to the idea of motive that had governed his adaptation of Belleforest's account of Hamlet's story, or Cinthio's of Othello's, or of the old play of King Leir, the same skepticism about human selves and lives. Once again, Shakespeare is loosening the connection between behavior and its causes as though he believes that such connection is unknowable. Holinshed's story, more coherent, in the usual sense, than Shakespeare's, multiplies explanations where Shakespeare reduces them. Shakespeare's Macbeth speaks once only of his ambition and deplores it as inadequate, because it is "vaulting," like a horseman who "o'erleaps [himself]." He declares that he has "no spur to prick the sides of [his] intent" and is fated to fall or fail for lack of such spur—perhaps a grievance of the kind that sustained the historical Macbeth. That his ambition is without justification might make him simply the victim of a ruling passion, and if he is the ambitious man as Othello is the jealous man, we expect this to be shown. But does Macbeth really have a clear desire for power or glory? Despite his obvious definition as someone ruined by compulsive yearning to get on, his supposed ambition is hard to verify. Lady Macbeth has to remind him of "the hope . . . / Wherein you dressed yourself," but we have seen no evidence of that hope. Macbeth has been called a man of imagination, but he is deficient in the imagination that dwells upon the bliss to be felt when the end is reached. As far as we can judge from what Shakespeare shows us, he does not dream about the gratifications of power and pomp. His crime does not spring from any vision of the crown, the "golden round" which gleams in his wife's imagination when *she* hears about the witches' prophecy. Nor does he appear ever to relish his success, unlike Richard III, who even enjoys as well his sinister plotting and murder, whereas Macbeth is horrified by his first crime. Shakespeare, as though collaborating with his character's reticence, denies us, by the compressed structure of the play, any view of the coronation scene where Macbeth's satisfaction might have been displayed. He makes it occur between the end of the second and the beginning of the third act.

Schoolroom teaching of Macbeth has generally exerted itself to mend what seems left out; the student is told that he is reading a morality play about the consequence of devilish ambition. Early stage productions actually rewrote *Macbeth* to make this more evident—just as Tate had rewritten *King Lear* to conform to his idea of correct poetic justice. William Davenant's 1674 rewrite, which aimed to "improve" Shakespeare by making Macbeth's ambition more obvious, changed "Hear it not, Duncan, for it is a knell/ That summons thee to heaven or to hell" to "O Duncan, hear it not, for 'tis a bell/ That rings my Coronation and thy knell." Like Davenant, David Garrick, in his acting version of the play, also saw the need to make Macbeth's ambition more distinct than Shakespeare had done, and his Macbeth concludes his own story:

'Tis done! the scene of life will quickly close.
Ambition's vain delusive dreams are fled,
And now I wake to darkness, guilt and horror.

Macbeth has not been actually rewritten this way since, but few of the play's best critics for almost four centuries have found it easy to admit that Macbeth's career cannot be described in this way. Like Hamlet resisting the Revenger model, Shakespeare's Macbeth may be thought of as *resisting* the conventional type of the Machiavellian ambitious man. Treacherous regicide that he is, he seems to perform his role under compulsion—committing murder, as Bradley observed, almost as though it were his "appalling duty" to do so. And he does not end by repenting his ambition. He merely blames the prophecies that misled him: "th' equivocation of the fiend,/That lies like truth." He seems to know no truth about himself, saying only, "I 'gin to be aweary of the sun/And wish th' estate o' th' world were now undone."

There is some temptation for the modern reader to get out of the difficulty by reading *Macbeth* psychologically and saying that the struggle between awareness and oblivion one finds in him is due simply to the fact that the play's puzzling protagonist is driven by unconscious rather than conscious desires. The fate to which he submits may be his own hidden nature. According to such a reading, the witches who give him their fatal guarantee may represent some *buried* wish—say, a parricidal passion he does not recognize in himself—and this may explain his weak sense of motive and his odd air of acting despite his knowledge that his acts are heinous. When Lady Macbeth admits that she has been unable to perform the murder herself because Duncan "resembled [her] father as he slept," she may be disclosing, it has been suggested, a dim sense that killing the king is parricide for her also. It is this realization, on some unconscious level, of his own oedipal anger and guilt that could, according to such diagnosis, explain Macbeth's mixed compulsion and horror. By this account, Macbeth's jump to the idea of murder when Duncan appoints Malcolm his heir is the outrage of the displaced son against the father who has favored a younger sibling. But such a reading cannot be taken literally. The construct of character which invites one to imagine an "unconscious" or a past psychic history capable of "explaining" Macbeth's behavior depends on a twentieth-century model—that of a patient undergoing psychoanalysis. But the reading that connects behavior to unconscious instead of conscious desire is only another version, after all, of the view that we do what we mean to even if we do not know what we mean. Shakespeare seems to have preferred to make a mystery of Macbeth's terrible urgency. I suspect that his distrust of conventional explanation would have extended, had he been acquainted with them, to the banal formulas of psychoanalysis.

Undertaking to watch the action of this play for some revelation of Macbeth's growth of purpose, we stop first, of course, at the opportunity to observe him when he hears the witches' prophecy. After he learns of his promotion to the titles of Glamis and Cawdor, Macbeth sees these fulfillments as guarantees of the witches' third promise, and is ready to expect that he might become king while looking the other way. "That trusted home/Might yet enkindle you unto the crown," Banquo remarks. "Enkindle" is more ambiguous than is generally noted. "Inflame with desire," the New Cambridge editor, A. R. Braunmuller, glosses, but Bradley interpreted it as less violent—"cause you to hope for," and Kittredge observed that Banquo may simply be warning Macbeth against dubious prophecies and false hopes. One can even find the sense to be still more passive if one is willing to think of Macbeth brought without his wish or act into the brightness of royalty like a fire lit by someone else—such a sense implying a future in which he might trust unperturbedly. Macbeth calls the Weird Sisters' prophecy a prologue to "the swelling act/Of the imperial theme," as though the future is already generated in the womb of time. Yet this anticipation makes Macbeth's "seated heart knock at [his] ribs/Against the use of nature" like a fetal monstrosity demanding to be born from within *himself*, and his visible disturbance puzzles Banquo. A "horrid image"—*perhaps* the image of what he might have to do to achieve this destiny—bursts upon his mind, and his

> Thought, whose murder yet is but fantastical,
> Shakes so [his] single state of man that function

Is smothered in surmise, and nothing is,
But what is not.

Coleridge wrote, "Every word of his soliloquy shows the early birth-date of his guilt." But if this is the first surfacing of the thought of Duncan's murder, we must take the syntax loosely, and some editors have suggested that the word *murder,* which appears here for the first time in the play, is only a description of the determined suppression of a still formless idea. In any case, Macbeth manages to banish it, after one frightened glance, with the hope that chance alone will crown him without his doing anything. His "Come what may, / Time and the hour runs through the roughest day" seems to signify submission to the foretold future rather than, as some have thought, an expectation of an opportunity to act. It is not till the next scene that Duncan designates Malcolm as his heir by giving him a title as good as Macbeth's, which Macbeth calls, "a step / On which I must fall down, or else o'erleap" — using again the image of leaping or vaulting over what must intervene or impede. It is his characteristic way of dealing with what he cannot bear to think about.

But even before this, watching him as he broods, Banquo observes, "Look how our partner's rapt," and once again there could be difference of interpretation among close readers. Does "rapt" mean the taking on of a new self, as one wraps a garment about oneself (a recurrence of Shakespeare's imagery of clothing so prominent in *King Lear*)? Does it mean that Macbeth is in a trance, enraptured, or put into ecstasy, by his inner vision? Or does it suggest "raped," or, more exactly, "seized," from the past participle of the Latin *rapere,* with the implication that Macbeth's will has been taken over by a force outside himself? The second meaning is primary; Macbeth will write his wife about the day when he "learned by the perfectest report [that the witches had] more in them than mortal knowledge," and how he "stood rapt in the wonder of it." But both the first or last meanings suggest that some external addition or intervention has created the self that calls itself Macbeth.

Murder, if on Macbeth's mind, is rarely on his tongue or his wife's. Lady Macbeth speaks of "that which rather thou dost fear to do, / Than wishest should be undone," and when the royal guest has retired, she refers obliquely to "this night's great business" or "this enterprise." When Macbeth himself recoils momentarily, it is with "We will proceed no further in this business." His "If it were done, when 'tis done, then 'twere well / It were done quickly" soliloquy at the end of Act I begins by referring to what is about to happen as an "it" repeated three times. The next sentence does begin

If th' assassination
Could trammel up the consequence and catch
With his surcease, success,

using two words, *assassination* and *surcease,* that hiss like snakes alongside *success* and seem to refer to the killing of Duncan. But again, there is syntactic ambiguity; "his" is not clearly a reference to the king, and it looks as though it is the ending of "consequence" he desires. Only in the rising climax of this speech does the word *murderer* emerge at last in the place of synonyms or pronouns as Macbeth reflects that he should "against [Duncan's] murderer shut the door, / Not bear the knife myself." Only his wife, who understands fully what they are about, realizes that he is slow to realize that his futurity cries "Thus thou must do."

So Shakespeare protects Macbeth for a while from our scorn by withholding from us any clear view of the germination of the plot to kill the king and gain the throne, almost as though there had never been a moment of decision making. It seems obvious that

Macbeth and Lady Macbeth *must* have put their heads together and made their dreadful plans. Yet any guesses about such an occasion become tangled in contradictions. Lady Macbeth reproaches her husband as he hesitates, claiming that he had already proposed "this enterprise" when neither "time nor place/Did then adhere, and yet you would make both"—before the king gave them the opportunity of his visit. She goes so far as to say, when she boasts of her own terrible resolution, that she would have dashed out the brains of her suckling babe, "had I so sworn/As you have done to this." But when had he sworn it? Shall we suppose that the murder of Duncan had been an idea they discussed before Macbeth's first encounter with the Weird Sisters—at some indefinite time when the conditions were not yet right? And when could the couple have had their discussion about what they would do when conditions became propitious? It is impossible to find a conceivable moment when the murder plot could have been developed by this pair, even though they act with speed and decision as though plans were already laid. Macbeth makes no reference to such an understanding in the letter his wife reads before his return home; this merely informs her of the prophecy he has been given of a "coming on of time" when he is to be hailed as king. There seems no time for a later letter from Macbeth before Duncan is at her door and she reels with the shock of his pat arrival and observes grimly to herself, "The raven himself is hoarse/That croaks the fatal entrance of Duncan"—a line which recalls with only the faintest irony Hamlet's demand for the commencement of "The Murder of Gonzago"—"the croaking raven doth bellow for revenge." She asks only to be filled enough with fiendishness to carry out a murder scenario too conventional to need recital.

The murder of Duncan is a terrible and perhaps inexplicable transgression of limits that brings the criminal into a world from which there is no return. Thomas DeQuincey, in his famous essay about the "knocking at the gate," perceived that where Macbeth arrived by killing Duncan was a place of transformative strangeness (which is why the porter, with his low jokes, is such a welcome glimpse of the world outside). This first murder is afterward what he is. He becomes the man who has assassinated his king, his cousin, the guest in his house. Macbeth himself does not "scan" or identify what he does until he does it. He says, "Strange things I have in head that will to hand / Which must be acted ere they may be scanned," referring to this priority of act (or the hand that does) to consciousness (or the eye that scans). The reversal of order between the two is something we hear about repeatedly. To quote him more fully in the comment he makes after the banquet attended by Banquo's ghost in Act III:

> I am in blood
> Stepped in so far that should I wade no more,
> Returning were as tedious as go o'er.
> Strange things I have in head that will to hand,
> Which must be acted ere they may be scanned. . . .
> Come we'll to sleep. My strange and self-abuse
> Is the initiate fear that wants hard use;
> We are but young in deed.

He realizes, now, that the process he is launched upon has just begun. He is but young in deed, and deeds are already making him a metamorphic person. Macbeth may now struggle to put a stop to the process that constantly thrusts him always onward toward new deeds and new states of being. We should not overlook the shifting pun in the opening line of his famous soliloquy uttered in the play's seventh scene, before he has killed anyone: "If it were done when 'tis done, then 'twere well / It were done quickly." The first occurrence of *done* means "finished" or "ended"; the second has the usual sense of "acted" or "performed"; the third, ambiguously, means either or both. The relation of doing to finishing is Macbeth's problem as he expresses his wish that "th' assassination / Could trammel up the consequence" and be the "be-all"—the accomplishing act—and, at the same time, the "end-all" that has no sequel. The great "quell" he and Lady Macbeth perform is, they hope, both a death and an end-making of itself. But as they will discover, all acts are incomplete, all trail after them some not-to-be-trammeled-up consequence. Macbeth wants time to have a stop and the murderous act to have no results beyond its immediate purpose. He is willing to "jump the time to come," to forget the futurity of hell—cutting himself off from any vision of the apocalyptic end of all when, indeed, human deeds will have their ultimate consequences and timelessness replace human time. On the hither side of eternity, "upon this bank and shoal of time," he fears the sequels of human history—but goes on. "I go, and it is done," he says as he enters Duncan's chamber, *done*, again, ambiguously meaning both the act and the vain hope of terminus. Nothing is proved less true than that it will be "done" in the second sense. He hears an unknown voice cry, "Sleep no more." The precipitance of his career will allow for no pause, no intervention of sleep's timelessness. Sleep that knits up the raveled sleeve of care—restores the garment of self—is never again to give relief to Macbeth or to his wife. Event must succeed event, now, without pause. Before too long even the dead seem enviable. Macbeth will say, "Duncan is in his grave. / After life's fitful fever, he sleeps well."

As Maynard Mack and others have observed, *deeds, do,* and *done* are words that repetitiously reverberate in this play as *honest* does in *Othello* and *nothing* in *King Lear*. But the meaning of this insistent repetition has not been sufficiently reflected on. There is, as we have seen, the constant reference to the dilemma for Macbeth of actions which cannot be said to be done or finished, sealed off from the flow of further and still further results. One must also notice that the primary sense of doing as action is reiterated again and again after the first witch declares on the blasted heath in Act I, "I'll do, I'll do, and I'll do." Lady Macbeth says, for example,

> Thou'dst have, great Glamis,
> That which cries, "Thus thou must do" if thou have it;
> And that which rather thou dost fear to do,
> Than wishest should be undone.

And soon, with an irony he cannot perceive, she offers Duncan on his arrival at her door "All our service, / In every point twice done and then done double" as return for the honor of his visit. Macbeth himself makes the declaration that he "dare[s] do all that may become a man; / Who dares do more, is none." This, as I have said, declares his essential male-warrior identity, but it also can be taken to mean that a man is brought into being by *doing* all that is appropriate to his manhood. This emphasis on *deed* in the play is all the more remarkable because it conflicts with Macbeth's own sensation, before the murder of Duncan, that he is invaded by unnamed thoughts and feelings—so that he loses all sense of outer action, which alone defines being. "Nothing is but what is not," he complains. Macbeth begins by admitting those "horrible imaginings" and the mere "surmise" that shake him so when he first hears the witches' prophecies. But he hastily dismisses these dreams and fears. His "If it were done" soliloquy is a weighing not so much of his own insubstantial feelings as of the universal *effects* of the murder he is about to commit. He longs to cease all thought, only to act. When the bell rings as he fortifies himself to follow the ghostly dagger, he reminds himself,

> Whiles I threat, he lives;
> Words to the heat of deeds too cold breath gives.
> I go and it is done.

The *done* in this last utterance before the murder is both the action that is to take place and the end-all never to be achieved.

Even though she had been the one who hallucinated the golden crown Macbeth might expect to wear, it had been Lady Macbeth who boldly began with a pragmatic skepticism about un-enacted ideas. She understood that desire was not enough. She told him in her thoughts,

> Thou wouldst be great
> Art not without ambition, but without
> The illness should attend it.

Macbeth's impediment was his inhibition against "play[ing] false" in order to "wrongly win"—a handicap surely absent from the makeup of a Machiavel who accepts the necessity of steps to be taken to achieve his goal. She would have to pour into him her own recognition that connected acts intervene between intention and attainment, conduct the ambitious man to the end which cries to him, "Thus thou must do." Accepting her own role, she called upon spirits that might empty her of reflection, filling her "from the crown to the toe topfull / Of direst cruelty" so that

> no compunctious visitings of nature
> Shake [her] fell purpose nor keep peace between
> Th' effect [that is, the act] and it.

She asked for an obscuring of consciousness so that her "keen knife see not the wound it makes," though in fact, she never used her knife. Their deed accomplished, Lady Macbeth invokes the punning alternate meanings of *done* when she tells her husband, "Things without all remedy / Should be without regard; what's done is done." But Macbeth acknowledges, now, the continuum of time when he tells her, "We have scorched the snake, not killed it." More deeds, beginning with the murder of Banquo, must follow.

Macbeth shrinks from full awareness of the horrors he performs. The "dagger of the mind" that appears before him when he is about to enter Duncan's bedroom "marshall'st [him] the way that [he] was going." It is not the murder weapon itself, but a prophetic image of the way that weapon is about to appear, dripping with gouts of blood, having done the deed Macbeth has feared to imagine. As though surprised by the reality of his act, he says, "This is a sorry sight" when he comes from killing Duncan, but now he cannot bear to describe the sight. Lady Macbeth thinks she can face the actuality better—and tells him, "A foolish thought to say a sorry sight." In killing his king almost without willing it, as it seems, he separates himself as murderer from the murder. Returning with the bloody daggers in his hands, he groans not so much at the murder itself as at the murmurs of Duncan's sleeping sons or the unconscious grooms. One cried "Murder!" in his sleep—that word again emerging, though not precisely designating the murder taking place while their eyes are shut—and one said, "God bless us." Macbeth cannot understand why he was unable to say "Amen" when the sleeping groom said, "God bless us," and this may indicate that, as a damned person, he cannot appeal to God. He may illustrate that condition Helen Gardner identified by saying that he is like one of the fallen angels described by theology as creatures incapable of repentance, and forever denied salvation. That Macbeth has lost connection with the mental sources of behavior is indicated by the strange moral oblivion of his report of the events in the murder-chamber. What is certainly evident is his division of mind which ever keeps him from realizing to full measure what he does.

The separation of awareness from doing is represented forcefully by the play's repeated imagery of dismemberment. I have referred to the image of the traitor's severed head carried aloft in ironic fulfillment of his desire to rise above the rest of men. But

Macbeth's severed head will, finally, also be the head of a man who did not want to see or give a name to the action of his body; it will be the head that contained "strange things that will to hand/ Which must be acted ere they can be scanned." Separating consciousness from act, making invisible to himself even his own desires, Macbeth cries,

> Stars hide your fires,
> Let not light see my black and deep desires,
> The eye wink at the hand. Yet let that be
> Which the eye fears when it is done to see.

At the beginning, it is as though Shakespeare wants us to share, for as long as we can, Macbeth's own submission to acts that he hardly seems to understand. He seems to weigh his decision for one crucial moment, forecasting accurately the universal censure the murder of Duncan might bring for "the deep damnation of his taking-off," but Lady Macbeth has reminded him to "be a man," and he is "settled and bend[s] up/ Each corporal agent to this terrible feat." Macbeth's murderous disloyalty is a disloyalty of the body to the mind, a cleaving apart of the murdering hand from the eye of consciousness that might include conscience or pity. The vision of a body chopped upon a butcher's block recurs in the play—in the witches' brew of dismembered animal and human parts, and elsewhere—and it is associated most of all with Macbeth, who so gorily "unseams" Macdonald before beheading him. But when, at the very end, he is referred to as a "dead butcher," the name fits more than literally because he has severed thought from act. The antique heroism of Pyrrhus or Fortinbras that sanctioned such separation is no longer operative.

That Shakespeare shields Macbeth from our revulsion for as long as possible makes for a disjunction also between *our* understanding and our direct impressions. It is not merely that we never hear him articulate his wicked intention to murder Duncan, never see the hatching of his plot — though his decision to have others destroyed afterward is articulated in our hearing. Why, it is sometimes asked, did the playwright decline to show this first murder scenically? He had certainly not hesitated to spill blood on the boards in earlier plays. Even in this play, the on-stage killing of Banquo and the cruel slaughter of Macduff's family soon make Macbeth's murderousness visible, but it is carried out by others on his behalf. In the case of Duncan we are outside a door passed through by both Macbeth and his Lady, and through which they both pass again, shaken, but only their bloodied hands make their work evident. This earliest of Macbeth's murders should make him more horrible to us than his subsequent ones do, for it is done with his own hands. Our sympathies should be with the gentle, trusting Duncan who has shown such gracious courtesy on arriving at Macbeth's castle and now lies slaughtered. Instead, they are with Macbeth, who staggers with horror at what he has done when he comes before us again with his terrible hands on exhibition — those hands which have somehow acted of themselves, as though his "eye" did not see them at their work. It is Macbeth's suffering we are compelled to feel participant in — almost against our will — and this makes him a tragic hero, after all. Macbeth's own revulsion and despair compel our sympathy. We sympathize with the terrified astonishment he feels, as we might feel at suddenly discovering ourselves the authors of cruel and wicked deeds. "What hands are here?" he asks as though he does not realize their attachment to himself. And he continues, "Ha! they pluck out mine eyes" as though the deed he has done annihilates his awareness. And yet, the deed signified by the irremovable blood on his hands is unalterable fact:

> Will all great Neptune's ocean wash this blood
> Clean from my hand? No: this my hand will rather

The multitudinous seas incarnadine,
Making the green one red.

As Macbeth approaches his second murder, the image of the bloody hand frees itself from his personal awareness so completely that it becomes an attribute of the night he invokes, like a metaphysical force, to obscure a cosmic eye of pity:

Come seeling night
Scarf up the tender eye of pitiful day
And with thy bloody and invisible hand
Cancel and tear to pieces that great bond
Which keeps me pale.

Seeling is a falconry term for the practice of sewing closed the eyelids of the bird being trained to the hood, and personified night is invoked to blindfold the awareness that is pity, something no longer purely his own but located in the universe at large in some way. This personification has, also, a bloody hand that is asked to destroy the universal force or a connection or restraint (exact interpretation is difficult) that holds him back from what he is about to do, performing itself an act of violent separation, a "tear[ing] to pieces."

Blood, the unstanchable presence of the wounded body, persists as testimony of the act of murder. The play's reference to blood begins early, with the report of the "bloody man," the mortally bleeding captain who relates the "bloody execution" of Macdonald by Macbeth and the further slaughter of the Norwegian enemy by Macbeth and Banquo, who seemed as though "they meant to bathe in reeking wounds/ Or memorise another Golgotha," a description that makes reference to Christ's wounds that flow without stop for mankind. Redemption and punishment are associations strangely mingled, as Macbeth is forced to admit, after Banquo's ghost has appeared at the banquet, "It will have blood they say: blood will have blood." And looking forward to the famous opening scene of the last act, we will see Lady Macbeth still unable to wash clean the bloodied hands with which she had emerged from Duncan's death-chamber. "Yet who would have thought the old man to have had so much blood in him?" she asks as she walks in her sleep, as though the flow of it, like the persistence of the past, cannot ever stop. In this mystical, half-symbolic, half-supernatural persistence of the blood on her hands, Shakespeare suggests the persistence of consequence, the persistence for eternity of what had been thought done when it was done. Her collapse is the collapse of a pragmatist who has not anticipated how the deed will stick upon her. The last words of hers we hear are, "what's done cannot be undone. To bed, to bed, to bed."

Yet Lady Macbeth had chided her husband for being like the proverbial cat who would eat fish but will not wet its feet, "letting I dare not wait upon I would." It was she who got Duncan's two chamberlains drugged with wine so that their daggers could be used for the murder while they slept, and when Macbeth emerged with the weapons still in his hands and wet with blood, it was she who was able to smear the innocent grooms with the blood of the murdered man and lay the daggers beside them. Her rationalism was seemingly greater than Macbeth's. "A little water clears us of this deed," she told him, although they will never be "cleared" of the deed and what follows from it. The completer skeptic, she was not persuaded that the air is crowded with invisible hosts—the witches never appeared to her—and she told her husband,

> The sleeping and the dead
> Are but as pictures; 'tis the eye of childhood
> That fears a painted devil.

She was not frightened by the superstition that the corpse of a murdered person bleeds in the presence of the murderer:

> If he do bleed,
> I'll gild the faces of the grooms withal,
> For it must seem their guilt.

Disbelieving in what comes after life, she cannot see ghosts. It is only Macbeth who is able to see Banquo's, which makes him remark so bitterly concerning the discontinuities he once believed in:

> The time has been
> That when the brains were out, the man would die,
> And there's an end. But now they rise again
> With twenty mortal murders on their crowns
> And push us from our stools.

That Banquo's ghost rises up from the grave is the refutation of Macbeth's desire to have things over with once and for all, and the fulfillment of his fear that this cannot be.

Before they have committed any murders what Macbeth and Lady Macbeth feel is something quite opposite—an impatience for a futurity which also denies the operation of time in its normal progress and ignores the steps that lead from one thing to another. When her husband first arrived home from warfare, ahead of Duncan, Lady Macbeth had expressed contempt for "this ignorant present" beyond which she felt already transported. She declared, "I feel now/ The future in the instant," despite her superior sense of the "illness" that must attend ambition, the process, however repulsive, that must intervene before the goal is attained. Even the jokes of the porter in the second act bear on the impatience the murdering couple share. There is the farmer "that hanged himself on th' expectation of plenty." He had not understood the mischances that may occur between expectation and achievement. The porter's bawdy reference to the effect of drink—that it "provokes the desire, but it takes away the performance"—refers to an unwelcome gap between anticipation and event. Unlike the hoarding farmer disappointed by a good harvest, or the man who fails at sex because he has drunk too much, the Macbeths attain their predicted triumph—he is the king he was promised he would be and she is queen. But in the hubbub that immediately resounds after the murder is discovered and the word *murder* now reverberates in earnest, Macbeth says,

> Had I but died an hour before this chance,
> I had lived a blessed time, for from this instant,
> There's nothing serious in mortality.
> All is but toys; renown and grace is dead,
> The wine of life is drawn, and the mere lees
> Is left this vault to brag of.

This eloquent statement of a kind of death, a stopping of time such as he has not foreseen, in which the "wine of life" is already drawn, seems to be uttered in a false pose of grief. But it may be an aside, sincerely expressing a sudden perception of his diminished future. He foresees already the time to come when all human history will seem to him a dull succession of disconnected days, the "tomorrow and tomorrow and tomorrow" of which he will speak in the most memorable literary statement of existential weariness.

After his murder of Duncan, we can only observe, in bafflement, how Macbeth's pitilessness increases once the first act of betrayal and self-betrayal is committed. Character, which one expects to find consistent, is constantly undone by new acts, though Macbeth, who tries never to look back, says, "I am afraid to think what I have done." He confesses to Lady Macbeth, "Look on it again I dare not." If he accepts the reality of his deed, he must forget the person he thought he was: "To know my deed, 'twere best not know my self." Each succeeding crime finds him less subject to those "compunctious visitings of nature" which Lady Macbeth once tried to cast out of herself. She succumbs more devastatingly than her husband to the effects of her participation in their common crime. Her fierce assault upon her own original nature with its women's breasts that once gave milk destroys her altogether, though she would, she has said, have "plucked the nipple from [her babe's] boneless gums" were such denial of female tenderness necessary. It is Macbeth, after all, who seems to succeed in achieving that thickening of his own blood which changes his nature almost physiologically. No longer can it be said of him that he is "too full o' th' milk of human kindness." He performs the same transformation as Lady Macbeth as though he, too, had once given suck to a babe but now is capable of destroying it.

Lady Macbeth may vainly say, "what's done, is done"; Macbeth must proceed to the murder of Banquo. Yet Banquo's death fails to make Macbeth "perfect;/Whole as the marble, founded as the rock"—and fixed in finality—for Fleance escapes unharmed. Before the third act is over the Scots nobles have become convinced of Macbeth's crimes. Accelerated almost unbearably now, the plot hurtles on, and though the witches seem to assure him of invulnerability, he has never been less sure that Fate will fulfill its promise without his stir. He hesitates about nothing any more, and, in the fourth act resolves to "take a bond of fate" and have Macduff killed as Banquo had been. But Macduff has escaped to England; Macbeth has not yet achieved that coincidence of intention and deed he craves. He has not been impatient enough.

> Time, thou anticipat'st my dread exploits;
> The flighty purpose never is o'ertook
> Unless the deed go with it. From this moment,

The very firstlings of my heart shall be
The firstlings of my hand.

Macbeth is more eager than ever to make deed coincide with intent, "to crown [his] thoughts with acts, be it thought and done."
So there follows the slaughter of Macduff's family. The calloused
Macbeth no longer quails at bloodshed: "This deed I'll do before
this purpose cool," he says.

Before that happens, Macbeth is given a view of the onward
progression of time—the forward motion of events producing their
consequences, which he has tried to deny—in the revelation by the
witches of a future beyond his own futile acts. On the one hand, he
is told, his delusions sustained, that time will, indeed, have a stop.
Although he must beware Macduff, "none of woman born / Shall
harm Macbeth," and

Macbeth shall never vanquished be until
Great Birnam Wood to high Dunsinane hill
Shall come against him.

But forced by his insistence to know the destiny of "Banquo's
issue" the witches call forth the procession of eight kings. The
spectral vision is a crushing disclosure of the continuity of time
Macbeth has been unable to halt, the continuity of legitimate lin-
eage. It is a biological continuity of parent to child—the continuity of blood—which flows onward from the murdered Banquo
in the veins of his descendants as a refutation of Macbeth's effort
to stop its flow. Macbeth will, in the next scene, attempt to cut off
the futurity of others by putting Macduff's children to death. But
though he has cut down Duncan and Banquo, he has failed to destroy their sons, Malcolm, who will succeed to the Scottish throne,
or Fleance, whose son will next wear the crown. Generation will
succeed generation of Stuart kings even to the present time of the

playwright and his audience—an expression of that concatenation of human time Macbeth has denied. Macbeth's rage against these heirs cannot be based on any hope of his own. As Macduff will say of Macbeth, flatly, when he learns of the murder of his own family, "He has no children." It is, perhaps, Macbeth's exclusion from the procreative process that gives further meaning to Lady Macbeth's "unsex me now," and her willingness to pluck her nipple from the mouth of a nursing babe, adding a special irony to the false pregnancy of that "swelling act of the imperial theme" which once had promised Macbeth so much.

Act V opens with that most famous of the play's scenes, Lady Macbeth's sleepwalking monologue in which she relives the moments that cannot be prevented from persisting out of the past. Her disease, as Macbeth recognizes, is incurable; it is simply the universal human disease of memory, which will not surrender the past to the present as she once desired. There is no way the physician can "pluck from the memory a rooted sorrow." But threatened now by the rebel Scots and their English allies, Macbeth barely can attend, and he sardonically asks the doctor to prescribe a purgative drug to expel his enemies. As his misfortune and disappointments multiply, he can only observe,

> I have supped full with horrors;
> Direness familiar to my slaughterous thoughts
> Cannot once start me.

He has no attention to spare even for the queen's death: "She should have died hereafter; / There would have been a time for such a word." Now, instead of desiring the future in the present, he wishes that the present might have been postponed. He who would have liked to make time sustain the moment of success against its inevitable aftermath understands that he is forever cut off by the past from outcomes he might have desired. He is said to feel "his secret murders sticking on his hands" like the bloody spots that seemed irremovable to Lady Macbeth. He says,

> That which should accompany old age,
> As honour, love, obedience, troops of friends,
> I must not look to have.

Life goes on for him without meaning or form as it "creeps in this petty pace from day to day / To the last syllable of recorded time."

To intervene before the end, Shakespeare gives us the portion of Act IV in which Macbeth's place at the center of the action is taken by others, and the effect of progressive process is felt. Scotland cannot heal itself but must depend on the aid of the saintly Edward the Confessor—the English king gifted with the royal touch that heals scrofula. We have a sense of the larger world, and the pace of time becomes more normal as we hear of those "cruel times" to which Ross refers in his melancholy conversation with Lady Macduff and which Macduff, in exile, describes

> New widows howl, new orphans cry, new sorrows
> Strike heaven on the face, that it resounds
> As if it felt with Scotland.

Macbeth, who "was once thought honest," is "this tyrant, whose sole name blisters our tongues," Malcolm and Macduff agree. But there is no certainty that a better condition will be restored even though the play seems to invite this expectation as the fall of Macbeth draws near. The playwright does not entirely forget Holinshed when he conveys in the fourth and fifth acts the *effects* of a prolonged reign as though to remind us of a normal way of thinking about time. In Shakespeare's account, Macbeth's rule has brought distress and disorder to the land as though years of oppression and corruption had passed. With the same trick of "double time" he used in *Othello,* Shakespeare exhibits degeneration the play's time scale does not really allow for. Close to the end, Macbeth tells his last loyal follower Seyton that his "way of life / is fall'n into the sere, the yellow leaf," as though one could behold in him "that time of life," as Shakespeare speaks of it in his seventy-third sonnet, when one is like a tree in autumn "when yellow leaves, or none, or few, do hang" upon its shaking boughs.

The ending of *Macbeth* is the bleakest in Shakespeare. Macbeth meets his death at the hands of Macduff with the fortitude which is all that remains to him of his once admirable personality—but without the illumination, however partial, that comforts us for the deaths of Hamlet, Othello, and Lear. It is Macduff who serves to restore the sense of the story to a degree by showing that cause has had effect and evil deeds must be paid for. But it remains dubious, I think, despite the wishful belief of most critics, that Macbeth is a morality play in which evil is finally put down by the forces of good. Even in *King Lear*, which seems to call for a redemptive "promised end," the sense of the irremedial dissolution of meaning persists. Similarly, *Macbeth* seems governed by a providential view of human events, a belief that divine intention operates in them—yet defeats this view. As we have seen before, the English stage provided patterns that Shakespeare found himself driven to fulfill, yet resisted. In *Macbeth* he invoked the most ancient and the most persistent dramatic idea in theatrical tradition, the idea that life is a contest between demonic and heavenly forces—and drains this idea of conviction.

Macbeth finds himself cast into the role long familiar in the traditions of religious drama in which an ambitious man submits himself to the devil's influence and falls to his doom of damnation—a pattern Marlowe had followed in his *Doctor Faustus*. Though there is no Mephistopheles in Shakespeare's play, Macbeth does give the impression of having given his soul away, being forever inaccessible to remorse or redemption. But Shakespeare has detached Macbeth from any primal contest of heaven and hell. The play does not illustrate the traditional providential contest of virtue and vice. There had been mystery plays in the Middle Ages about such events as Christ's Harrowing of Hell, in which Christ entered Hell's castle through a "hell-gate" guarded by a devil-porter and rescued the souls of prophets and patriarchs—which might, it has been thought, have given a suggestion to Shakespeare for the cleansing of Scotland by Macduff and Malcolm. Such interpretation finds in Macduff a hero as invulnerable to ambition as a wicked Macbeth is ambition's embodiment. But on the whole, the mis-fit rather than the fit of these precedents reveals the playwright's resistance to them, and his resistance to platitude. *Macbeth* may seem, superficially, to refer itself to a tradition of plot demonstrating the way the sacred order of things is disrupted and then restored. But at the same time, a contrary rhythm is introduced.

Goodness as the opposite of evil is, as I have said, only weakly represented in the character of Duncan, who vanishes so early from the scene. Banquo, who is described by Holinshed as Macbeth's trusted friend to whom he confided his plan to kill Duncan, is of more stalwart virtue in Shakespeare than history describes him—but some hint of his complicity remains. At the end of Act II, Ross and Macduff were ready to suspect Malcolm and Donaldbain of Duncan's murder, and the mysterious Old Man has to censure them: "God's benison go with you; and with those / That would make good of bad, and friends of foes!" Ross, in particular, will seem more self-preserving than anything else when he leaves the doomed Lady Macduff with the curious remark,

> I dare not speak much further,
> But cruel are the times when we are traitors
> And do not know ourselves, when we hold rumour
> From what we fear, yet know not what we fear,

But float upon a wild and violent sea,
Each way and none. I take my leave of you;
Shall not be long but I'll be here again. . . .
I am so much a fool, should I stay longer.
It would be my disgrace and your discomfort.

Finally, neither Malcolm nor Macduff is a reincarnation of the Christ of the Harrowing of Hell, and any reminder of such typology can only be ironic. We have expected them to be the worthy redeemers of Scotland, and so, we are forced to assume, they probably will prove. But the atmosphere of the play remains darkened, and we cannot entirely recover from the impression given that nothing stays stable. Seldom properly examined by critics is the strange exchange between Malcolm and Macduff in the third scene of Act IV, a scene that challenges easy assumptions of a providential outcome. Cut off from their own suffering country among strangers living under a better rule, Macduff and Malcolm feel the unreality and ambiguity of exile. Duncan's son tests Macduff by painting himself as worse than Macbeth, more

> bloody,
> Luxurious, avaricious, false, deceitful,
> Sudden, malicious, smacking of every sin
> That has a name,

until the honorable Macduff recoils in horror. The scene works in two directions. In the end, it validates Macduff as the virtuous avenger and Malcolm as a worthy heir, yet in the course of Malcolm's false self-incrimination we have a vision of possibility. The view of himself that Malcolm presents to Macduff is a pretense—but, like Macduff, we bring ourselves to reject it with difficulty. Macduff cannot easily find his balance after Malcolm's removal of his villain's mask. "Such welcome and unwelcome things at once, / 'Tis hard to reconcile," he says, as we might well say ourselves after this episode in which doubt seems to submerge the action.

What kind of a king Malcolm could prove in the future beyond the play remains an open question. All we have seen of him before this is that moment after Duncan's murder when, understandably unheroic, the boy prince resolves on flight. He does not stay to be killed like Macduff's brave child, who calls his murderer a "shag-haired villain" before he dies. There is the haunting possibility that Malcolm's false self-portrait may prove true and that disorder will set in again, when he comes to the throne, as it had after Macbeth became king. Macduff, appearing so ready to be politic, to countenance one after another of Malcolm's pretended faults, momentarily appears to be corrupt himself. He has already seemed uncertainly honorable in the bitter comment of his abandoned wife:

> His flight was madness. When our actions do not,
> Our fears do make us traitors . . .
> To leave his wife, to leave his babes,
> His mansion, and his titles in a place
> From whence himself does fly?

Malcolm seems right to doubt Macduff's virtue for having left his children and wife in the "rawness" of disordered Scotland—and only when he learns of their death does Macduff blame himself. Reverting to typology, D'Avenant not only simplified and rationalized the character of Macbeth in the seventeenth century. In his efforts to impose a moral coherence on Shakespeare, he omitted most of this testing scene and the scene in which the abandoned Lady Macduff condemns her husband so irrefutably.

Shakespeare's play is sparing of religious reference, and Macbeth's idea of time's unfolding does not reach to any vision of divine retribution. His consciousness takes little account from first to last of the eye of heaven—not even, perhaps, when he sees himself on the bank and shoal that separates man from eternity. Before he has committed any crime, we remember, he has said that he would be willing "to jump the life to come"—that is, forget God's judgment of murder and the punishment of hell—if there were some way to prevent consequences "here." Macbeth acknowledges to himself that Duncan's virtues

> Will plead like angels, trumpet-tongued against
> The deep damnation of his taking-off
> And pity, like a naked newborn babe
> Striding the blast, or heaven's cherubim, horsed
> Upon the sightless couriers of the air,
> Shall blow the horrid deed in every eye,
> That tears shall drown the wind.

But in this famous, visionary passage, Macbeth refers to *human* pity, and to a universal *human* perception of the murder he is about to commit, though the wonderful lines are drenched in the imagery of religious revelation. He continues up to the brink of the murder to be aware of Duncan's virtues and his own obligations as kinsman and subject of the anointed king who has "borne his faculties so meek, hath been/ So clear in his great office" that his death will arouse pity and indignation. But personified pity is merely *compared to* the angels or cherubim who might beckon the human spirit from a baroque ceiling. His own objections do not spring from religious or even moral compunction but are purely prudential. He tells his wife,

> We will proceed no further in this business.
> He hath honour'd me of late; and I have bought
> Golden opinions from all sorts of people,

Which would be worn now in their newest gloss,
Not cast aside so soon.

This pragmatic acknowledgment that success in killing Duncan would only bring dishonor and defeat in the end does not amount to much. He abandons the argument of prudence when Lady Macbeth observes that logic has nothing to do with his hesitation, and he asserts only his Fortinbras-like resolution.

But if the spiritual presence of divine solicitude is hardly present, what of the witches who might be thought of as demonic agents of seduction, though they make no contract with Macbeth and besides their skills as diviners of the future have only trivial faculties for working mischief in human lives? It has never been clear whether they should be played as grim sibyls or ridiculous crones. The night of the murder is called Hecate's hour, the time of wicked dreams, when, "withered murder . . . towards his design/ Moves like a ghost"—murder made an abstract personification, and so displaced from direct reference to Macbeth's will. The passage strengthens the appearance that powers outside himself have "rapt" Shakespeare's character in their talons like predatory birds. Macbeth may have been seized and held fast by those "spirits/ That tend on mortal thoughts" Lady Macbeth calls upon as she waits for Duncan's arrival. She calls them "murd'ring ministers" as though they, rather than herself and Macbeth, are the agents of murder, though she has invited them, like a witch offering herself to an incubus, to "take [her] milk for gall," finding sustenance for evil at her breast. How literally does Shakespeare intend us to take this as the intervention of supernatural agents who collaborate with the perverted human will?

That Macbeth is a man who does not seem capable of his crimes has made it seem to some that Shakespeare wanted to show that evil springs from some unknowable universal demonism that invades the human heart and against which the will is defenseless. But the play gives little evidence of the presence either of transcendent good or transcendent evil. The "masters" of the witches, the "spirits" upon whom Lady Macbeth calls are not evident in the action of the play. Is the mysterious force of destiny represented by the spooky trio Macbeth met on the unlocalized heath? Shakespeare follows Holinshed in naming them Weird Sisters, and *weird* still had, in Shakespeare's time, its Old English or Middle English sense of Fate—which would make them like the Norse Norns or Atropos, Clotho, and Lachesis, the Greek spinners and cutters of the thread of life. Yet they parody or trivialize the grim prototypes of mythology they suggest. Are they merely mischievous old women able to make an audience laugh as well as shudder? They were surely meant as contemporary reminders of crazed or malicious womanhood that, in the early seventeenth century, could be discovered among the demented or eccentric elderly in any English village, and who were subject to trial and execution if village hysteria rose high enough. They could toss a boat in a tempest, but not make it sink.

Still, those who have seen the witches as central to the play have been right after all. It is not accident that they appear alone on the stage before the human personages—not, like the ghost in *Hamlet*, which presents itself after we meet the living interpreters who will speculate about its nature and intention, never to be absolutely sure of its reality or whether it is benign or demonic. But uncertainty about the witches' powers—whether to cause the future or merely to read it—remains at the heart of the play and corresponds to uncertainty concerning Macbeth himself—whether he is the maker of his fate by his own choice or not. And as I have observed, it was the gift of prophecy as well as that of determination that made witches dangerous in the eyes of Shakespeare's contemporaries. Holinshed wrote that "the common opinion was, that these women were either the weird sisters, that is (as ye would say) the goddesses of destinie, or else some nymphs or feiries, imbued with knowledge of prophesie by their necromanticall science." Prophecy, a presumption to know the future, may have been the more interesting of their two faculties to Shakespeare, for in this play, though they have little power to make things happen, they can be said to represent Macbeth's illusion of foreknowledge. The fact that, though they were female, they were generally played by men, and that they wore beards, could make them merely comic but also increased their ambiguity as Tiresias-like prophetesses. The uncertainty with which they are associated is also suggested by their strange language, which refuses to award absolute meaning to human events. Their "fair is foul, and foul is fair" forecasts a rhythm of reversal such as might occur in the history of nations as well as in personal life—and a universal relativism in which what is lost is won and what is won is lost. The imagery of overturn with which they are associated corresponds to the idea of social insurrection but also suggests the general instability of order in the universe and in man and suggests a skeptical metaphysics of off-and-on truth.

There is the passage of time but no true dramatic meaning for the

> poor player
> That struts and frets his hour upon the stage
> And then is heard no more.

As he had done in depicting Hamlet's theater interests, moreover, Shakespeare may have been thinking of his own theater career in a way that reminds us that we are watching a play—and that a play is always a failed attempt to make life seem meaningful. He may have been thinking himself of how life's failure to compose itself as more than "tomorrow and tomorrow" defies the dramatist, or of the way, as an actor, he had been sometimes reminded of how human behavior is itself a matter of roles and costumes put on or taken off. Maybe the playwright who never addresses us directly permits a rare glimpse into his own thought at its most skeptic extreme when he makes Macbeth observe that one's life really has no recognizable plot but is only

> a tale
> Told by an idiot, full of sound and fury
> Signifying nothing.

We do not generally ask *why* Shakespeare has constructed *Macbeth* as he has. But in writing this tragedy, Shakespeare may express his own uncertainty of how one event brings on another, how events move along through time, the way each occurrence, therefore, *takes* time and prepares the next. The very structure of this play may declare the elusivenesss of meaning and the disconnectedness of the events of our lives.

The "petty pace" of which Macbeth comes at last to speak is, paradoxically, expressed even in what has come before in a plot of "fiery speed," as Bradley called it. The duration of the action in *Macbeth* can only be a few months. On the day following Duncan's murder, the two royal princes flee, and Macbeth goes to Scone to be crowned. But almost immediately we learn that Malcolm is in England and Donaldbain in Ireland, and we overhear Banquo say to Macbeth, under his breath, "Thou hast it all now," on the very day he himself will be murdered. The day after, Macbeth goes to see the Sisters again, after which he promptly hears of Macduff's flight and decides on the murder of his family. Between this event, in the fourth act, and the scene in which Macduff hears about it there can only be a brief interval, and directly after follow the events of the last act that lead to Macbeth's death. There was, as I have observed, good political reason for Shakespeare to have eliminated Holinshed's leisurely, peaceful postlude to Macbeth's regicide and seizure of power. There is a thrilling dramatic intensity achieved by the swift succession of events. But the change of pace has other effects as well. We, too, as we see or read *Macbeth,* must be affected by its compulsive mood which rushes us along so quickly as to make us as indifferent as Macbeth himself to the step-by-step logic of temporal progress.

The gaps that elide the realist progression of dramatic plot in the play do not seem mistakes or accidents. They have been thought to be flaws the genius playwright could not have been responsible for—evidence that what we have is only a cut version of what he wrote; *Macbeth* is one of the shortest of Shakespeare's plays, little more than half the length of *Hamlet.* The brilliant textual critic J. Dover Wilson was sure that what we have was reproduced not from Shakespeare's manuscript but from a "prompt copy" abbreviated for production. The Folio contains our only text of the play, and the Folio was printed after Shakespeare's death—which favors the view that it is an editing-down of a vanished original. The argument goes that a lost early scene could have strengthened our impression of Macbeth's character and intentions. It is even suggested that scenes besides the one in which Duncan's death is first contemplated by the Macbeths must also have been taken out of what Shakespeare composed—the scene of Macbeth's coronation, some scene in which Banquo clearly withdraws his allegiance from Macbeth, a scene in which Macduff parts from his wife, a scene in which the so-called Third Murderer, who suddenly appears to participate in the murder of Banquo, is explained. But is what we have merely a mutilated remnant of some more coherent composition by Shakespeare?

On the whole, I think not. Kenneth Muir, in his Arden edition, was right to insist that the play we know would suffer from addition of the missing parts Dover Wilson regretted. The editor of the more recent Oxford edition of the play, Nicholas Brooke, believes that our *Macbeth* is a theater product but a good one, deriving from a copy of the author's manuscript which had been cut in performance *skillfully,* by whatever hand—a much better example of such a process than the "bad" First Quarto of *Hamlet.* Whether or not it is a prompt copy, a deliberate intention, it can be said, compresses the action—and this intention may have been evident even in an earlier vanished text. And Shakespeare himself could have made or approved cuts—if they had occurred—as well as made other changes as his script traveled through successive performances, reinforcing his radical vision. In any case, we need not deny the wholeness of what we have. Its elisions are what it is about; they seem to rebuke our inveterate demand for explanation of everything. Macbeth's mingling of compulsion and unawareness becomes, perhaps, even a projection of the writer's own mingled mood, his desire and reluctance to see this murder-tale in the conventional way. He removes linkages we think indispensable. He huddles the time scale so that we see events as though they were nearly simultaneous. The evolution of effects from causes, so fundamental to our sense of the meaningfulness of life and the basis of human responsibility, seems to drop out of a history that sometimes seems a sequence of disjointed happenings.

If *Macbeth* illustrates any other theory of history, it may be a cyclical one which suggests that there is no absolute forward movement but only an alternation of phase. Cyclicity restores some constancy of character for Macbeth when, finally, he dies on the battlefield with heroism, though a reviled, beheaded traitor, like the man he once killed. "Bloody instructions . . . being taught, return / To plague the inventor," as he feared they would. His murder of Duncan instructs Malcolm and Macduff. When Macduff comes back on stage with Macbeth's severed head on his lance and

Malcolm speaks his closing word about "this dead butcher," we are reminded that these liberators of the realm have become butchers themselves. Macbeth's disjunction of hand and eye may be an experience the new monarch will discover in his turn. And perhaps, this rhythm suggests, those who have brought Macbeth down will be also brought down in turn. The act of blood breeds other acts of the same kind. The chain whose first links were forged in the beginning of the play may continue to connect itself to the future. A new generation may repeat everything, as Malcolm's false—and yet, perhaps, not false—prediction about his own future reign suggested.

Epilogue

The Roman Frame

Framing the four great tragedies I have just discussed, *Julius Caesar* and *Antony and Cleopatra* seem to separate *Hamlet, Othello, King Lear,* and *Macbeth* from Shakespeare's earlier and later works yet have a special relation to what they enclose, as well as to the plays they fence off. Most critics have found more difference than likeness between these two and the tragic four bounded by them. Like the series of English "history plays" that had just culminated in *Henry V* when Shakespeare wrote *Julius Caesar,* these linked representations of the greatest crisis of Roman times are based closely on recorded history. They reproduce history's accidents and gaps and the unexplained as well as the disputedly explained character of past happenings. Are they, then, simply "history plays" also? Or shall we call the Roman plays Shakespearean tragedies, although in neither is our interest kept uninterruptedly fixed on a single, salient character whose struggles and their outcome give definition to some idea of human experience—as in the four central plays? Caesar, despite the play's title, is present for only half of *Julius Caesar.* Brutus says at Philippi,

O Julius Caesar, thou art mighty yet.
Thy spirit walks abroad and turns our swords
In our own proper entrails.

But it is not true that Caesar's ghost, or even the "Caesarism" that
will have its revenge upon his murderers and take over the empire,
holds the center of the play to the end. One might as justifiably say
that the ghost who initiates the revenge plot is the hero of *Hamlet*.
More likely it is Brutus, the almost-Hamlet of *Julius Caesar*, who is
the earlier play's hero. Yet there is a distance between the suggestive
but fragmentary dramatic presence of Brutus and that of Hamlet.
Hamlet's is the longest part for an actor in all of Shakespeare, and
his own speeches dramatize a complex effort of self-realization that
is merely implied in Brutus.

To say what *kind* of a play *Antony and Cleopatra* is—history,
tragedy, or something else—has always seemed even more difficult than to tie a generic label on *Julius Caesar*. The second of the
pair of Roman plays seems to undertake to show the spiraling disorder consequent upon the regicide of Julius Caesar, disorder that
multiplies its effects in the relation of the avengers. It locates a
transcendent love affair within this political context, a love affair
that negates politics. But like the many messengers and commentators in the play itself, we can only guess at the motives and "true"
natures of the principal actors. Antony and Cleopatra almost never
express themselves in those self-exploring soliloquies the preceding tragedies have made so much of. We find ourselves outside the
cave of tragic personal mystery. With its double ending in the separated deaths of the lovers, the play feels epic rather than tragic.
United in death on Cleopatra's monument, Antony and Cleopatra
provide monumental spectacle instead of that disclosure of private
truth gained from our last view of Othello and Desdemona on their
deathbed.

And yet despite this difference in tone, I am going to argue for the deep relation of this play and its Roman predecessor to the four supreme works written in such an astonishing rush between 1599 and 1606. Out of the very contradictions and gaps of veritable ancient history, the refusal of modern as well as ancient historians to reach consensus and to simplify and summarize what has been so differently interpreted, there emerges in both *Julius Caesar* and *Antony and Cleopatra* an acceptance of the difficulty of knowing the truth about even the most famous real persons. The indeterminateness that puzzles and challenges us in *Hamlet* and continues to be felt in *Othello, King Lear,* and *Macbeth* is forecast in *Julius Caesar* and has an outcome in the ironic acceptance of *Antony and Cleopatra.*

When Shakespeare wrote *Macbeth* his mind must have gone back to the start of his tragic period with *Julius Caesar.* In both plays the ruler of the state is murdered by the man who had seemed most loyal to him and whom he had most favored. In both, the consequence of a ruler's assassination is a succession of disasters and civic turmoil. A conspicuous bloodiness links them as well. Macbeth and Lady Macbeth unforgettably gazing at their own dripping hands after the murder, and haunted forever by the mental connection of hand and blood, remind one of the conspirators who bathe their hands in the blood gushing from the body of murdered Caesar. But Shakespeare also allows us to feel that not only Brutus but even Macbeth, who claims none of Brutus's devotion to republicanism, is a villain *malgré-lui.* We are allowed to think that he, too, might have been entitled to claim some justification for his crime, though he seems simply driven by an inevitability he cannot withstand.

Shakespeare's ambiguous presentation of his Scottish king-killer derives in part, I have suggested, from contemporary political issues — that is, from the unresolved tensions about royal succession and the contest between England's new king and his enemies, some of whom even plotted his murder in 1606. These were conditions which divided English opinion concerning the killing of a king, which had always been thought the worst of political crimes. The English public could not help thinking again of 1599, when the Earl of Essex, Elizabeth's troublesome favorite, had been on his way back from his campaign against the Irish rebels, and hopes had been high in some quarters that he might even be the queen's successor. Essex's failure, his fall from favor, his wildly imprudent rebellion against the queen, and his eventual execution for treason provided a demonstration of the perils of political ambition and insurrection against legitimate royal authority. Yet there had been some, including, probably, some in Shakespeare's own circle, who had believed that Elizabeth was a tyrant and that rebellion might sometimes be necessary. It is a concession that lurks behind the condemnation of regicide in *Macbeth*. *Julius Caesar,* written directly after *Henry V,* with its tribute to Essex as well as its warning concerning the impermanence of power seized illegitimately, had already been poised upon the balance of this political dilemma.

The uncertainty that underlies our response to Macbeth is inherent in the subject of Caesar's assassination. The murder performed in 44 B.C. before the full audience of the Roman Senate, and even the plot that led to it, are so thoroughly known that one might suppose there could be nothing to dispute. But in fact, interpretation has divided itself since Caesar fell bleeding from his twenty-three wounds. Caesar himself would always be viewed in opposite ways, either as one of the greatest men who ever lived or as a tyrant who threatened the political ideals of the Roman republic. In Thomas North's 1579 translation into English of Plutarch's famous "Parallel Lives" Shakespeare read of Caesar's "covetous desire to be called king which gave the people just cause and next his secret enemies honest colour, to bear him ill will." But Plutarch also called Caesar a "merciful physician whom God had ordained of special grace to be Governor of the Empire of Rome." Other ancient and modern writers whom Shakespeare might have glanced at contributed to the picture that was at least as two-sided as Plutarch's. Suetonius had multiplied Caesar's personal faults or weaknesses — finding him an adulterer, a sodomite, a pillager of foreign cities for personal gain — yet stressed his tenderness to his friends, his clemency even to his enemies. His military and administrative abilities, his role as a man of destiny were always praised. Montaigne, whom I have been quite sure Shakespeare read, was unable to deny "the incomparable greatnesse and invaluable worth of his mind . . . his moderation in his victorie [and] resolution in his adverse fortune" all "eclipsed by this furious passion of ambition."

Even more ambiguously, Brutus was regarded in this split tradition as *either* a noble republican *or* a traitor among traitors. If Caesar was a tyrant, Brutus was a lover of liberty, an idealist; if Caesar was a godlike statesman and architect of empire, Brutus was a self-justifying villain. Plutarch praises Brutus for his "marvelous noble mind" that set the public good even above the love and admiration he sincerely had for Caesar. Others viewed him as did Dante, centuries later, who in his *Inferno* praised Caesar as the founder of a world empire and put Brutus and Cassius in the lowest depth of hell. Shakespeare, as one might expect when one recalls the way the major figures in his tragedies often refuse to conform to any fixed definition, seems to have found this conflicted picture quite congenial. As we have seen, he was ready to take the skeptic view of the constancy of selfhood — as Montaigne did — and to create in his next play a character, Hamlet, who perfectly illustrates it.

Perhaps responding to the contrary suggestions of tradition, he makes his Caesar an indeterminate figure — in the end an enigma who, though he is gone midway in the play, leaves a legacy of doubt clinging to our memory of him. Whether he is in any sense either the potential tyrant or the admirable ruler it is impossible to decide. The Caesar we hear and see in the play is an illustration of the process by which the idea of an essential inner man is sacrificed to his role as he becomes embodied royal authority. He speaks almost entirely in the third person—something that Othello will only do when he has lost his sense of an inalienable self. To the soothsayer who hails him at the Lupercalia, Caesar says, "Caesar is turned to hear." This may be, some think, a sign of his pompousness. But it is really only the first note of that denial he makes of any private being. He becomes another witness to his own appearance.

With impersonal intelligence the mind of Caesar grasps the nature of those, like Cassius, who represent a danger to him, but observes, "I rather tell thee what is to be feared / Than what I fear, for always I am Caesar." His character as Caesar is without intermission. He is Caesar and nothing else *always*, no longer like ordinary men who may vary from themselves. In his dismissal of Metellus Cimber's suit for the pardon of his brother, he says,

> I could be well moved if I were as you:
> If I could pray to move, prayers would move me.
> But I am constant as the northern star,
> Of whose true-fixed and resting quality
> There is no fellow in the firmament.

Again, this may be seen as pomposity, but it expresses Shakespeare's understanding of the way Caesar's private being is submerged, with his own complicity, into his role as the first of mankind. In his comparison of himself to nature's inexorable law he becomes what he describes—as Othello will fulfill his awesome promise to be, in the execution of his murderous intent, like

> the Pontic sea
> Whose icy current and compulsive course
> Ne'er keeps retiring ebb but keeps due on
> To the Propontic and the Hellespont.

We may call it preposterous bravado he expresses, but it is, again, the image of *a* Caesar which utters words that almost tempt us to laugh at their presumption.

> Caesar should be a beast without a heart
> If he should stay at home today for fear.
> No, Caesar shall not. Danger knows full well
> That Caesar is more dangerous than he.
> We are two lions littered in one day.
> And I the elder and more terrible,
> And Caesar shall go forth.

Even with his wife, Calphurnia, Caesar cannot stop making himself into something mythic. When she begs him to stay at home, he says, "Caesar shall forth." And when she speaks to him of the unnatural events that portend danger and even when the augurers advise him not to go to the Capitol that Ides of March day, he insists,

> What can be avoided
> Whose end is purposed by the mighty gods?
> Yet Caesar shall go forth, for these predictions
> Are to the world in general as to Caesar.

Of course, this depersonalization is fatal. He refuses to listen to Artemidorus, who wants to forewarn him of the conspirators' plot and urges that his "suit" is one "that touches Caesar nearer" than any other. According to Plutarch, Caesar accepted Artemidorus's note, but, being jostled in the crowd as he entered the Senate, he never got to read it. But Shakespeare sees another opportunity to exhibit Caesar's elevation above ordinary fear: Caesar refuses the note and tells Artemidorus, "What touches us ourself shall be last served."

It is this process that gives meaning to Cassius's image, "he doth bestride the narrow world/ Like a colossus, and we petty men/ Walk under his huge legs," and to Cassius's efforts — however mean-spirited — to bring him into the company of common mankind by recollections of his human weakness. Cassius brings up Caesar's proneness to "the falling-sickness" — probably epilepsy — his near-drowning in the Tiber, his fever in Spain when "he did shake. 'Tis true, this god did shake." It is the way Iago feels about Othello, whose stately dignity and elevated language offend him. Caesar's historical fainting fits may even have suggested Othello's seizure at the crisis of his anguish of doubt. But precisely because Caesar himself never in our hearing has admitted the presence of the vulnerable mortal encased in his armor of divinity, his last words are so moving a concession of surprise and grief, "Et tu Brute? Then fall, Caesar." Shakespeare adapted these famous words from Suetonius; in Plutarch, Caesar dies silently, though with an eloquence of gesture: "For it was agreed among them, that every man should geve him a wound, because all their partes should be in this murther: and then Brutus him selfe gave him one wounde about his privities. Men reporte also, that Caesar did still defende him self against the rest, running everie waye with his bodie, but when he sawe Brutus with his sworde drawen in his hande, then he pulled his gowne over his heade, and made no more resistaunce."

Caesar's transformation into a representation of impersonal power and nothing else is feared by Brutus. He admits that he has, till now, known

> No personal cause to spurn at him
> But for the general. He would be crowned:
> How that might change his nature, there's the question.
> It is the bright day that brings forth the adder,
> And that craves wary walking. Crown him that,
> And then I grant we put a sting in him
> That at his will he may do danger with.
> Th' abuse of greatness is when it disjoins
> Remorse from power.

Absolute power will corrupt or, rather, replace a former "nature" with a new one different from that of the man against whom Brutus can, as yet, make no reproach. But even from the start, Caesar is subject to the conflicting perceptions of others. The play begins with Rome's divided response to his triumphant elimination of his rival Pompey. Seen by the tribunes Flavius and Murellus as a signal of dangerous ambition, this victory of Caesar's is cause for celebration by the unstable commoners who had once adored the defeated triumvir. What we are provided with in this way is a forecast of the famous scene in which Brutus and Marc Antony address the populus with equally persuasive though contrary word-portraits of the dead Caesar. It is usual to say that Antony's emotional pentameters denying Caesar's ambitiousness make a better argument than Brutus's prose affirmation of it; but this is not really true. Both speeches are momentarily effective without being absolutely logical—and illustrate how a public figure is without essentiality. Is there a "real" Caesar to be seen in the play? Or is he, like all famous men, the product of the publicist's rhetoric, or the historian's or biographer's art of portraiture, as well as of his own crafting of an expedient self?

Brutus seems also to have an ideal, public personality, that of the "Soul of Rome" Ligarius calls him. But his appearance of patriotic single-mindedness may be a matter of reputation, not something essential. Caska says, in evident envy though with some effect,

> O he sits high in the people's hearts:
> And that which would appear offence in us
> His countenance, like the richest alchemy,
> Will change to virtue and to worthiness.

Brutus is useful to the conspirators not because of what he may essentially be but because of the way he is seen by the citizens of Rome. The action of the play itself provides some basis for the double view which makes him alternately the "noblest Roman of them all" and the worst traitor, who gave Caesar the unkindest cut of all "about his privities." He himself seems uncertain even at the start concerning the virtue of the act he is about to commit along with Cassius and the rest. Before he finally joins himself to the "faction," he thinks of their conspiracy as having a "monstrous visage" masked "in smiles and affability." The contrast anticipates Hamlet's horrified wonder that Claudius "may smile and smile, and be a villain," but also the way this event will always be viewed in opposed ways by history.

Brutus *wants* to think of the murder almost religiously. In this mood he resembles Othello declaring, "It is the cause, it is the cause, my soul," as he prepares to kill Desdemona. Brutus announces that he and his confederates are "purgers not murderers." He tells Cassius, "Let us be sacrificers, not butchers." But whereas Othello resolves, "I'll not shed her blood / Nor scar that whiter skin of hers than snow," the ritual murder of Caesar exhibits its paradoxical nature by the evident fact that it *is* bloody butchery. With a strange self-betrayal of language, as though he foresees and accepts the work of swords, the effect of wounds, Brutus seems actually to look forward to the stabbing and hacking described by Plutarch. At the same time, he resolves,

> Let's kill him boldly, but not wrathfully:
> Let's carve him as a dish fit for the gods,
> Not hew him as a carcass fit for hounds

—suggesting that Caesar's body could be imagined as sacrifice on an altar. Our imagination is even more shocked at Brutus's words as the egregiously gory execution consummates itself:

> Stoop Romans, stoop,
> And let us bathe our hands in Caesar's blood
> Up to the elbows and besmear our swords.
> Then walk we forth even to the market-place,
> And waving our red weapons o'er our heads
> Let's all cry. "Peace, freedom and Liberty."

The effect upon beholders, as Plutarch described it, was the reverse of what Shakespeare's Brutus seems to have expected: "At the beginning of this sturre, they that were present, not knowing of the conspiracie were so amazed at the horrible sight they sawe: that they had no power to flie, neither to helpe him, not so much, as once to make any outcrie. They on thother side that had conspired his death, compassed him in on everie side with their swordes drawen in their handes, that Caesar turned him no where, but he was striken at by some, and still had naked swords in his face, and was hacked and mangeled amonge them, as a wilde-beaste is taken of hunters." Shakespeare remembers this passage in composing Antony's words:

> Here wast thou bayed, brave hart,
> Here didst thou fall. And here thy hunters stand
> Signed in thy spoil and crimsoned in thy lethe,

which compares the assassins to hunters bloodied by their dead quarry—a scene reducing Caesar's body to a "carcass fit for hounds," after all.

Everything, we are persuaded by this play, depends on how it is played and how it is viewed. The contrast between Brutus's and Antony's funeral orations is purely rhetorical. Though Antony calls himself "a plain blunt man," his oration in pentameters is the style of the rule of empire to come, more extravagant in visual imagery, full of prosodic devices compared with Brutus's plain prose argument. But plain-speakers are not always to be trusted either; they, too, are stylists—a realization that will emerge in the controversy over style that Shakespeare admits into *King Lear.* And in *Julius Caesar,* too—as, shortly, in *Hamlet*—Shakespeare's sense of the theatrical is present to bring out the relativity of event to the viewpoint taken by a playwright or the audience, and the borrowed veracity of played roles. There is that eerie exchange between Cassius and Brutus which makes one feel that the dead historic personages are looking at *us:*

> CASSIUS. Stoop then and wash. How many ages hence
>   Shall this our lofty scene be acted over
>   In states unborn and accents yet unknown?
> BRUTUS. How many times shall Caesar bleed in sport
>   That now on Pompey's basis lies along,
>   No worthier than the dust?
> CASSIUS. So oft as that shall be,
>   So often shall the knot of us be called
>   The men who gave their country liberty.

But as everyone in the theater audience knows already—for it is familiar history—no such outcome is to follow. Rather than preserving the sacred republican ideal, Caesar's death breeds chaos in the mob that tears to pieces Cinna, the poet, a prelude to turmoil and war. Future ages came to view the assassination with mixed responses.

Brutus is already a Shakespearean protagonist, a little like Hamlet in his acceptance of an obligation of action—revenge in Hamlet's case, tyrannicide in Brutus's—by which he is forced to formulate his indefinite self. In response to Cassius's probing at the start of the play, Brutus speaks of "conceptions only proper to myself." His resistance resembles Hamlet's rebuff to his mother, "I have that within which passeth show," an ambiguous statement that, as I have noted, either means that he hides his inner mind or denies that he thinks anything that can be expressed outwardly. And yet, however doubtful or inconstant is his true interiority of character, Brutus is a man to whom ideas, as one find them in books, are important—as they will be shortly to Hamlet. There is that moment when, sleepless in his tent on the eve of Philippi, he does not go out to roam the battle line like Henry V before Agincourt but seeks a book he has been reading and even chides his servant for not finding, before he discovers it in the pocket of his nightgown; he is someone, like Hamlet, always reading. Shakespeare may have inserted this little scene to remind us that Brutus is a man about whom Plutarch says that he had "framed his manners of life by the rules of vertue and the studie of Philosophie."

But not only is there a relation between Hamlet and Brutus, but in Othello we have something of Brutus's susceptibility to persuasion by Cassius, though it is not Brutus but Caesar who is the object of Cassius's murderous rancor. Of course, it is true that the declared animus of Shakespeare's Cassius against Caesar is his doctrinal republicanism, an ideal that Iago would not have been interested in. Nor does Shakespeare tell us, as Plutarch does, that, like Iago, Cassius had hoped for a promotion given to someone else, in Cassius's case an appointment Caesar awarded instead to Brutus. Cassius's attitude—like Iago's—seems, really, more a matter of temperament than anything else. As Caesar notes, Cassius "reads much," just as Brutus does, but he is also "a great observer [who] looks/Quite through the deeds of men," as Brutus does not, and he is one of those men who can "never be at heart's ease/Whiles they behold a greater than themselves." If he does have a philosophy, it seems the skepticism that he shares with Iago. Othello's grand self-fabrication in exalted language that has some precedent in Caesar is vulnerable to the skepticism to be found first in Cassius. Like Iago scornful of Othello's inflation, he would bring down the demigod who is only a mere man like himself. But besides philosophy, what he feels is a bitter irritability. He can never have loved Caesar, as Brutus did.

Like Iago, Cassius does not regard human essentiality as something destined, and comparing Caesar to Brutus, he says,

> The fault, dear Brutus, is not in our stars
> But in ourselves, that we are underlings.
> "Brutus" and "Caesar": what should be in that
>   "Caesar"?
> Why should that name be sounded more than yours?

—and reminds Brutus of his namesake and ancestor, the founder of the Roman republic in 509 B.C., whose character could be recovered in the living Brutus. Iago, as we know, will say, "'tis in ourselves that we are thus, or thus" and "Our bodies are gardens, to the which our wills are gardeners." As for the stars, Cassius is also to be echoed, of course, by Edmund, who will insist, "I should have been that I am had the maidenliest star in the firmament twinkled on my bastardizing." Skeptic Cassius also understands that appearance is what one is, and that one must look in the mirror to see what others see to find a self. He offers to be such a mirror for Brutus— to show Brutus what he really is or can be. Brutus asks,

Into what dangers would you lead me, Cassius,
That you would have me seek into myself
For that which is not in me?

Cassius answers,

Therefore, good Brutus, be prepared to hear.
And since you know you cannot see yourself
So well as by reflection, I your glass
Will modestly discover to yourself
That of yourself which you yet know not of.

And Cassius proceeds to tell him of this inwardness which is more potentiality than visible being: "I know that virtue to be in you Brutus, / As well as I do know your outward favour." That he has a self to discover is the burden of the forged messages Cassius puts into Brutus's windows: "Brutus, thou sleep'st; awake and see thyself."

As the manipulator of the other man, Cassius employs a method that is an anticipation of Iago's. Leaving Brutus to reflect upon the argument against Caesar, he remarks to himself,

Well Brutus, thou art noble: yet I see
Thy honourable mettle may be wrought
From that it is disposed. Therefore it is meet
That noble minds keep ever with their likes;
For who so firm that cannot be seduced?
Caesar doth bear me hard; but he loves Brutus.
If I were Brutus now, and he were Cassius
He should not humour me.

Many critics think Cassius is saying that if he were Brutus he would not allow himself to be "humoured" by *Caesar* (who loves him as he does not love Cassius) and prevented from acting against him.

But it is plausible that what he is really remarking is that he, if he were Brutus, would not permit himself to be "humoured" by a *Cassius*. He also knows that he can circumvent Brutus's attachment to principle ("for who so firm that cannot be seduced?") because he, himself, is not a "noble mind." Brutus is such a mind, and would be luckier if he could count on nobility like his own in his companions. But Cassius, like Iago, is not ashamed to be devious. Whereas Plutarch says merely that various unknown persons threw provocative notes into Brutus's windows, Shakespeare's Cassius fakes a set of such notes and tosses them into the windows himself. Cassius, like Iago, takes some pride in his own realism in taking advantage not of Brutus's base but of his "noble" qualities. He thus anticipates Iago's

> The Moor is of a free and open nature
> That thinks men honest that but seem to be so,
> And will as tenderly be led by th' nose
> As asses are.

Iago will also recall that mental change-of-places by which Cassius reveals his own distinction, "Were I the Moor, I would not be Iago."

If, indeed, Cassius reads much, as Caesar says, what he reads is likely to be the philosophy of Epicurus, the Montaigne of ancient times. As Shakespeare could have discovered in Plutarch, Cassius called himself an Epicurean. What that meant to Plutarch and to Shakespeare was not that Cassius was someone fond of good food and other pleasures (a temperament hardly to be identified with his "lean and hungry look"!). Shakespeare knows this commonplace version of the philosopher's views and will have it in mind when, in *Antony and Cleopatra,* Pompey imagines Antony's "Epicurean cooks [who] sharpen with cloyless sauce his appetite." But here he has before him Plutarch, who explains Cassius's character by reference to Epicurus's philosophic skepticism. This is the way Plutarch represents Cassius's response to Brutus's account of his vision of Caesar's ghost:

> Cassius beeing in opinion an Epicurian, and reasoning thereon with Brutus, spake to him touching the vision thus. In our secte, Brutus, we have an opinion, that we doe not always feele, or see, that which we suppose we doe both see and feele: but that our senses being credulous, and therefore easily abused (when they are idle and unoccupied in their owne objects) are induced to imagine they see and conjecture that, which they in truth doe not. For, our minde is quicke and cunning to worke (without eyther cause or matter) any thinge in the imagination whatsoever. And therefore the imagination is resembled to claye, and the minde to the potter: who without any other cause than his fancie and pleasure, chaungeth it into what facion and forme he will. And this doth the diversitie of our dreames shewe unto us. For our imagination doth uppon a small fancie growe from conceit to conceit, altering both in passions and formes of things imagined. For the minde of man is ever occupied, and that continuall moving is nothing but an imagination. But yet there is a further cause of this in you. For you being by nature given to melancholick discoursing, and of late continually occupied: your wittes and sences having bene overlabored, doe easilier yeelde to such imaginations. For, to say that there are spirits or angells, and if there were, that they had the shape of men, or such voyces, or any power at all to come to us: it is a mockerye.

Shakespeare's Cassius draws back from the unflinching skepticism expressed in this passage when he tells Messala at Philippi,

> You know that I held Epicurus strong
> And his opinion: now I change my mind
> And partly credit things that do presage,

like the eagles that had accompanied Brutus's troops but abandoned them and were replaced by crows. Plutarch himself admits that during those last desperate days, various occult signs of this sort "beganne somewhat to alter Cassius minde from Epicurus opinions." But it is evident that up to this penultimate moment Cassius, as both Shakespeare and Plutarch saw him, was someone who had absorbed the skeptical materialism central to the thinking of the Greek philosopher.

Epicurus, as the Renaissance understood, had been a materialist who believed the universe consisted only of bodies and the void of space, even the soul being just some sort of matter distributed in little bits throughout our material selves and dissolved and vanished with the rest of us at death. If one thought this, of course, one ceased to believe in immortal essences and other kinds of supernatural existence as well as in various ideal concepts without material basis—the kind Iago would scoff at. Epicurus's idea that nothing can come out of nothing and nothing passes into nothing had long challenged the precarious faith of believers, as Shakespeare knew. He was to make the *ex nihilo* problem significant, as we have seen, in *King Lear*. Disbelief in the supernatural monitoring of the stars or of the rest of nature in the form of prodigies and omens, is a particular mark of skeptic materialism— as Shakespeare went on to depict in the character of his Edmund, who expressed such contempt for the astrological superstition of Gloucester. It is anticipated in Cassius's own earlier statement that it is not the *stars* but themselves men should blame for being underlings. This self-reliance that suggests that the unaided human will is the maker of fortune will be the source of Iago's Machiavellianism, expressed in his "Our bodies are gardens, to the which our wills are gardeners." That Cassius "hears no music," as Caesar remarks, is a comment that reflects the Platonic notion that music was an expression of the divinely ordered harmony of man and nature which skeptic Iago would be likely to deny; one would expect that Iago, too, has no ear for music. The consequence, as Shakespeare expresses it in *The Merchant of Venice,* is that "the man that hath no music in himself./Is fit for treasons, stratagems and spoils."

Skepticism, a feature of Cassius's personality, appears pervasively in the play to provide the suggestion that life in general is not easily read. All the warnings of soothsayers and augurers are, in fact, validated by events. Calphurnia's dream that Caesar's statue spouted blood and "many lusty Romans/Came smiling and did bathe their hands in it" is truly predictive. But a different reading is offered by the conspirator Decius, with deliberate intent to mislead—"that all great Rome shall suck/Reviving blood" from Caesar, and it is no less plausible before the event. Despite all reference to portents in the unnatural weather and bizarre animal behavior, Cicero tells Cassius in the storm that "men may construe things after their fashion/Clean from the purpose of the things themselves." It is Caesar himself, finally, who takes the attitude of the skeptic stoic who will not necessarily deny the possibility that such signs and wonders may have meaning but refuses to try vainly to anticipate and avoid what will happen, "seeing that death, a necessary end,/Will come when it will come." It is an attitude not unlike Hamlet's acceptance of the unknown but inevitable coming of death when he tells Horatio, "We defy augury. If it be now, 'tis not to come. If it be not to come, it will be now. If it be not now, yet will it come." Likewise it echoes the "ripeness is all" we hear in *King Lear.* It is, perhaps, Shakespeare's most considered wisdom, a resignation that surrenders any expectation of certain knowledge, but is, still, a response to skepticism.

Macbeth had ended with its hero/villain's death and replacement by Malcolm on the throne of Scotland, with Macduff as his staunchest friend and defender. But as I have suggested, there is some implication that history's wheel will continue to turn and life repeat itself. The avengers will themselves, perhaps, become enemies. As the ambiguous third scene in Act IV allows one to imagine, all the excesses and errors of tyranny may be repeated once again. Macbeth's replacement of Duncan had led to a chain of further murders, beginning with the murder of his partner, Banquo, and degeneration in society at large. So, it might be forecast, Macduff and Malcolm will remove the usurper only to bring on a fragile order subject to its own entropy. *Antony and Cleopatra*, written so directly after Macbeth, seems a sequel to it, as well as to *Julius Caesar*. It goes beyond the dissolution of empire already visible in the earlier Roman play and exhibits an entropic era beyond the death of Brutus and Cassius and the triumph of Caesar's avengers. A renewed fragmentation of authority appears in the fractious new times of Antony and his chief rival, but after Actium and the capture of Alexandria, the pieces all belong to Octavius Caesar.

As every educated theatergoer of Shakespeare's time knew, beyond the final curtain of Shakespeare's play lay the age named for this heir of Julius Caesar, who will soon be given his new title of Augustus by the Roman senate. Contemplating the joined corpses of Antony and Cleopatra at the close of the play, the future world leader acknowledges, "No grave upon the earth shall clip in it/ A pair so famous." His own future fame, amounting to deification, is not hinted by Shakespeare, though Virgil and Horace and Ovid had exerted their talents to celebrate the man who proceeded to organize and dominate a world empire for nearly fifty years. Perhaps, looking about him in the reign of England's James I, Shakespeare found some correspondence with the insecurity of the pre-Augustan period and no immediate prospect of an English Augustus. In any case, Shakespeare found himself confronted by a bifurcated historic tradition—as he had in dealing with Julius Caesar's assassination. Even in ancient times there had been those, like Tacitus, who saw the Augustan age as the final suppression of the vestiges of republicanism.

Shakespeare's image of the man still called, simply, Caesar is not the focus of his sense of historical ambiguity. The future Augustus is almost a minor character in *Antony and Cleopatra,* already assuming the imperial impersonality that was exhibited by Julius in the earlier play when he appears in the fourth scene to say, "It is not Caesar's natural vice to hate / Our great competitor." His is almost a choric voice that reflects upon the changeableness of reputations that makes every politician either a great man or failure in the record of history:

> It hath been taught us from the primal state
> That he that is was wished until he were,
> And the ebbed man, ne'er loved till ne'er worth love,
> Comes dearest by being lacked. The common body,
> Like to a vagabond flag upon the stream,
> Goes to and back, lackeying the varying tide
> To rot itself with motion.

The sense that human beings, like their fortunes, are variable as the tides is the subject he reflects upon at this point, as he recalls an earlier, heroic Antony visible during the military campaigns: this Antony had borne famine, and, "though daintily brought up," had drunk horse's urine and grazed like a stag on wild berries and the bark of trees, and even eaten "strange flesh, / Which some did die to look on." Antony had been a man whose very name, as his officer Ventidius will later say, had become "the magical word of war."

In this play it is Antony who is the striking example of a hero with two faces, neither of which excludes the other from our view. Plutarch describes Antony as someone whose "manly look" reminded others of traditional representations, stamped on old coins, of Hercules (from whom his family claimed to be descended). He seems to have been both notorious and popular. Plutarch takes grudging note of Antony's "foolish bravery" and of his generosity. But he expresses astonishment that "things which seem intolerable in other men"—his ceaseless pursuit of the pleasures of food and drink and sex, and his undignified informality of dress ("his cassocke gyrt downe lowe upon his hippes, with a great sword hanging by his side, and upon that some ill-favoured cloke") did not prevent many from adoring him. His downfall, it was generally agreed, was the result of his infatuation with Cleopatra, which caused him to abandon all purpose and responsibility as a leader of men and culminated in the crazy folly of the battle of Actium, when his own ships fled from battle after hers. From the point of view of such interpretation, of course, the love of Antony and Cleopatra is contemptible. Whatever role Cleopatra played in Antony's collapse and defeat makes these events, as Shaw observed, the story of "the soldier broken down by debauchery, & the typical wanton in whose arms such men perish." But there was also the idea that this love affair was the madness of two gods, an Olympian passion that had achieved a superb elevation no less poetic than sensuous. Or as Dryden expressed it in the title of his own revised version in 1678, "All for Love, or The World Well Lost."

The very form of *Antony and Cleopatra* seems to express a fractured world. It is a play that has often been found to be without a strict plotline. Johnson complained: "The events of which the principal are described according to history, are produced without any art of connection or care of composition." One does not have to agree with Johnson's deprecation to see what put him off, though it need not do so for us. As he had already done in *King Lear,* Shakespeare takes the progress of his play from place to place, from one set of characters to another, and does not confine it to a single action in the classic way—but sets into motion a shifting system of moments that reflect upon one another, of appearances that give off sometimes one, sometimes another light. It is a play concerned not only with its titular pair of principals but with a world shuddering with contentions. These extend beyond the contest between Rome and Egypt in an opposition between duty and pleasure—so often identified as the dynamics of the play. While attention is lobbed back and forth between East and West, the fortunes of empire remain a vibrating presence. From Alexandria, where Antony has been dallying with Cleopatra, he is called back to Rome by news of the death of his wife, Fulvia, and also because of the seizure of sea power by the son of that Pompey whom Julius Caesar had defeated at the start of the earlier Roman play. Perhaps to remind the audience, again, of the instability of popular favor, we hear that the younger Pompey is now a favorite of Rome's "slippery people," as his father had been before Julius took over. From Pompey in Sicily we go to Rome, where a peace is patched between Caesar, Lepidus, and Antony and sealed by Antony's marriage to Caesar's sister, Octavia, and then a truce is established with their enemy at a banquet on Pompey's galley. Some of this history has seemed irrelevant to critics concentrating too exclusively on the relation between the Antony and the beguiling queen of Egypt. How is that love story served, it is asked, by such a scene as the opening of Act III, in which Ventidius celebrates victory over the rebellious Parthians somewhere in the area of today's Iraq and follows their fleeing forces into Mesopotamia and Media? But the scene reminds us of the widespread disruptiveness against which the imperial design weakly holds. The triumvirate of rulers breaks apart despite a brief reconciliation and Antony's political marriage. The truce with Pompey is short-lived. The inconsequential Lepidus will soon be squeezed out, despite his fawning deference to his partners. The bond between Antony and Caesar begins to unravel, and we hear Antony complain that his young colleague has publicly deprecated him in the Senate. Antony is soon back in Alexandria in a new military as well as erotic alliance with Cleopatra, and war between him and Caesar renews itself. With the naval defeat at Actium, in which Antony flees after Cleopatra's ships "like a doting mallard," all is not quite over but soon will be. Antony still fights the "boy" Caesar and wins on land but loses again at sea. When Caesar hears of Antony's death, he understands it to be the end of an era, and, as though recalling the apocalyptic prodigies that accompanied the death of Julius Caesar, he says,

> The breaking of so great a thing should make
> A greater crack. The round world
> Should have shook lions into civil streets
> And citizens to their dens. The death of Antony
> Is not a single doom; in the name lay
> A moiety of the world.

As in his history plays, Shakespeare has traced a historical trajectory in *Antony and Cleopatra.* But as in those earlier studies of English history that retain the indeterminacy of the chronicle record on which they are based, he allows for accident and the inexplicable. He does not try to mend the gaps and obscurities in historical accounts. In this tragedy, as in *King Lear* and even in *Macbeth,* he permits the world-without-end feeling of chronicle to penetrate his story with its reminder of time going on and on, as the history plays had done. He surrounds his chief figures with a multitude of minor characters, moreover, so that this sense of a vaster world is always present. But the play does not wrap the human story in any atmosphere of cosmic participation as in the earlier tragedies. Caesar's remark that there should have been some universal "crack," and lions in the street at the death of a man who was half the world is ironic now when nothing of the sort takes place as it had at the death of Julius Caesar. The universe at large, natural as well as human, is simply spectatorial. Gone are all the references to weather that in *King Lear* or *Macbeth* suggested the collaboration of nature in the human tragedy. All the action is bathed in the equable Mediterranean sunlight of a universe simply indifferent.

So, despite the richness of his scenic fictionizing, Shakespeare sometimes seems willing even to make the causes of events more obscure than Plutarch, his chief historical source, had done. An example is his treatment of Antony's marriage to Octavia. Plutarch describes it as a political act designed to strengthen Antony's renewed bond with Caesar, but he also implies that it was entered into with some sincere commitment on Antony's part. Seeming to have put Cleopatra out of mind, Antony moved with his new wife to Greece, had a daughter by her, and lived domestically in Athens, generally enjoying himself in his usual way by giving big parties and holding open house for eight years or so. When he fell out again with Caesar, Octavia, who had now borne him a second child and was again pregnant, made a trip to Rome to bring her brother and husband together again, and had some success. But finally Antony went to Syria to mop up the rebellious Parthians and found himself near Alexandria. And *then,* Plutarach writes, "beganne this pestilent plague and mischiefe of Cleopatraes love (which had slept so long a tyme, and seemed to have bene utterlie forgotten, and that Antonius had geven place to better counsell) againe to kindle, and to be in force, so soone as Antonius came neere unto Syria. And in the end the horse of the mind, as Plato termeth it, that is so hard of rayne (I meane the unreyned lust of concupiscence), did put out of

Antonius' heade all honest and commendable thoughtes," and he sent for Cleopatra and welcomed her with "no trifling thinges" but the gift of Phoenicia, Cyprus, parts of Arabia, and Syria and other eastern provinces of the empire. Shakespeare, however, makes no mention of the time Antony enjoyed with Octavia or of his children by her; he tells Cleopatra that he returned to her from Octavia leaving his pillow "unpressed." The play makes renewed dissension between Antony and Caesar seem almost immediate after the marriage. And when Octavia promptly arrives in Rome to mend the breach with her brother, supposing her husband still in Athens, Antony and Cleopatra are already, Caesar tells her, sitting together like a royal couple on chairs of gold in the marketplace of Alexandria. Plutarch's account of the reawakening in Antony—after a long interval—of the repressed "horse of the mind" is not implausible, though it is an example of the way behavior may follow from obscure compulsion rather than conscious motive. But it isn't the way Shakespeare tells it. Shakespeare's collapsed sequence makes Antony's marriage to Octavia hardly explicable even as politics if it was to be so immediately abandoned and a cause of Caesar's renewed hostility.

Cleopatra's behavior is even more mysterious. What really happened at Actium is difficult enough to understand; the contest had been in the balance when Cleopatra inexplicably turned her ships and fled, and Antony, unbelievably, fled after her. But Cleopatra's role after this was ambiguous, and Shakespeare does not remove the ambiguity. The ambassador from Egypt brings separate messages to the victor. Antony desires simply to "live a private man in Athens," but Caesar is told:

> [Cleopatra] does confess thy greatness,
> Submits her to thy might, and of thee craves
> The circle of the Ptolemies for her heirs.

Caesar, sensing an opportunity, sends Thidias, to whom Cleopatra treacherously says about her relation to Antony, "mine honour was not yielded,/ But conquered merely." She lets Caesar's ambassador kiss her hand and declares her submission. Again, as after Actium, Antony suspects her treachery and roars, recalling her former liaison with assassinated Julius, "I found you as a morsel cold upon/ Dead Caesar's trencher." Is he wrong to suspect her of making up to the winner? "Not know me yet?" she cries. "Coldhearted toward me?" he responds. Nothing could be more touching than their mutual confession of need for the other. And Antony is cheered and will fight again after they have "one other gaudy night."

But the swings of doubt and recovery continue. After a land victory Antony is somehow (we *don't* know how!) persuaded to confront Caesar again at sea and meets predicted defeat. Again he bitterly blames Cleopatra, calling her "triple-turned whore." Even now there is no end to the turnabouts. Cleopatra has fled to her monument; Antony receives false news of her death; the suicide that would close his story does not quite come off; he learns that she still lives and has himself carried to her monument to be reconciled with her and to die. But her own death is reserved for the very end of the next, the last act. It is a finality she achieves for herself only after successive scenes in which it is difficult to distinguish ruse from sincerity in her duel with Caesar. She seems resolved upon suicide, but she parleys for her son's inheritance and declares her submission to the conqueror either with irony or duplicity. When seized by his guards she does try to kill herself, and though prevented, she learns that he has no other intent than to parade her through Rome in his triumphal train. But she still listens to Caesar's false amiability and offers her treasury—or half of it—though to what purpose unless for survival she has reserved the mass she calls "lady trifles" isn't in the least clear. (She *says* it is to provide gifts for Octavia and others when she is his prisoner in Rome.) And then, after all, she cheats Caesar by her suicide of what he wants more than her wealth. The denouement of *Antony and Cleopatra* is not a single untying of the knot but peripeteia upon peripeteia. This, of course, is the way history tells the tale, without much more explanation than Shakespeare offers with a constant denial of the inevitability of tragic plot. In duplicating the refusal of history either to provide full explanation or to make an end, Shakespeare seems to be willing to avoid the closure of tragedy for as long as possible—as had been the case in the deferred finale of *King Lear.*

The effect of the play, with its many scenes, is like that of modern radio or television posting of the episodes of an extended war. Many of the scenes feel like news flashes of battles or diplomacy we are not able to witness directly. Interpretation of past action is the main business of the dialogue, more prominent than the direct interaction by which events progress. This relayed information and analysis is offered not only in the place of such an obviously unstageable public occurrence as the sea battle of Actium. The love of Antony and Cleopatra itself, though centrally evident before our eyes, is continually also an object of description. The reporters or commentators upon it are mostly the crowd of minor characters— Antony's and Caesar's and Cleopatra's entourages and a series of anonymous messengers who discuss things that have already happened. But we also hear reflections from other major characters to whom news and rumors of off-scene conditions have arrived. And spectatorial distancing does not stop even there. In our direct sight and hearing, Antony and Cleopatra *themselves* seem to be witnesses of their own feelings, they seem to describe themselves self-consciously so that we do not often get the sense of unmediated self-revelation, the bursting forth of the inner self, however reduced and stripped of pretense, which is felt in the ending of *King Lear*. Their speeches are nearly always for an auditor, the lover or someone else; there are few that can be called soliloquy. There is even a discrepancy often to be observed between what we hear Antony and Cleopatra say about themselves and what they actually do that further ironizes the idea of inarguable truth. And their *acts* themselves often remain opaque. They often seem exhibitions they have themselves arranged.

A contest of interpretation is announced in the opening scene with a summary judgment, offered by Philo, one of Antony's own henchman, and introduced by a "Nay, but . . ." as though he demurs something already said—signifying already that his subject has other sides. He speaks of his general's "dotage," of "the triple pillar of the world transformed/Into a strumpet's fool." Yet in a moment the fool and the strumpet appear, and Antony expresses the superb exaltation of his and Cleopatra's love, the triple pillar collapsing and the arch of empire fallen into the Tiber:

> Let Rome in Tiber melt and the wide arch
> Of the ranged empire fall! Here is my space.
> Kingdoms are clay; our dingy earth alike
> Feeds beast as man. The nobleness of life
> Is to do thus, when such a mutual pair
> And such a twain can do't.

Cleopatra becomes, for a moment, herself a skeptic critic of this exaltation when she comments to herself,

> Excellent falsehood!
> Why did he marry Fulvia and not love her?
> I'll seem the fool I am not. Antony
> Will be himself.

But she will not sustain this skepticism. Meanwhile, the voices of Philo and his friend Demetrius close the moment as it began, and Demetrius says that Antony "approves the common liar"—that is, justifies the derisive view of him current in Rome.

Such alternation continues. Throughout the Roman world Antony's life with Cleopatra is commented on. In the fourth scene of the play, Caesar and Lepidus react to a bulletin just received from Alexandria, and Caesar says

> He fishes, drinks, and wastes
> The lamps of night in revel; is not more manlike
> Than Cleopatra, nor the queen of Ptolemy
> More womanly than he.

Immediately, there is news about pirate threats, and, in Lepidus's presence still, Caesar mentally appeals to the absent Antony— "Leave thy lascivious wassails"—and invokes an opposed portrait by recalling the earlier Antony. Similarly, the triumvirate's adversary, Pompey, in Sicily, opens Act II by remarking, "Mark Antony / In Egypt sits at dinner, and will make / No wars without doors," and sends his mental message to Cleopatra,

> Salt Cleopatra, soften thy waned lip!
> Let witchcraft joined with beauty, lust with both,
> Tie up the libertine in a field of feasts,
> Keep his brain fuming. Epicurean cooks,
> Sharpen with cloyless sauce his appetite,
> That sleep and feeding may prorogue his honour
> Even till a Lethe'd dullness.

Meanwhile, one commentator sustains for a while a transcendent image of the lovers, who are the god and goddess of sensuous beauty and love in some sphere outside ordinary mortal conditions. When Antony resolves to go to Rome in the second scene of the play, it is Enobarbus who says, "Cleopatra, catching but the least noise of this, dies instantly; I have seen her die twenty times upon far poorer moment." To Antony's somewhat resentful, "She is cunning past man's thought," his temporary adoption of the adversarial view, Enobarbus responds in the same imagery of cosmic nature that the lovers use themselves: "Alack, sir, no, her passions are made of nothing but the finest part of pure love. We cannot call her winds and waters sighs and tears; they are greater storms and tempests than almanacs can report. This cannot be cunning in her; if it be, she makes a shower of rain as well as Jove."

Enobarbus's recollection of Cleopatra on her barge at Cydnis, when Antony first wooed her, is closely inspired by Plutarch's details but given a supreme poetic shaping by Shakespeare. It is like a Renaissance painting of the goddess Venus or like that glorification attempted in her own royal appearances by the queen called Gloriana by the Elizabethans:

> The barge she sat in, like a burnished throne
> Burned on the water. The poop was beaten gold;
> Purple the sails, and so perfumèd that
> The winds were lovesick with them. The oars were
>   silver,
> Which to the tune of flutes kept stroke, and made
> The water which they beat to follow faster,
> As amorous of their strokes. For her own person,
> It beggared all description: she did lie
> In her pavilion—cloth of gold, of tissue—
> O'erpicturing that Venus where we see
> The fancy outwork nature. On each side her
> Stood pretty dimpled boys, like smiling Cupids,
> With divers-coloured fans, whose wind did seem

To glow the delicate cheeks which they did cool,
And what they undid did.

But Enobarbus will abandon Antony when his folly in the real world goes too far. He comes to share that skepticism about poetic afflatus that we have seen in Iago and in Cassius. He is a detached observer, despite his admiration—one whose observing intelligence cannot help its distrust of such exaltation in the long run. It is he who informs us that Octavia "is of a holy, cold, and still conversation," and that Antony "will to his Egyptian dish again." He advises Cleopatra not to insist on taking part in Antony's military operations, but when the disaster he fears takes place at Actium, he becomes critical of Antony and tells Cleopatra not to blame herself. When Antony then declares his intention of challenging Caesar to single combat, he remarks on the foolishness of the gesture which will only be met with contempt. He is poorly impressed by Antony's lugubrious self-pity that makes his followers weep. He recognizes that Antony is a sinking ship he himself should quit. Yet having done so, he is filled with remorse when Antony sends treasure after him. "O Antony, / Nobler than my revolt is infamous," are his words before he kills himself. But curiously, we are not put off by Enobarbus's changes of attitude. He never appears to be treacherous or an opportunist. He admires the glorious pair but abandons them, out of worldly wisdom. That both attitudes contend in the play as a whole makes him central, almost an authorial spokesman, and in the end, he regrets his own skepticism out of feelings that survive his Iago-knowledge of love as "merely a lust of the blood, and a permission of the will."

As they see each other even Antony's and Cleopatra's views are changeable. In his disillusion, Antony will say,

I made these wars for Egypt, and the queen,
Whose heart I thought I had, for she had mine—

Which whilst it was mine had annexed unto't
A million more, now lost—she, Eros, has
Packed cards with Caesar and false-played my glory
Unto an enemy's triumph.

A mutual change of view takes place, particularly in those scenes when Antony blames or suspects Cleopatra and duplicates the language of "the common liar," or when she upbraids him for what she fancies is his neglect or unfaithfulness. Much of this has a comic tone. In *Othello,* a comic subpattern could sometimes be felt in the irrationalities of the jealous husband, as we have seen, but in *Antony and Cleopatra* jealousy is patently antitragical. Cleopatra's agitation has a farcical extravagance. She rages about Fulvia, quizzes and abuses the messenger from Rome who brings news of her lover's new marriage, and, oscillating between uncertainties, supposes either that her rival is beautiful or homely. Antony's jealous fury also calls for a whipping of the messenger in the case of Thidias, with whom, he believes, he catches Cleopatra flirting. And he is more denunciatory than any of their critics when he blames her for the second naval failure, calling her a "witch" who has sold him to the "Roman boy." The jealous impulse that overturns perception in *Othello* and suggests a skeptic doubt of the reliability of all perception contributes, to a less tragic degree, to the instability of appearances in *Antony and Cleopatra.*

The comparison of life to a theatrical performance, which Shakespeare has resorted to before in *Hamlet* and *Macbeth,* comes to mind too in *Antony and Cleopatra,* as it did in *Julius Caesar.* Brutus and Cassius reflected on the many future times Caesar would bleed in sport as his death would be reenacted on the stage, and they expected—deludedly—the applause of future generations. Cleopatra is less hopeful of general judgment as she anticipates the representation of her great love affair:

> Saucy lictors
> Will catch at us like strumpets, and scald rhymers
> Ballad us out o' tune. The quick comedians
> Extemporally will stage us and present
> Our Alexandrian revels; Antony
> Shall be brought drunken forth, and I shall see
> Some squeaking Cleopatra boy my greatness
> I' th' posture of a whore.

Once more, the theater metaphor reminds us of the view Shakespeare seems to have had that human acts are *acting*—the representation of ourselves in one or another role we willingly or reluctantly find ourselves taking on—and that our performances are received by audiences according to their inclinations. In her early scenes before us, we see Cleopatra instruct her messengers in representing her variously:

> If you find him sad,
> Say I am dancing; if in mirth, report
> That I am sudden sick.

How, indeed, the play seems to ask, should we take the Alexandrian revels about which there is so much debate? Cleopatra, particularly, underlines the theatricality of her behavior by her conscious staging of effects, as in her magnificently mounted appearance on her barge on the Nile when Antony fell in love with her. Her death, too, is a carefully staged tableau. "I am again for Cydnis," she says, and we recall Enobarbus's description. Now, again, she poses on her monument with the asp at her breast and calls for her royal robe and her crown. Charmian, assisting her, says, "Your crown's awry; Ill mend it and then play." Having chosen how to die she shows no alteration of her famous beauty: as Caesar's guard remarks,

> She looks like sleep,
> As she would catch another Antony
> In her strong toil of grace.

Suicides are often staged with a posthumous audience in mind, of course. Even Antony knows this, though he bungles his own performance. The devoted Eros cannot be persuaded to do the job for him—and kills himself instead. Nor does the great Roman soldier quite manage the thing when he falls on his own sword—and, though he is mortally wounded, no one around will dispatch him. He is carried, bleeding, to Cleopatra and heaved up to her on the monument. But dying at last, he sees himself in a prescribed pose, just the same. His last words are a properly Roman epitaph:

> Lament nor sorrow at, but please your thoughts
> In feeding them with those my former fortunes,
> Wherein I lived the greatest prince o' th' world
> The noblest; and do now not basely die,
> Not cowardly put off my helmet to
> My countryman—a Roman by a Roman
> Valiantly vanquished.

But Antony's image has been undercut by humiliations and errors too many times for this epitaph to stand without irony's erosion. His character remains unstable, finally expressed in his own remark to Eros as he observes the changing forms of clouds:

> Thy captain is
> Even such a body. Here I am Antony,
> Yet cannot hold this visible shape, my knave.

Enobarbus praises Cleopatra for her "infinite variety," but her protean variousness, fascinating as it is, makes her an inhuman creature without fixed attributes.

Despite all doubts and contradictions, however, a magnificent music of hyperbole, as has often been noted, sustains the love of Anthony and Cleopatra against worldly practicality and skeptic realism. Cleopatra, having railed at Antony's departure for Rome in the first act, will remind him, "Eternity was in our lips and eyes,/ Bliss in our brows' bent." Even at the depths of despair, as he contemplates his own suicide near the end of Act IV, he continues to conceive of his love and Cleopatra's as something anticipated by ancient high poetry and myth, and rivaling the most famed:

> I come, my queen. . . . Stay for me.
> Where souls do couch on flowers, we'll hand in hand,
> And with our sprightly port make the ghosts gaze.
> Dido and her Aeneas shall want troops,
> And all the haunt be ours.

Cleopatra rises to heights as great when Antony, dying, arrives at the monument:

> O sun
> Burn the great sphere thou mov'st in; darkling stand
> The varying shore o' th' world.

—as though the death of Antony would be a cosmic catastrophe, causing the sun to burn out its sphere and the earth to be plunged in darkness. Her imagery is cosmic to the last when she tells Dolabella,

> His face was as the heav'ns, and therein stuck
> A sun and moon, which kept their course and lighted
> The little O, the earth. . . .
> His legs bestrid the ocean, his reared arm
> Crested the world; his voice was propertied
> As all the tunèd spheres, and that to friends;

But when he meant to quail and shake the orb,
He was as rattling thunder. For his bounty,
There was no winter in't; an autumn 'twas
That grew the more by reaping. His delights
Were dolphin-like; they showed his back above
The element they lived in. In his livery
Walked crowns and crownets; realms and islands were
As plates dropped from his pocket.

And then, her extravagance, her defiance of the probable, fails
her, and she asks Dolabella, "Think you there was or might be such
a man / As this I dreamt of?" To which he answers, "Gentle madam,
no." And Cleopatra seems to answer for the poet, who pitches the
impossible against the real:

You lie up to the hearing of the gods.
But if there be or ever were one such,
It's past the size of dreaming. Nature wants stuff
To vie strange forms with fancy; yet t'imagine
An Antony were Nature's piece 'gainst fancy,
Condemning shadows quite.

Shaw, after offering his reductive negative view, went on to say,
"Shakespeare finally strains all his huge command of rhetoric and
pathos to give a theatrical sublimity to the wretched end of the
business, and to persuade foolish spectators that the world was well
lost by the twain. Such falsehood is not to be borne except by the
real Cleopatras and Antonys (and they are to be found in every
public house) who would no doubt be glad enough to be transfig-
ured by some such poet as immortal lovers." This is curiously both
right and wrong. Shakespeare does "strain" all his poetic force to
exhibit sexual passion at its most glorious, man and woman glori-
fied by emotions that take them out of time and place—the dream

of poets and of lovers whose imaginations outdo nature. But we are compelled to see the shadow of the real that haunts the hyperbolic language of this glorification.

The hyperbole of Antony and Cleopatra acknowledges, as soon as it is uttered, the gap between the demonstrable and the truths affirmed in the absence of proof. Yet there is no anguish in this acknowledgment of the kind felt in the tragedies considered in my earlier chapters. There is even comedy in the persiflage, full of hyperbole, that flourishes in Cleopatra's court—a comedy that makes exaggeration a representation of the ludicrousness of our emotional postures. The tradition of romance, as Shakespeare had himself exploited it in his earlier plays, applies the language of hyperbole to the subject of love, most of all, and even in his most romantic comedies, Shakespeare had seen the gulf of doubt yawning beneath the "shaping fantasies" of lovers and poets who, as Theseus says in *Midsummer Night's Dream,* join the madman in seeing "Helen's beauty in a brow of Egypt." *Romeo and Juliet,* saturated as it is with hyperbolic language, had asserted the absolute of love and its impossibility in the world into which it is born.

Antony and Cleopatra closes Shakespeare's tragic period in the complex mood of hyperbole with acceptance of the role of belief—though it may be no more than illusion—*and* of the skepticism that undoes it. It is the paradox of hyperbole to invoke both doubt and belief at once, for hyperbole makes its assertion by affirming the impossible. When Antony says, "There's beggary in the love that can be reckoned," and Cleopatra responds with "I'll set a bourn how far to be beloved," Antony tells her, "Then must thou find a new heaven, new earth," an echo of the apocalyptic language in Revelations: "And I saw a new heaven, and a new earth." The reference to the hyperbole of religious faith is appropriate, for what he would assert is a necessary faith in what cannot be proven, our only rescue from absolute skepticism.

Selected Bibliography

SHAKESPEARE'S SOCIAL AND INTELLECTUAL MILIEU

Archer, Ian W. *The Pursuit of Stability: Social Relations in Elizabethan London.* Cambridge: Cambridge University Press, 1991.

Beier, A. L. *Masterless Men: The Vagrancy Problem in England, 1560–1640.* New York: Methuen, 1987.

Cassirer, Ernst. *The Individual and the Cosmos in Renaissance Philosophy.* Trans. Mario Domandi. Philadelphia: University of Pennsylvania Press, 1972.

Finlay, Roger. *Population and Metropolis: The Demography of London, 1580–1650.* Cambridge: Cambridge University Press, 1979.

Greenblatt, Stephen. *Renaissance Self-Fashioning: From More to Shakespeare.* Chicago: University of Chicago Press, 1980.

Kantorowicz, E. H. *The King's Two Bodies.* Princeton: Princeton University Press, 1957.

Kastan, David Scott. *A Companion to Shakespeare.* Oxford: Blackwell, 1999.

Kittredge, George Lyman. *Witchcraft in Old and New England.* Cambridge: Harvard University Press, 1929.

Klaits, Joseph. *Servants of Satan: The Age of the Witch Hunts.* Bloomington: Indiana University Press, 1985.

Levao, Ronald. *Renaissance Minds and Their Fictions.* Berkeley: University of California Press, 1985.

Palliser, D. M. *The Age of Elizabeth.* 2d ed. London: Longman, 1992.

Popkin, Richard H. *The History of Skepticism from Erasmus to Spinoza.* Berkeley: University of California Press, 1979.

Rider, Frederick. *The Dialectic of Selfhood in Montaigne.* Stanford: Stanford University Press, 1973.

Rosen, Barbara. *Witchcraft in England, 1558–1618.* Amherst: University of Massachusetts Press, 1969.

SHAKESPEARE'S WORLD OF LITERATURE AND THE THEATER

Baris, Jonas. *The Antitheatrical Prejudice.* Berkeley: University of California Press, 1981.

Barker, Francis. *The Tremulous Private Body.* London: Methuen, 1994.

Belsey, Catherine. *The Subject of Tragedy: Identity and Difference in Renaissance Drama.* London: Methuen, 1985.

Empson, William. *The Structure of Complex Words.* London: Chatto and Windus, 1970.

Findlay, Alison. *Illegitimate Power: Bastards in Renaissance Drama.* Manchester: Manchester University Press, 1994.

Goldberg, Jonathan. *James I and the Politics of Literature: Shakespeare, Donne, and Their Contemporaries.* Baltimore: Johns Hopkins University Press, 1983.

Jardine, Lisa. *Still Harping on Daughters: Women and Drama in the Age of Shakespeare.* New York: Columbia University Press, 1989.

Neill, Michael. *Issues of Death: Mortality and Identity in English Renaissance Tragedy.* Oxford: Clarendon, 1997.

Parker, Patricia. *Shakespeare from the Margins: Language, Culture, Context.* Chicago: University of Chicago Press, 1996.

Sanders, Wilbur. *The Dramatist and the Received Idea: Studies in the Plays of Marlowe and Shakespeare.* Cambridge: Cambridge University Press, 1968.

Spivack, Bernard. *Shakespeare and the Allegory of Evil.* New York: Columbia University Press, 1958.

Woodbridge, Linda. *Vagrancy, Homelessness, and English Renaissance Literature.* Urbana: University of Illinois Press, 2001.

CRITICISM

Adelman, Janet. *The Common Liar: An Essay on Antony and Cleopatra*.
New Haven: Yale University Press, 1973.

Barton, Anne. *Essays, Mainly Shakespearean*. Cambridge: Cambridge
University Press, 1994.

Booth, Stephen. *King Lear, Macbeth, Indefinition and Tragedy*. New
Haven: Yale University Press, 1983.

Bradley, A. C. *Shakespearean Tragedy: Hamlet, Othello, King Lear,
Macbeth*. 1904. Rpt., New York: Meridian, 1955.

Bradshaw, Graham. *Misrepresentations: Shakespeare and the Materialists*.
Ithaca: Cornell University Press, 1993.

―――. *Shakespeare's Scepticism*. New York: St. Martin's, 1987.

Calderwood, James L. *Shakespearean Metadrama*. Minneapolis: University of Minnesota Press, 1971.

Cavell, Stanley. *Disowning Knowledge in Six Plays of Shakespeare*. Cambridge: Cambridge University Press, 1987.

Coleridge, Samuel T. *Samuel Taylor Coleridge: Shakespearean Criticism*.
2 vols., 2d ed. Ed. T. N. Raysor. Totowa, N.J.: Biblio Distribution
Center, 1974.

Dollimore, Jonathan, and Alan Sinfield, eds. *Political Shakespeare: Essays
in Cultural Materialism*. 2d ed. Manchester: Manchester University
Press, 1994.

―――. *Radical Tragedy: Religion, Ideology, and Power in the Drama of
Shakespeare and His Contemporaries*. Durham: Duke University
Press, 1984.

Eagleton, Terry. *William Shakespeare*. Oxford: Blackwell, 1987.

Elton, William. *King Lear and the Gods*. San Marino: Huntington
Library, 1966.

Felperin, Howard. *Shakespearean Representation: Mimesis and Modernity
in Elizabethan Tragedy*. Princeton: Princeton University Press, 1977.

Fiedler, Leslie. *The Stranger in Shakespeare*. New York: Stein and Day,
1972.

Goldman, Michael. *Shakespeare and the Energies of Drama*. Princeton:
Princeton University Press, 1972.

Greenblatt, Stephen. *Shakespearean Negotiations: The Circulation of Social Energy in Renaissance England.* Berkeley: University of California Press, 1988.

Howard, Jean. *The Stage and Social Struggle in Early Modern England.* New York: Routledge, 1994.

Johnson, Samuel. *Johnson on Shakespeare.* Ed. Arthur Sherbo. New Haven: Yale University Press, 1968.

Kahn, Coppélia. *Man's Estate: Masculine Identity in Shakespeare.* Berkeley: University of California Press, 1981.

Kastan, David Scott. *Shakespeare and the Shapes of Time.* Hanover, N.H.: University Press of New England, 1982.

Knight, G. Wilson. *The Wheel of Fire.* 1930. Rpt., New York: Meridian, 1957.

Kott, Jan. *Shakespeare Our Contemporary.* Trans. Boleslaw Taborski. Garden City, N.Y.: Doubleday, 1964.

Mack, Maynard. *Everybody's Shakespeare: Reflections Chiefly on the Tragedies.* Lincoln: University of Nebraska Press, 1933.

———. *King Lear in Our Time.* Berkeley: University of California Press, 1965.

Miola, Robert. *Shakespeare's Rome.* Cambridge: Cambridge University Press, 1983.

Parker, Patricia, and Geoffrey Hartman, eds. *Shakespeare and the Question of Theory.* London: Routledge, 1985.

Rabkin, Norman. *Shakespeare and the Common Understanding.* New York: Free Press, 1954.

———. *Shakespeare and the Problem of Meaning.* Chicago: University of Chicago Press, 1981.

Righter, Ann. *Shakespeare and the Idea of the Play.* 1962. Rpt., Westport, Conn.: Greenwood, 1977.

Salingar, Leo. *Dramatic Form in Shakespeare and the Jacobeans.* Cambridge: Cambridge University Press, 1986.

Snyder, Susan. *The Comic Matrix of Shakespeare's Tragedies.* Princeton: Princeton University Press, 1979.

Stoll, Elmer Edgar. *Art and Artifice in Shakespeare: A Study in Dramatic*

Contrast and Illusion. 1933. Rpt., New York: Barnes and Noble, 1951.

Traversi, Derek. *Shakespeare: The Roman Plays.* Stanford: Stanford University Press, 1963.

EDITIONS

Antony and Cleopatra. Ed. David Bevington. The New Cambridge Shakespeare, Cambridge University Press, 1990.

Hamlet. Ed. G. R. Hibbard. The Oxford Shakespeare, Oxford University Press, 1987.

Julius Caesar. Ed. David Daniell. The Arden Shakespeare, Thomas Nelson, 1998.

King Lear. Ed. R. A. Foakes. The Arden Shakespeare, Thomas Nelson, 1997.

Macbeth. Ed. A. R. Braunmuller. The New Cambridge Shakespeare, Cambridge University Press, 1997.

Othello. Ed. E. A. J. Honigmann. The Arden Shakespeare, Thomas Nelson, 1997.

Hosley, Richard. *Shakespeare's Holinshed: An Edition of Holinshed's Chronicles, 1587.* New York: Putnam, 1968.

Montaigne, Michel de. *The Essayes of Montaigne, John Florio's Translation.* New York: Modern Library, [1933].

Plutarch. *Selected Lives from the Lives of the Noble Grecians and Romans, Compared Together by That Grave Learned Philosopher and Historiographer Plutarch of Chaeronea.* Trans. James Amyot and Thomas North. Ed. Paul Turner. Carbondale: Southern Illinois University Press, 1963.